● ANTWERP

BRUSSELS

RUDOLF BERTHOLD'S
AREAS OF OPERATIONS

● Champenoux

● Nancy

Parroy Forest

● Saarburg
● Bühl

● Embermenil

● Lunéville

Iron Man

This book is dedicated to my friends Christa and Franz Rothenbiller, who have helped me to learn more about the intricacies of German language and culture. Their informal, patient lessons during nearly thirty years of sister-city exchanges have greatly benefitted my research.

Other books by Peter Kilduff

The Red Baron

That's My Bloody Plane

Germany's Last Knight of the Air

U.S. Carriers at War

A-4 Skyhawk

Germany's First Air Force 1914-1918

Richthofen – Beyond the Legend of the Red Baron

Over the Battlefronts

The Red Baron Combat Wing

The Illustrated Red Baron

Talking With the Red Baron

Red Baron – The Life and Death of an Ace

Black Fokker Leader

Hermann Göring – Fighter Ace

IRON MAN

RUDOLF BERTHOLD:
GERMANY'S INDOMITABLE WORLD WAR I
FIGHTER ACE

Peter Kilduff

Grub Street • London

Published by
Grub Street
4 Rainham Close
London
SW11 6SS

British Library Cataloguing in Publication Data
  Kilduff, Peter.
  Iron man: Rudolf Berthold: Germany's indomitable
  fighter ace of World War I.
  1. Berthold, Rudolf. 2. Fighter pilots–Germany–
  Biography. 3. World War, 1914-1918–Aerial operations,
  German.
  I. Title
  940.4'4'943'092-dc23

ISBN-13: 9781908117373

Cover design by Sarah Driver

Book design and artwork by:
Roy Platten, Eclipse – roy.eclipse@btopenworld.com

Printed and bound by MPG Ltd, Bodmin, Cornwall

Grub Street Publishing only uses
FSC (Forest Stewardship Council) paper for its books.

CONTENTS

Foreword		7
Chapter 1	First Blood	11
Chapter 2	From Peace to War	19
Chapter 3	Service for the Nation	29
Chapter 4	Pistols to Machine Guns	40
Chapter 5	The Fighter Ace Era Begins	51
Chapter 6	Early Air Combat Success	63
Chapter 7	Leadership in the Air	79
Chapter 8	Stormy Times	101
Chapter 9	Beginning of the End	113
Chapter 10	The Final Battle	127
Appendix I:	Aerial Victory List of Rudolf Berthold	138
Appendix II:	Daily Victory and Casualty Lists of JG 2 Units	141
Endnotes		173
Bibliography and Sources		185
Index		189

FOREWORD

I first became aware of the fighter ace Rudolf Berthold through one of his former flying comrades, the late Oberst der Reserve a.D. [Colonel, Reserves, Retired] Paul Strähle, some forty-five years ago. At that time, a few hundred World War I aviation veterans were alive in Germany and one of them, the late Oberstleutnant der Reserve a.D. Hanns-Gerd Rabe, put me in touch with Strähle, the first German fighter pilot I came to know. Strähle and I had a lively correspondence while I was gathering material to write an article for the old *Cross & Cockade Journal*. Consequently, he invited my wife Judy and me to his home in Schorndorf, Germany in May 1967, just before his seventy-fourth birthday.

I was impressed that Paul Strähle had endured numerous aerial combats and shot down fifteen of his opponents over a seventeen-month period. At one point he interjected:

> 'You should have met my old boss. He flew during most of the war, won the highest medals, brought down forty-four British and French aeroplanes, was shot down several times himself and went on to fly with a paralysed arm. *Er war der Eiserne der deutschen Jagdflieger!* [He was the Iron Man of German fighter pilots!]'

I listened carefully as he described serving under Berthold, who then commanded Jagdstaffel 18 and was preparing Strähle to move up and lead a unit of his own. He told me about Berthold's various wounds and touched briefly on the dark side of medical treatment that drew '*der Eiserne*' into drug abuse. We finished the evening on a cheerful note with a nice glass of Swabian wine, but I was left with many unanswered questions about Rudolf Berthold.

Sadly, little historical material about Berthold survived the World War II bombing of the Reichsarchiv in Potsdam and it was difficult to learn more about his life, struggles and achievements. However, the final years of the Cold War in the late 1980s gave me access to Berthold-related resources in a former East German archive, while I was researching other World War I flyers. That material and the subsequent discovery of Berthold's personal war diary in the Bundesarchiv freed me from relying on the few books that had long represented his story – and not always accurately or completely. Now, with better facts at hand, I am glad to offer a new look at Rudolf Berthold's life and am grateful to John Davies at Grub Street for providing the opportunity to do so.

Rudolf Berthold triumphed in at least forty-four aerial combats. Archival material and map study now make it possible to examine those and related combats and to suggest which air units and even individual airmen *most likely* fought against each other. Such encounters are a significant component of researching World War I aviation history, in which an aerial victory, *luftsieg* or *victoire aérienne* decided the fate of so many combatants. In recent years, this form of research has become more conclusive with the help of books such as *The French Air Service War Chronology 1914-1918*, *The Jasta Pilots*, *The Sky Their Battlefield*, and other valued standard reference texts published by Grub Street, which are included in this book's bibliography. I am indebted to the authors of those books for their labours in compiling such works.

Photographs have been important to my research and I am grateful to friends and colleagues who have generously shared images for this book: Rainer Absmeier, Dr. Lance J. Bronnenkant, Helge K.-Werner Dittmann, Trevor Henshaw, Dr. Volker Koos, the late Heinz J. Nowarra, Colin Owers, Alex Revell, Greg VanWyngarden and Tobias Weber.

While researching and writing this book, I received help from many people and note with gratitude the kind efforts, encouragement and information provided by the following people and their institutions: Brigitte Bänsch, Alexandra Nothdurft and Renate Wünschmann, Stadt Erlangen; Karin Binder, Stadtgeschichte Wittenberg; Thomas Binder, Stadtarchiv Kamenz; Dieter Dureck, Landesamt für Gesundheit und Soziales, Berlin; Wesley Henry and Brett Stolle, National Museum of the U.S. Air Force; Achim Koch and Michael Weins, Bundesarchiv Militärarchiv; Dr. Eberhardt Kettlitz, praeHistoria Büro für Archäologie und Geschichte; Stephan Kühmayer, Deutsche Dienststelle (WASt); Oberstleutnant Harald Potempa, Militärgeschichtliches Forschungsamt; Dr. Wolfgang Mährle, Judith Bolsinger and Manfred Hennhöfer of the Landesarchiv Baden-Württemberg; Dr. Uwe Müller, Stadtarchiv Schweinfurt; Schulleiter Heinz Pfuhlmann, Franz-Ludwig-Gymnasium Bamberg; Annemarie Renz-Sagstetter, Stadt Bamberg; Pfarrer Wolfgang Scheidel, Evangelische Gemeinde Ditterswind; Claudia Veit, Stadtarchiv Passau; Dr. Clemens Wachter, Universitätsarchivar, Friedrich-Alexander-Universität Erlangen-Nürnberg; and Dr. Robert Zink, Stadtarchiv Bamberg. Last but not least, Kimberly Farrington and Ewa Wolynska of the Elihu Burritt Library of Central Connecticut State University exemplify the valued help I have received from my alma mater.

Other valued friends and colleagues who have helped in many ways include: Rainer Absmeier, Trudy Baumann, Dr. Lance J. Bronnenkant and his exhaustive research into German wartime images, Christophe Cony, Russell Folsom, Norman Franks, Russ Gannon, Trevor Henshaw, Reinhard Kastner, Andrew Kemp, Paul S. Leaman, James F. Miller, Nicolas Philippe, Thorsten Pietsch, Julian J. Putkowski, Alex Revell, Oberleutnant Sebastian Rosenboom, Claudia Schünemann, Gunnar Söderbaum, Dr. James Streckfuss, Dr. Hannes Täger, Lothair Vanoverbeke, and Aaron Weaver.

My sincere thanks also go to this cadre of friends: Ronny Bar for his excellent colour artwork portraying aircraft flown by Rudolf Berthold, Judy and Karl Kilduff and my long-time friend and mentor David E. Smith for their helpful review of and comments on the manuscript, my cultural mentor Klaus Littwin for helping me understand German linguistic nuances and providing valuable assistance in locating important research sources, Dr. M. Geoffrey Miller for providing his medical expertise, long-time friends Oberbürgermeister i.R. Prof.Dr.(h c) Franz J. Rothenbiller and his wife Christa for their valued help in deciphering significant documentary material, the late Oberst der Reserve a.D. Paul Strähle for relating his experiences of service under Rudolf Berthold's command, and Stewart K. Taylor for sharing his encyclopaedic knowledge of British Commonwealth flight operations in World War I.

I am very grateful for the friendship, interest and support of these very helpful people.

Peter Kilduff

Rudolf Berthold joined the ranks of nationally-known German airmen when this postcard view of him appeared in early 1916. The photo, taken over a year earlier, shows him wearing an observers' badge, along with his 1st and 2nd Class awards of the Iron Cross. (Lance J. Bronnenkant)

CHAPTER ONE
FIRST BLOOD

*'I came about vertically behind the Frenchman, dived down and got …
right on his heels. My machine gun began its monotonous tack-tack-tack.
It did not take long before [he] went over onto his left side, emitting smoke …'*[1]

RUDOLF BERTHOLD

By October 1915, armies on both sides of the Western Front had long been dug into fortified trenches winding some 700 kilometres from Belgian coastal sand dunes in the north to mountain peaks in southeast France. But the stalemate that frustrated ground commanders for over a year did not hamper Oberleutnant [First Lieutenant] Rudolf Berthold, who flew his big two-engine biplane bomber high over British and French troops, easily out of range of soldiers' guns. Further, he had two gunners on board to help fight off aerial opponents.

The twenty-four-year-old pilot exulted in his advantages of range and height. Writing about his bombing flights over a British barracks complex at Abbeville, France, some thirty-five kilometres east of the English Channel coast, Berthold was pleased that his adversaries must have 'looked on in amazement when they saw the first German [G-type [2]] aeroplane over their encampment …'

> 'During the second flight the British soon tried to bring us down, as both of my propellers later showed traces of explosive ammunition … I also flew out over the sea. The broad sheets of water passed big and powerful below me. War and mankind were forgotten there.'[3]

At that time, Berthold flew an AEG G.II,[4] which, in the words of one German aviation expert, 'proved to be … a most efficient bombing aeroplane, easy to fly and maintain and of a robust construction that endeared it to … hard-working three- to four-man crews.'[5] But the bigger AEGs also attracted smaller, faster and more manoeuvrable British and French aircraft whose pilots sought to shoot down the bombers before they dropped their lethal loads – or could return to their bases for more bombs and ammunition.

Combat in the Air

On the bright, clear morning of Saturday, 2 October 1915, Rudolf Berthold and his two observer/gunners headed for Abbeville again, but were interrupted by a British biplane. As the two aeroplanes drew closer Berthold recognised his adversary as a Vickers F.B.5, a rear-engine two-seat fighter aircraft in which the pilot sat behind the operator of a Lewis

Mk I machine gun on a flexible pivoted mounting[6] that gave it a wide field of forward fire. British flyers called the aeroplane the 'Vickers Gun Bus'[7] for good reason.

A British report for that day described the encounter:

> 'Lieut. [Herbert T.] Kemp and Capt. [Cecil W.] Lane of 11 Squadron [were] in a Vickers[8] when patrolling north of Arras at 9:45 a.m. at a height of 10,000 feet, [they] observed a hostile machine crossing the line three miles away. Lt. Kemp succeeded in heading off the enemy aeroplane which then turned toward the Vickers and the two machines approached each other [head] on. Capt. Lane opened fire at eighty yards' range. The hostile aeroplane immediately dived almost under the Vickers and a drum [of machine-gun ammunition] was emptied into it while [it was] diving. The Vickers then dived down after the hostile machine, firing three more drums into it at close range. The hostile aeroplane, which was an Albatross [*sic*], crossed the line, diving to earth at a very low altitude.'[9]

The British gunner's drums each held forty-seven rounds of 0.303-calibre (7.7-mm) ammunition.[10] But the cumulative force of the four drums – more than 180 bullets – at such close quarters had a devastating effect on the German bomber. Rudolf Berthold wrote in his diary:

A Vickers F.B.5 of the type that attacked Berthold's AEG G.II during a bombing mission. (Kilduff Collection)

'Suddenly I see explosive tracer flashes ahead of our aeroplane. A Vickers pursues us. I would have preferred any other aeroplane to this manoeuvrable little Englishman. Nevertheless, we charge at him! He has seen us and now turns toward us. I know that if it should come to an aerial combat, I will be at a disadvantage as the handling ability of my two-engine bird is inferior. Should I fly away? No! It is preferable to be overcome in combat. After all, I have two observers who know how to shoot.

'The enemy fires ... and I continually hear the shots hitting our wings. Then, the main fuel tank is smashed to pieces! Shards of fabric flutter from the wings and I make a banking turn. Alongside and behind me I hear my observers firing away. Suddenly, the observer to my right collapses and goes pale, as if he is hit. I realise it is also quiet in the back. I still hear the tack-tack-tack of the enemy's machine gun. The upper part of my rear observer's body falls onto the edge of his station.

'Then both of my engines quit. In one moment the front of my bird is pointing downward. In the next I sideslip, at first downward, then over onto the left wing. The engines howl into life, the wings bow, the aeroplane goes almost straight down. Thank God, I got away from the opponent. Now I hold the control column tightly in my hand and the aeroplane responds to me. At a certain altitude, I pull out slowly.

This view of Berthold's AEG G.II 26/15 on the ground shows a pilot and three observer/gunners, but he usually flew with only two crewmen. (Tobias Weber)

'A glance to the rear shows that my observer is alive, he has just blinked his eyes, but the forward gunner is dead. Where to now? To the nearest aeroplane depot, where there is a doctor. How slowly the aeroplane seems to creep along ... Finally we come in to land! I have no idea what happened after that. The following morning, the rear observer died.

'The [second] dead man was my dear old friend Grüner. I can barely comprehend it; he was not scheduled to fly, but he pleaded with me so earnestly that I could not refuse him.'[11]

Anatomy of an Air Combat

This encounter needs to be examined, as the preceding account is flawed. First, Berthold's narratives often conveyed an overblown sense of drama. Second, this text, from Berthold's *Persönliches Kriegstagebuch* [personal diary], seems to have melded the narratives of two fights between his AEG G.II and different Vickers F.B.5 aircraft on separate occasions. The 'diary' summarised his activities over time; it did not chronicle daily events.

In this case, Berthold stated that on the morning of 2 October, 'the entire region ... lay in a dense coat of fog ... Half an hour later the fog lifted ... and an hour later I was ready to take off. As the fog still lay to the south, we flew in a northerly direction'[12] from a German airfield near St. Quentin toward Arras, some sixty kilometres to the northwest. Conversely, a British source reported that the weather for that area was 'fine all day'.[13] And, while Berthold was most likely attacked that day, he escaped from his pursuer. His unit, Feldflieger-Abteilung [Field Flying Section] 23, reported no casualties that day[14] – and certainly none related to either of Berthold's observer/gunners, Leutnants [Second Lieutenants] Josef Grüner or Walter Gnamm.[15]

But five weeks to the day later, on Saturday, 6 November, Berthold and his crew paid for their incursion over the front lines. On a day when Royal Flying Corps

Ltn Josef Grüner, Berthold's friend and observer/gunner, who was mortally wounded in the air combat of 6 November 1915. (Heinz J. Nowarra)

weather officers reported 'fog and clouds, with observation very difficult',[16] Ltn Grüner was fatally wounded in an air fight north of Péronne. The twenty-two-year-old observer died at Etappen-Flugzeug-Park 2 [Advanced Area Aeroplane Depot 2] at Château de Grand Priel, twenty kilometres east of Péronne.[17] German records list Grüner as the only FFA 23 crewman to perish in combat that day[18]; there is no record of Gnamm[19] or any other FFA 23 observer/gunner being wounded.[20]

A British report for that day noted that a Vickers F.B.5 of 11 Squadron was attacked by what the RFC crew of 2/Lt Robert E.A.W. Hughes Chamberlain and 2/Lt Edward Robinson described as a 'Fokker biplane with [observer] and machine gun ... north of Péronne'. The pair misidentified their opponent, as, up to this time, the Fokker aircraft company produced only single-seat aircraft; however, other aspects of their account – such as flexible machine guns on the German aircraft – are consistent with features of Rudolf Berthold's AEG G.II.

Hughes Chamberlain and Robinson stated that they did not see the German aircraft until it was 150 yards away.

> '... It [then] dived from 200 feet above them and opened fire at 100 yards. By the time [we shot at it] the enemy machine crossed in front of the Vickers at fifty yards' range and in this position twenty-five rounds were fired at it. The [German] then circled left, passing the Vickers at 150 yards' range, firing from the side in bursts of fifteen to twenty rounds. The remainder of the [Vickers'] first drum was fired into it and, by the time a new drum had been fitted, the range was reduced to twenty-five yards. The Vickers was [approaching] head-on and, at this range, half a drum was fired into the [German], which continued [to respond with] a rapid fire.
>
> 'The enemy then circled 'round for position to cross the Vickers' front but, anticipating it, the Vickers fired one drum at the [observer] and pilot at fifty feet. The enemy machine dived steeply, followed by the Vickers and in this position another drum was got off. The [German aeroplane] disappeared in a bolt of clouds at 3,000 feet above Aizecourt ...'[22]

The last portion of Berthold's narrative fits the combat described immediately above. Apparently, he managed to disengage from his intended victim over Aizecourt-le-Bas, northeast of Péronne and less than twenty kilometres from the aeroplane depot at Château de Grand Priel. But that short, desperate flight to save his comrade was in vain. Rudolf Berthold had been a reconnaissance and bomber aircraft crewman with FFA 23 since August 1914[23] and during many long flights over the lines – often with only a rifle or a pistol for self-defence – he had not lost a crewman. It was as if that status represented some mystical bond.

Friendship Forged in Combat
Moreover, Rudolf Berthold and Josef Grüner had much in common, which led to their becoming close friends. Both men were born in villages in northern Bavaria and earned regular army commissions as regimental officer candidates, rather than through the more prestigious Bavarian cadet system. Indeed, they had trained in infantry regiments outside

of the Kingdom of Bavaria, Berthold with a Prussian unit residing in a Saxon duchy and Grüner with a regiment in the Kingdom of Saxony.[24] Like Berthold, Grüner had been active in the German youth movement and showed strong patriotic feelings.[25]

Above all else, they shared a craving for battle action that earned them awards for their bravery. Both men earned the Iron Cross 1st and 2nd Class medals early in the war and Grüner was the first of the pair to receive a high Saxon award. In his case it was the Ritterkreuz II. *Klasse des Albrechts Orden mit Schwertern* [Knight's Cross 2nd Class of the Albert Order with Swords], which he received on 15 July 1915.[26]

Im Luftkampf starb den schönsten Soldatentod der

K.S.Leutnant Joseph Grüner

Ritter des Eisernen Kreuzes I. und II. Klasse und Inhaber des Ritterkreuzes II. Klasse des Albrechtsordens.

Als Vorbild soldatischer Pflichttreue und unerschrockener Tapferkeit bleibt er uns für alle Zeit unvergesslich.

Seber,

Hauptmann und Führer einer Feldflieger-Abteilung im Westen.

11,332

FFA 23's obituary notice for Ltn Josef Grüner included the Prussian and Saxon awards he had earned. (Stadtarchiv Passau)

After Grüner's death, however, Berthold felt a deep loss and, in a move rare for him, took home leave to mourn his close friend. He did not go to his family for solace; rather he spent time alone, perhaps to wonder whether he had been bold or foolhardy by charging at and flying so close to his adversary. Also, there was the inexplicability of survivor's guilt: with so many enemy bullets directed at the aeroplane, why had Grüner been hit and not Berthold? He wrote in his diary:

'I cannot rightly recall what happened in the following weeks. Almost aimlessly I wandered around Germany. Everywhere I looked I saw in my mind's eye the cockades of the Vickers, I saw my observer hanging over the edge of the aeroplane. All I thought about were vengeance and combat! Sleep soundly, my friend Grüner, you will be avenged!'[27]

Berthold's First Aerial Victory

But Rudolf Berthold had to wait more than two months for his triumph. By this time he flew a Fokker E.I Eindecker [monoplane], armed with a fixed Parabellum IMG 08 machine gun[28] and synchronised to shoot 7.92-mm ammunition through the propeller arc. This gave it the forward-firing advantage of British and French rear-engine fighter aircraft – with greater speed and manoeuvrability.

A Fokker Eindecker of the type flown by Rudolf Berthold when he achieved his first aerial victory. (Kilduff Collection)

On Wednesday, 2 February 1916, Berthold and Ltn.d.Res Ernst Freiherr [Baron] von Althaus[29] attacked a pair of French aeroplanes within German forward lines and shot down both of them. Consequently, Berthold's 'kill', a Voisin LA rear-engine biplane brought down near Chaulnes, was officially credited as his first aerial victory. Althaus' victim, a Nieuport Type XIV or XV two-seater,[30] crashed and burned about fifteen kilometres away, near Biaches, and was recorded as his third victory.[31]

Berthold's diary entry that day detailed this momentous event in his military career:

'The weather was bad today: low clouds, rain. About 3 p.m. came an urgent telephone alert: A big French aeroplane was reported to be over Péronne [almost twenty km away]. Althaus and I were just having coffee, as the others had gone for a walk. Both of us rushed out … and got right into our "birds".

'By this time it was raining again. We tore down the middle of the 'field … and right into the rain. Althaus was off to my right. We could not see much. Then finally toward the west, over the lines; there was a big hole in the clouds! We flew at 2,000 metres altitude.

'We were flying in a north-westerly direction, when suddenly I saw two small black spots that swiftly become bigger. They were aeroplanes! I pulled up my bird and took them on. Then they saw Althaus first as he flew lower than me … I had not been spotted because I placed myself in front of the sun, which had fortuitously come out.

'What happened now was a few minutes' work! I came about vertically behind the Frenchman, dived down and got right behind him as he put himself close behind Althaus, right on his heels. My machine gun began its monotonous tack-tack-tack. It did not take long before the Frenchman went over onto his left side, emitting smoke and crashing. I went howling down after him.

'A glance toward Althaus showed … his opponent also going down. We had disposed of both of them. Nevertheless, we still had to be aware; one never knows where the next enemy fighter may come from … In fact, once again, my Frenchman righted himself

17

around. Again he fired a burst from his machine gun and then he tumbled down. I saw him disappear behind a small wooded area. At the last moment, I pulled my machine up; otherwise I would have crashed into the woods.

'There was ...a heavy mist everywhere; it was like looking into a wash basin! Therefore I flew straight and began climbing. I noticed that I was flying very far to the west. From time to time my engine quit, due to either a sticky valve or an oil-fouled sparkplug. I was in a fine mess! Should I land on the other side of the lines? Not for all the world, so I pushed on! At last my engine ran perfectly again.

'There glistening before me was a silver stripe: the Somme river. Heading off in an easterly direction, I was not far from my airfield. I landed successfully and Althaus was waiting for me at the 'field, he had been worried. Now there were only congratulations and an account of his fight, which was extensive! My mechanics, fine fellows, were beside themselves with joy! We stuck together in happiness and sorrow: pilots, mechanics and "birds", like a little family.

Voisin LA (serial number V.1321) of Escadrille VB 108 was brought down intact and recorded as Rudolf Berthold's first victory. (Greg VanWyngarden)

'Then the report came that our forward-most troops had already confirmed by telephone – the downing of both aeroplanes; they were just behind our frontlines. Half an hour later, cars were heading for them. I did not go with them, as the sight was too depressing. I walked away quietly, but inwardly I was free! My dear friend … Grüner, now you have been avenged!'[32]

CHAPTER TWO

FROM PEACE TO WAR

*'For trouble does not come out of the earth, and misfortune
does not sprout from the field; rather, mankind is born to
misfortune, just as birds soar, flying upwards.'*

JOB 5: 6-7

Oskar Gustav Rudolf Berthold, later known as Rudolf, was born at about 6:00 p.m. on Tuesday, 24 March 1891[1] in Ditterswind, a village nestled in a forest valley in the part of north-western Bavaria known as Lower Franconia. He was the sixth child born into the family of *Oberförster* [Chief Forester] Oskar Berthold, who lost his first wife four years earlier. Anna Ida (née Hofmann) died at age thirty while giving birth to their fifth child, who also died.[2] For a time, Oskar, still in his mid-thirties, returned to his original homeland in the Province of Saxony, where he grieved and ultimately met and married Helene Stief. She was three years Oskar's junior and began his second family by having Rudolf. Three other children followed.[3]

Oskar Berthold proved to be a good husband for Helene. He was the son of a building contractor, but, rather than join his father's company, he had trained for a career in forestry. In addition to directing timber harvesting and protecting wild game, he also managed and dealt with people; for, in a small community, a man in his position served as both game warden and local law enforcement officer.[4] Thus, Oskar Berthold's talents were put to good use in Bavaria, where he was hired by Oskar Freiherr [Baron] von Deuster, a landed nobleman with a large estate surrounding his Ditterswind residence. The elder Berthold enjoyed considerable prestige, which was reflected in his family's lifestyle.

The forest and the fields became the Berthold children's playground and they learned to appreciate the animals and plants under their father's care and administration. It became a milestone for the children when they were allowed to individually accompany their father on game stalking pathways in advance of Freiherr von Deuster's hunting parties for various guests.[5] On such occasions, Rudolf and his brothers gained an early familiarity with and respect for the rifles that were among the tools of their father's trade.

In early September 1897, Rudolf Berthold, then six years old, was enrolled in Ditterswind's *werktagschule* [elementary school]. Like so many boys that age, he was occasionally boisterous and impulsive, but he stuck to his lessons and advanced through his classes. Young Rudolf developed an early interest in German history and, given to flights of fancy, he saw himself leading 'a courageous troop, fighting for the Fatherland'. Outside of school, Rudolf's great joys were sojourns into the forest, competitive sports and playing war games with other boys in the village.[6]

Oskar Berthold was responsible for the area around the Ditterswind residence of Oskar Freiherr von Deuster. (Heinz J. Nowarra)

Away to School

Following Rudolf's tenth birthday, in 1901, his parents had to start thinking about his future. At age eleven, for example, he could apply for entrance to the Bavarian military cadet system and receive a good education for the next eight years at state expense and gain the prospect of service as an officer and perhaps a career in the army.[7] But, despite his early leaning toward a life in uniform, Rudolf was enrolled as a first level student in the *Humanistische Neue Gymnasium* [New Secondary School for the Humanities] in nearby Bamberg.

At the time, two army regiments were garrisoned in Bamberg: the 5th Infanterie-Regiment Grossherzog Ernst Ludwig von Hessen[9] and the horse-mounted 1st Ulanen-Regiment Kaiser Wilhelm II., König von Preussen. On various occasions, Bamberg's streets were filled with local infantrymen and cavalry men all decked out in colourful dress uniforms and the school boys joined the crowds to witness the grand spectacle. Rudolf was so motivated by the visual power of row upon row of soldiers that even 'when he went on vacation and searched again for the places of his early childhood, the ... love of his homeland grew all the more and he took a solemn oath that, when the hour required it, he would be a defender of the homeland, not merely a son of it.'[10]

During his time in Bamberg, according to Rudolf's school reports, he displayed 'good aptitude ... great diligence and orderly behaviour ... [and earned] special recognition for his ... self-control.'[11] When asked what his personal motto would be, fourteen-year-old Rudolf, no doubt inspired by his early military interests and exposure to an oft-heard line from the Roman lyrical poet Horace, responded 'without a moment's hesitation: "It is sweet and honourable to die for the Fatherland!"'[12]

Rudolf completed the fifth level at the gymnasium in Bamberg in the summer of 1906. The following September he was one of thirty-seven boys accepted into the sixth level at the *Königliches Humanistische Gymnasium* [Royal Secondary School for the Humanities] in the Lower Franconian industrial city of Schweinfurt.[13] The following year, as Rudolf graduated to the following class, he was joined at the school by his younger brother Wolfram.[14] Wolfram had a gentler nature (he went on to study theology at Erlangen University[15]) and, given Rudolf's athletic prowess and nearly total absence of fear, Wolfram was well looked after and was not concerned about the inevitable schoolyard bullies.

During the winter of 1909, Rudolf transferred to the *Altes Gymnasium* [Old Secondary School] in Bamberg, which offered a better course of study for the military career he was always thinking about. The move proved to be beneficial:

'As with earlier courses, Rudolf was outstanding in history and in gymnastics, and did well in natural science and in language subjects (except in the French language). He also mastered the *prima* [senior year examination] diligently and energetically so that ... on 14 July 1910 he received the *reifezeugnis* [matriculation certificate], which, in consideration of good works, was achieved without his having to take an oral examination. Also during his final year, Berthold ... had the cheerful disposition of youth, which was displayed to the fullest among like-minded people and his peers ... and also did not exclude the beer parties of his student friends; rather, he got to know this ... side of student life from his own experiences.'[16]

A school chum, Hanns Fiedler, recalled a classroom incident in their final days in Bamberg that portended Berthold's aptitude for military life. Their much respected and feared teacher was completing a discussion of Friedrich Schiller's play *Wallensteins Tod* [Wallenstein's Death], which should have interested Berthold, as it was about the Thirty Years' War general, Albrecht von Wallenstein. But when called upon to recite a famous verse, Berthold paused. He could not recall it. Rather than admit defeat, he began with what he remembered, the first few lines:

'"There are moments in the life of a man,
Where he is closer to the spirit of the world than ever ..."

After that, Berthold coolly improvised lines that somewhat imitated Schiller's style. Then he cleverly ended with an actual line from the play: '*Und Ross und Reiter sah man niemals wieder*' [And one never again saw horse and rider], after which his classmates burst into laughter at his daring ruse. By then the teacher was onto the game, but apparently was impressed by his pupil's poise, self-confidence, courage and ability to think on his feet in a tight situation; he said nothing and continued with the lesson. Fiedler believed that Berthold could never be happier than he was at that moment, having come through such a 'stormy voyage' unharmed – and without being made to look foolish before his peers.[17]

Thus, Berthold's 'gymnasium days ended harmoniously. Now nothing stood in the way of fulfilling the dreams of his youth. The passionately desired profession of a military officer was open to him.'[18]

Entering the Army

By the time that nineteen-year-old Rudolf Berthold completed his public education, the most common way for him to obtain a regular army (vs. reserve) commission was to enlist in a regiment as an *avantageur* [officer candidate]. After that, he and other graduates of secondary school education in his cohort would spend eighteen months, preparing: 'for officer rank through the equivalent of "on the job training ... [after which] the officers of [the] regiment voted on their acceptability."'[19]

Although raised and educated in Bavarian communities, Berthold decided to begin his military career with a regiment based in Wittenberg, a city best known for its role in the beginning of the Protestant Reformation. In the early twentieth century, Wittenberg was in the Prussian-administered Province of Saxony,[20] bordering the larger Kingdom of Saxony. Most likely, Berthold's choice of a regiment was influenced by its garrison being in his parents' homeland. His father 'hailed from Brehna near Bitterfeld, while his mother came from Alperstedt near Erfurt.'[21] And he chose a unit with a rich heritage: Infanterie-Regiment Graf Tauentzien von Wittenberg (3. Brandenburgischen) Nr. 20, named in honour of the Prussian field commander whose soldiers wrested the Wittenberg area from Napoleon's army in 1814.[22]

It is easy to imagine that Rudolf Berthold would have been keen to add to the unit's further glory. And it is just as easy to appreciate the following scene, described as occurring in Wittenberg on a national holiday to honour the kaiser, Saturday, 27 January 1912:

> 'Today Wittenberg celebrates, like all cities and villages of the German Reich, in the traditional manner the festival on the kaiser's birthday …
>
> 'A young leutnant of the *"Tauentziener"* in full dress uniform strides through the city centre's bustling streets. Brand-new are the shoulder boards on his officer's overcoat. Happiness and pride radiate in the facial features of the slender manly figure. After [eighteen months'] time as a *fähnrich* [army ensign], Rudolf Berthold this morning received his officer's commission from his regimental commander. Now the dream of youth has come true ...'[23]

Nurturing Patriotism

Shortly before Berthold was commissioned, the German government began encouraging development of a national youth movement. Called the Jungdeutschland-Bund [Young Germany Federation], it became a widespread patriotic activity for youngsters. Berthold supported it enthusiastically, as an expression of his 'love of homeland in marches and scouting activities ... [as] the first spiritual elements of [a] magnificent German people's army.'[24] Not surprisingly, he was elected leader of the Wittenberg branch.[25]

As it turned out, Rudolf Berthold's local involvement with a national youth group became compatible with his military service, as a driving force for the Bund was newly-retired Generalfeldmarschall [Field Marshal] Wilhelm Leopold Colmar Freiherr von der Goltz. The sixty-eight-year-old career soldier had served most recently as an advisor to the Turkish army during the 1908 revolution of the progressive, modernist members across Ottoman society known as the Young Turks. According to a contemporary biographical sketch of von der Goltz:

Celebrating his early success, Rudolf Berthold posed for this formal view with his father, Oskar, in autumn 1914. (Lance J. Bronnenkant)

'It did not escape him that the new [Turkish] rulers lacked practical experience and daily practice in their new professions. But he hoped that their patriotism, their fervour and their intelligence would compensate for it.'[26]

When he returned home in 1913, von der Golz heard from ranking War Ministry members of their concern that Germany's youth needed to become physically and mentally prepared for war; to be imbued with the spirit he reported witnessing in Turkey. Consequently, 'in order to awaken in the … current generation the spirit of warlike capability and to have it become accustomed to soldierly discipline and toil, he returned to national service and helped to develop the Jungdeutschland-Bund; he became its first chairman.'[27]

The Bund grew into an umbrella organisation for all groups of young men who were keen on physical fitness training, as noted in its founding statement of December 1911: 'We need a strong race for the future of our people. Only a militant youth ensures the state and nation of a happy future. History teaches [this lesson] for all times …'[28] Ultimately the head of eleven regional associations folded into one national organisation, von der Goltz said that, through the Jungdeutschland-Bund, German children would be raised: 'in a martial spirit and inspired … from the earliest age with a love for the Fatherland, for which they might have to sacrifice.'[29]

While leading the local branch of the Bund, Rudolf Berthold further refined his leadership and motivational talents:

> 'Every secondary school pupil and apprentice of a similar age … wanted to join in when his companions marched out to the sound of pipes and drums behind the powerful [symbol of the] black-white-red banner. Every Saturday and Sunday they went out in city neighbourhoods, at first in small and then in larger gatherings. And in the middle of the youths marched the very embodiment of an officer, a leutnant of the Tauentzeiner-Regiment: Rudolf Berthold.
>
> 'From the beginning, leading this group of youths was a well-loved responsibility. To help implant a national awareness in the youth, which was attracted early to a vigorous defence of the Fatherland, that was … a welcomed and heart-warming fulfilment of the, at times, systematic and tedious service with the troops ... Berthold maintained his stature among the impetuous youths … He recalled the war games of his youth in Ditterswind and so for him there was no nicer Sunday [outing] than a field exercise with the Jungdeutschland-Bund.'[30]

The Bund was so effective that, at the outbreak of World War I, it 'numbered three-quarters of a million members' – all well-motivated recruits for the army and navy.

In the Fliegertruppe
Meanwhile, as Berthold settled into his new profession, he became aware of other military service opportunities. One of them was the Fliegertruppe [flying service], which had been under development since 4 July 1910 and became part of the German army organisation

on 1 October 1912.[32] Berthold was devoted to his family and wrote many letters home, detailing his experiences. But, as an army career itself was a dangerous undertaking, he would not have wanted to worry his parents and siblings further by mentioning a nascent interest in such a perilous activity as flying in a fragile wooden-framed machine covered with fabric. Consequently, he noted only that, in the summer of 1914, he had been given a 'special assignment' to a flying school[33] not far from his regiment. In fact, Berthold had volunteered to receive flight training.

The Fliegerschule der Halberstädter Flugzeugwerke [Flying School of the Halberstadt Aeroplane Works] was an early centre of German aviation activity. The factory produced license-built versions of the Bristol two-seat mid-wing monoplane and the school offered instruction to prospective civilian and military airmen. Among its pre-war pupils was Leutnant Oswald Boelcke, who later became an early developer of air combat tactics and one of Germany's highest-scoring fighter aces. Boelcke attended the school at about the same time as Rudolf Berthold and described to a friend a nearly idyllic setting for pupils:

Berthold's mother, Helene, seen here later in life, after two of her sons and her husband had died. (Heinz J. Nowarra)

'We are on duty only in the morning; the afternoons are completely free – for playing tennis, lying about in the sun or going to the mountains. One could not think of a more pleasant assignment.

'If only the duty were not <u>so</u> agreeable and, preferably, we were pestered to do a bit more. Of course, when we have good flying weather, we are awakened at 3:30 a.m. and are supposed to begin work at 4:00 – if only there were something to do and we did not have to stand around endlessly without purpose and wait!

'We have four instructors here, each of whom has a training aeroplane (... with two steering columns, one ... controlled by the instructor, the other by the pupil) and three pupils whom he instructs one after the other. Our machines are 70-horsepower Bristol-*Taube* [*sic*] types, which, for training, have the one good quality of being rather slow. But at times they have a bad habit of not wanting to do anything at all: when the weather is warm or the engine is not quite first-rate, then the beasts cannot carry two men higher than five to ten metres and they only taxi around on the ground, whereby one learns nothing at all about flying.

'Occasionally the pilot becomes fed up after instructing only one pupil. Thus, at times one stands around for four hours and barely has a turn – and that always makes me enormously angry.'[35]

At first, neither Boelcke nor Berthold understood the full impact of events on Saturday, 27 June 1914, when the Austrian Archduke Franz Ferdinand and his wife Sophie were murdered in Sarajevo, the Bosnian capital. During the following weeks, however, the assassination of the heir to the Austro-Hungarian throne helped to catalyse underlying conflicts between the Triple Alliance of Germany, Austria-Hungary and Italy, and the Triple Entente of Britain, France and Russia. When Germany's Kaiser Wilhelm II pledged loyalty[36] to his Habsburg counterpart, two of Europe's oldest royal houses stood shoulder to shoulder. Thus reinforced, the government of Austria's Kaiser Franz Joseph I imposed harsh demands on Serbia, which was seen as responsible for events in Bosnia, and that move resulted in military plans being strengthened across Europe.

Boelcke remained at Halberstadt without interruption, while Berthold's aviation training was nearly cancelled as a result of these developments. On 1 July Berthold was recalled to his regiment in Wittenberg, where he noted: 'For months I had not marched a single step or taken part in a field manoeuvre. Now, sometimes my feet did not want to go; one unlearns how to march too quickly. In aviation service one sits either in an aeroplane or in a car...'[37]

Berthold was required to take part in two weeks of infantry drills before he could return to Halberstadt – and now he was further behind his peers in the training cycle. But, while some conditions remained the same, the mood among his regimental comrades had changed, as he wrote in mid-July:

'In the *Kasino* [officers' mess] there is only one topic of discussion: war ... This time we all agree that it will come to this. My thoughts race ahead. Will we prevail? Full of confidence, we will confront the future ... We suspect and feel and know that it will explode – and yet everything is so peaceful ... Our drills are the same as every other year at this time, yet everything has an entirely different appearance ... We still use practice ammunition.'[38]

On Friday, 17 July, Rudolf Berthold was formally transferred from his regiment to the Fliegertruppe. With his service status now permanent, he could concentrate on the true passion of his military life. He poured out his feelings into his diary:

'I had to return to the flying school at Halberstadt ... I still had to take my first and second pilots' examinations. Until now I had been trained as an observer. But I wanted to steer the aeroplane myself! I can no longer climb into an aeroplane with anyone else; in my mind, I am steering and become restless when I notice uncertainty in a pilot. Perhaps that comes about because my old training pilot secretly taught me how to fly ...

'I believe that very few are really aware of how beautiful flying is. With a little pressure on the control column I guide the aeroplane and compel it to do my will, within the forces of nature, and to dare to do battle with those forces. I envy the pilots who, completely trained, have their aeroplanes.

'Very few of them truly make the best use of their domain; they are satisfied when they have made some circuits around the airfield during calm weather and are gazed at as dashing fellows by the crowd. My fingers itch to be at the controls: I want to fly high, far away, where no one sees me, alone with my bird. I want to leave all the pettiness behind me, I want to be free and surpass the birds in flight ...'[39]

Three days later Berthold was back in Halberstadt. He viewed the, by now inexorable, path to war with widely-mixed emotions, at once seeming not to comprehend what was going on and, in the next moment, eager for it to happen. He wrote:

'The training aeroplanes were out on the airfield. A peculiar feeling came over me: Patched up in every spot, they did not look really ready for war. There were few pupils here ... One flew especially well: Boelcke. He was ready and waiting to be recalled to his aviation unit. One look at him shows that he flies because it makes him happy. Boelcke has already passed his second examination; however, in the event of mobilisation, I will definitely be an observer ... What a shame that out of consideration for the equipment, in fear of every crack, it was flown so little. That makes me sad ... if only I were away from here!'[40]

Mobilising for War
Berthold got his wish following the defining event on Tuesday, 28 July, when the government of Austria-Hungary declared war on Serbia. Allegedly, the action was taken to exact retribution for the assassination of Archduke Franz Ferdinand, but it only gave Russia a reason to mobilise. In turn, Germany also militarised, which filtered down to effect Berthold by ending his plans to become a pilot, as he wrote in his diary:

'The situation has become serious. We have just received the mobilisation order. All of the officers have been recalled to their regiments by telegraph. Boelcke and I depart. I have my orders as an observer ...

'I am supposed to report to Grossenhain. I stop on the way at my garrison in Wittenberg ... The streets are swarming with people ... My regiment is to move out the next day ... I can stay only a few hours. I bid farewell to all.

'Who knows if I will see any one of the dear, old comrades again ... All are so happy at the prospect of victory! I love flying and, yet, what I would give if I could move out with my old, dear regiment ... The glass of Sekt [sparkling wine] that I swiftly toss down at my comrades' departure tastes quite tart, as a few furtive tears have fallen into it ...'[41]

Germany supported Austria by declaring war on Russia on Saturday, 1 August, and on France two days later; on the latter date, erstwhile German-Austrian ally Italy proclaimed its neutrality. Germany's subsequent violation of Belgian impartiality was one stated reason for Great Britain to declare war on Germany and Austria-Hungary on 4 August.

During all the commotion of that first day of war, Rudolf Berthold continued his hectic train ride to the Royal Saxon Air Base at Grossenhain.[42] There he would be assigned to one of the squadrons being organised to bring the new dimension of aviation to Germany's military might.

Berthold was by nature an emotional person and, at times, had to work hard at self-control. His diary entry for 1 August showed that his jumbled feelings were finally settling down, as his firm sense of military orderliness took over:

'The farewell in my garrison still had me trembling as I arrived in Grossenhain. The journey was terrible. The general state of war affected everything. The train leaving Wittenberg was overfilled and I had to stand. How I longed to be back with my comrades. But a sense of duty dispelled all soft feelings; now I had to be firm with myself!'[43]

CHAPTER THREE
SERVICE FOR THE NATION

'As soon as it can happen, I want to become a pilot.
Should my ability, my will, always be dependent on another person?
Should the weakness of one person hinder my strength …?'[1]

RUDOLF BERTHOLD

The first few days of World War I were a kaleidoscope of events for Rudolf Berthold. When he departed Wittenberg on that fateful Saturday, 1 August 1914, the streets overflowed with streams of soldiers. They were heading off to trains that would carry them to battlefront staging areas. All were swept up in the passion of the moment.

But, when Berthold arrived in Grossenhain that evening, the city appeared to be a ghost town. After a night during which nervous excitement hardly let him sleep, he was roused and inspired by the sound of Sunday church bells. After breakfast, Berthold's spirits soared further upon seeing, as he wrote in his diary:

> '... an infantry battalion passing by. What a happy and refreshing sight! They are singing, marching with flowers in their buttonholes and on the bayonets of their rifles! They are invincible in their hopes! Despite the seriousness of the situation, they have happy, sparkling eyes. It was as if everyone was part of a big family... As if awakened by a knock at the door, I snap out of my musings … My service for the nation begins.'[2]

Berthold marvelled at the soldiers and cavalrymen he had seen in Wittenberg – all distinguished by orderly rows of uniform designs and colours. Such pageantry and splendid heraldry had drawn him to military service. But, arriving at the Grossenhain airfield a day later, he saw various modes of attire; the Fliegertruppe was so new that it did not have a distinctive uniform. The variety of regimental dress worn by men reporting to the airfield made it hard to comprehend that all of them belonged to a cohesive aviation entity.

While Prussia dominated the German empire since it came into being on 18 January 1871, the Kingdoms of Bavaria, Saxony and Württemberg – and most of the lesser states – continued to send their own regiments into the field and retain links to them. The Kingdom of Prussia wisely allowed this expression of regional heritage and the subsequent mixture of disparate uniforms worn by aviation personnel during the war. In keeping with this sense of military autonomy, the Grossenhain facility was dedicated as a Königlicher Sächsischer Fliegerhorst [Royal Saxon Air Base].[3]

Feldflieger-Abteilung 23 Goes to War

Officially, Berthold was still attached to the 3. Kompanie des Flieger-Bataillons Nr. 1 [3rd Company of Aviation Battalion No. 1], which was also assigned to Saxony.[4] There were five Flieger-Bataillons[5] and all became gathering points for men to be assigned to various aviation units. After reporting to the airfield, Berthold was assigned as an aviation observer to Feldflieger-Abteilung 23 [Field Flying Section 23]. That unit, along with FFAs 24 and 29 and Etappen-Flugzeug-Park 3 [Advanced Area Aeroplane Depot 3][6], were among thirty-four FFAs and eight EFPs established by the Inspektion der Fliegertruppen [Inspectorate of the Flying Service] to provide aerial reconnaissance and bombing for German armies in the field.[7]

FFA 23 was commanded by thirty-two-year-old Oberleutnant [First Lieutenant] Otto Freiherr Vogel von Falckenstein.[8] A pre-war flyer he, in 1911,[9] completed the aviation course at Döberitz, on the western edge of Berlin, and participated in early air events.[10] Vogel von Falckenstein had also been one of three company leaders of Flieger-Bataillon 1 when it was established at Döberitz.[11] Hence, FFA 23 had a seasoned, knowledgeable and well-connected pilot in command.

But, the brisk and effective type of organisation that Berthold witnessed among ground troops dispatched from Wittenberg did not carry over to Germany's new aviation branch. To begin with, FFA 23's standard allotment of six aeroplanes[12] consisted of Mars-Taube [Dove] monoplanes produced by the Deutsche Flugzeugwerke [German aeroplane works] – abbreviated as DFW – in nearby Leipzig. Their low speed made them popular among student pilots, but made them unsuitable for wartime flight operations. The Flieger-Bataillon provided commanding officers for many of the first military field aviation units[13] and FFA 23 leader Vogel von Falckenstein drew on contacts with his former superiors to obtain expedited delivery of more modern replacement machines.

Thus, on the sixth day of mobilisation, Friday, 7 August 1914, FFA 23 headed off to war with new DFW two-seat biplanes.[14] At that point, the efficient German railroad system was sending 550 trains per day[15] to German cities closest to the frontlines in Belgium and France.

A DFW Mars-Taube monoplane, the type first assigned to FFA 23. (Heinz J. Nowarra)

FFA 23's men, aircraft and equipment were on one of those trains, travelling westward across Germany to Montjoie [now called Monschau], south of Aachen, near the Belgian border. FFA 23 was assigned to the German 2nd Army,[16] commanded by Generaloberst [Colonel-General[17]] Karl von Bülow. The 2nd Army was part of a broad 'wheeling' movement intended to sweep through northern Belgium, into central France and then, in concert with Generaloberst Alexander von Kluck's 1st Army, to surround Paris.[18]

At various points during the journey, Berthold wrote in his diary:

'We were on the train for forty-eight hours, which seemed endlessly long … Finally we approached our destination. There was hours-long waiting before we disembarked. One military transport after another plodded through the unloading. The evening sky was blood-red. The muffled rumbling of the cannons gave us an inkling of the severity of the firing at Liège that had begun.'[19]

On Sunday, 9 August, FFA 23 was ordered to send up two-man crews to reconnoitre the area south of Maastricht in the Netherlands, being careful not to violate Dutch neutrality, and over the heavily-defended Belgian fortress cities of Liège and Namur and then south to Dinant to determine the locations of any Belgian or French forces opposing the steadily-advancing German 1st and 2nd Armies that made up the right flank of the invasion force. But once again the new aviation branch experienced growing pains; disassembled aeroplanes and support equipment were not as easily put into action as ground troops and horses. Berthold described the situation:

'Unloading proceeded with feverish haste. Each two-man aircrew competes with the other because each wants to achieve the first flight over the enemy … Some of us already know one another from our peacetime service. The abteilung is made up of six aeroplanes, an Abteilungsführer [literally section leader, actually commanding officer] and adjutants, seven pilots[20] and as many observers.[21] They are really nice fellows. Our leader, Vogel von Falckenstein, has a true Prussian soldier's disposition and is an accomplished old pilot. Everything went so smoothly thanks to his aviation experience and his tireless efforts …'[22]

By Saturday, 15 August, the aircraft were assembled and housed within large hangar-tents on the newly-cleared airstrip. Nearby, smaller tents for aircrews and ground support staff were erected. Later that day, Rudolf Berthold and Leutnant Johannes Viehweger, a pre-war pilot,[23] made FFA 23's first flight over the battlefront. They were armed with a pistol and a rifle for Berthold's use. As the observer, he was in charge of the aeroplane and directed the pilot where to fly; he was also responsible for the aeroplane's defence. He described the mission:

'It was bad weather today, but we advanced to the Meuse river. How proud I am … to be the first observer in the abteilung who has flown ahead of our cavalry and brought back the first report about the enemy! The bullet holes in the wings show that it was not easy for us to be over the enemy territory; we flew an all too straight course [with no zigzagging]. The Army High Command was surprised; they had, perhaps … not given aviation too much credit. Therefore, our flight showed that the aeroplane, through its reconnaissance capability, must have an important significance for the ground troops.

'The flight itself was beautiful, but difficult. Our airfield at Montjoie is in the worst spot imaginable. Big forests stretch out to the south, to the east and west are steep slopes and to the north there is a village … The day came with Belgian fog. One had to recognise it: inscrutably it crept coldly under the skin. We waited for hours, but the fog would not clear. Finally, toward noon, it lifted and cloud formations appeared. Liberated, my pilot and I breathed sighs of relief, hauled the aeroplane out of the hangar-tent, and an hour later we found ourselves over the Ardennes forest, heading toward the French town of Givet, along the Meuse river.

'It was very difficult to gain orientation. At the outset, at 1,000 metres altitude, we had a clear view, but all we saw was forest, endless trees, no railroad line, no river, no valley. For a time, dense fog obstructed every distant view. Then I said to myself: keep going at any cost … And finally the forest below again appeared through the haze. Glittering railroad tracks showed their trail. Far below us, along the Meuse, I saw the enemy working feverishly. It seems that we caught them by surprise, as they still lacked a large body of troops. I assessed the situation and made a sketch of it.

'The engine was running well. The wind was very gusty. My pilot was good at the controls. I pointed my hand to the north. There – with a loud crash – a small white cloud appeared and then another! There was a strange bang in the left wing – we were hit by shrapnel! An anti-aircraft shell almost got us! After a three-hour flight, it was time to go back home, as we had everything we needed.'[24]

Early FFA 23 air operations were carried out with DFW B.I two-seat biplanes with their distinctive 'banana' wings. (Heinz J. Nowarra)

Down Behind Enemy Lines

Two days later, Berthold and Viehweger made a flight to determine whether Belgian or French forces were moving along the Meuse river, where they would come under fire by German forward artillery batteries. Mist, fog and low clouds at about 400 metres obscured any long-range view. But the Army High Command pressed Oblt Vogel von Falkenstein to have his airmen obtain the information. Berthold and Viehweger were in the air only a short time when they became lost. Ever a perfectionist, the observer blamed their sad state on his pilot, later writing in his diary:

'My pilot did not concentrate on my instructions; I had studied the map very carefully so that we could not fly off course. But in order to avoid the clouds, the pilot withdrew ever further to the south and finally had to land and, of course, it was on such a bad piece of ground that the aeroplane's entire undercarriage was bent out of shape ...'[25]

Berthold was enraged by the turn of events, fearing most of all they would be captured. But the first people they met were local villagers, speaking German but probably from Malmédy, a multi-lingual area between Germany and Belgium. The villagers said they saw no German soldiers, but that French cavalrymen were moving through the woods. That was enough for Berthold to lead the dejected Viehweger out of the area.

The two men moved across open fields demarcated by wire fences which, as they passed by and over the barriers, tore at the soft fabric of their flight suits and slowed them down. Berthold was in no mood to talk, but later confided to his diary:

'We were very hungry and had only a belly full of rage. And all that due only to the fleeting mood of a pilot found to be wanting. As soon as it can happen, I want to become a pilot. Should my ability, my will, always be dependent on another person? Should the weakness of one person hinder my strength, which knows no barrier? ... Indeed, I had much time to think about that, for the way back appeared to be endlessly long. The thorns snagged many pieces from my tunic. The forest was so dense.'[26]

By now, their FFA 23 comrades knew that, if Berthold and Viehweger were still alive, they were probably down behind enemy lines. While the rest of the unit moved north that day to a better airfield, closer to Liège, the missing crew would be listed as the unit's first casualties, a distinction that was anathema to the ambitious Berthold. He later became known for his explosive temper and, on this occasion, his unshakeable faith in his own sense of mission enabled him to keep his angry feelings to himself. But, eventually, he must have found a way to voice his disappointment; he never flew again with Viehweger.

As the sun began to set, the two airmen's fortunes brightened. Berthold wrote:

'Toward evening we dared to walk closer to the main road; I had my revolver ready to fire. Carefully, we looked all around us. Then, on the road, like a manifestation of our homeland, came a German bicycle patrol feeling its way along! We dashed forward. There was a hoorah from both sides. Saved! ...

'Our first concern was about our aeroplane. The patrol leader provided the necessary people and then we searched for our bird ... A group of hussars [light cavalry] had found my jacket, which I had thrown away, and saw the abandoned aeroplane. They surmised that we were the crew ... We then explained everything.

'We dismantled our aeroplane for transport to the new airfield. After a full day's journey in a car provided by the 3rd Army commanded by Crown Prince Wilhelm we ended up in Liège. We were greeted joyously by our comrades ...'[27]

Back at their unit, Berthold and Viehweger learned that they were not FFA 23's only casualties on 17 August. Ltn Aribert Müller-Arles and his pilot, Ltn Hans-Joachim von Seydlitz-Gerstenberg, were brought down over French territory. Müller-Arles was severely wounded and taken prisoner. He remained in French captivity until 6 September 1917, when he was interned in Switzerland[28] on humanitarian grounds. Seydlitz-Gerstenberg escaped and made his way back to FFA 23.

From Belgium into France

The German advance proceeded rapidly through Belgium and reached the fortress of Maubeuge, along the Sambre river in northern France, on Sunday, 23 August.[29] The next, day FFA 23 Abteilungsführer Otto Vogel von Falckenstein flew over the advance route as far as Philippeville and Beaumont near the Belgian-French border to confirm the enemy forces' retreat. He selected Ltn Rudolf Berthold to be his observer.[30]

On 26 August, the day that the five Belgian forts at Namur fell, Vogel von Falckenstein again flew over French territory and took Berthold with him. They flew beyond Maubeuge to Valenciennes,[31] the next major objective of the advancing German forces, and returned with useful information. Not so lucky that day, however, was a second FFA 23 crew, which was brought down at Ville Dommange, near Reims, within French lines. The observer, Oblt Karl von Gross,[32] was captured and subsequently died at Villers-aux-Noeuds, in French captivity, on 20 September 1914.[33] There is no mention of von Gross's pilot, who may have escaped to

Oblt Otto Karl Ferdinand Freiherr Vogel von Falckenstein, FFA 23's first commanding officer, flew several missions with Rudolf Berthold. (Tobias Weber)

German lines; thus, no casualty report would have been necessary.[34]

Berthold was assigned to fly with twenty-seven-year-old Oblt Otto Freiherr Marschalck von Bachtenbrock[35] to observe the progress of retreating French troops on Monday, 31 August. The two men flew again on 1 and 3 September[36] and, on the latter occasion, Berthold reported the retreat had deteriorated into chaotic disarray.[37] He wrote:

'We stride from victory to victory. How happy I am when, through my flights, I can help! Now I fly reconnaissance in any weather and keep the Army High Command well informed. My aeroplane is the only one that is always ready to take off. The opponent does not show up at all. Where are the French aerial performers? ... The enemy retreat back to St. Quentin is orderly. Twice a day I determine the movement of the columns. We are hard on the enemy's heels: La Fère and Laon have fallen.'[38]

By late August and early September, the German advance to the Marne river seemed to portend success for the invasion plan and a conclusion of hostilities in France. Berthold's view from the air – far more accurate than any traditional cavalry reconnoitring – reinforced hopes for German success. He wrote:

'Every day I have flown reconnaissance missions. First we followed the retreating enemy incessantly to St. Quentin. They were on forced marches ... and I was amazed by the relatively good bearing of the retreating French columns ... But the soldiers were scarcely across the Marne river when there was no longer any restraint: without discipline they threw away their weapons and knapsacks and fled into the countryside ... I went down to 100 metres' altitude and wrote and sketched what I saw ... The Army High Command's order was clear: "Relentless pursuit!"'[39]

The Battle of the Marne

Other events, however, quickly changed the course of the fighting and led to a reversal of German fortunes. Many books and studies have examined that aspect of World War I combat; for this book it is necessary to note only that, on the westward-moving German right flank, Generaloberst von Kluck's 1st Army and Generaloberst von Bülow's 2nd Army became separated in early September,[40] thereby enabling fresh French troops to advance northward and exploit the gap between the armies in a way that spared Paris from being enveloped by German forces. Consequently, the German drive was halted.

Rudolf Berthold had a unique vantage point to witness the Marne battle's effect on the German advance. But, equipped only with high-powered binoculars and no radio equipment, he could only look on as French reinforcements were transported to Provins, some seventy kilometres south-south-east of Paris. There, the soldiers were formed into columns and led northward less than twenty-five kilometres to La Ferté-Gaucher, a staging area from which to begin their thrust into the gap. Berthold ordered his pilot to return to their airfield quickly so he could deliver his report. Back at the field headquarters, a sceptical staff officer asked him: "Have you perhaps mistaken retreating French troops for advancing soldiers?"[41]

Berthold kept his anger to himself, but later wrote:

'I fumed with rage. At my urging, another aeroplane was sent out; it completely confirmed my observations. I could not keep still and flew yet again: my second report gave an even clearer picture. Ever more Frenchmen had poured into the gap between the 1st and 2nd Armies ... In my third report I stated: "The opposition has passed through and is already behind our lines."'[42]

Berthold and his pilot, Otto Marschalck von Bachtenbrock, took off again and made an extensive reconnaissance beginning in the 1st Army sector to the north. After they returned three hours later, Berthold was ordered to report directly to Generaloberst von Bülow. The seventy-one-year-old general, a Franco-Prussian War veteran,[43] listened intently as Berthold stated: 'The opposition is advancing with strong columns between the 1st and 2nd Armies. It is heading north and has already crossed over the Marne.'[44]

On Sunday, 13 September 1914, Berthold was again summoned to Generaloberst von Bülow's headquarters. By then, the original plan had been abandoned[45] and German general staff planners were adjusting to new developments. But for Rudolf Berthold this meeting with the general was a joyous occasion, as he was presented with the Iron Cross 2nd Class, which 'in the first year of the war ... was a highly-regarded military award'.[46]

Berthold immediately recognised the design of the badge, a cross *pattée* with arms that are narrow at the centre and broaden out at the perimeter; the design had been used for nearly eight centuries by the Teutonic Knights, who displayed it on their shields, breastplates and banners. The Iron Cross became the emblem of a military award when instituted by Prussian King Friedrich Wilhelm III on 10 March 1813 for his subjects who were fighting Napoleon Bonaparte; the award was renewed on 19 July 1870 by King Wilhelm I during the Franco-Prussian War, and on 5 August 1914 by Kaiser Wilhelm II.[47] Even though the 1st and 2nd Class awards were issued to officers and enlisted men alike, as well as some civilians of all German states,[48] the ribbon issued with the medal bore Prussia's colours of black and white. Variations of the same cross *pattée* also graced the fuselages and wings of German aircraft during World War I.

Back at his airfield, Berthold's immense pride in this great honour was so great that he even noted the time, 8:00 p.m., on the letter he wrote home:

'An hour ago I received the Iron Cross 2nd Class. Apart from General von Bülow, I am the first [person in the 2nd Army] to wear this ... solemn badge. It had just arrived from supreme headquarters. I still cannot grasp that it is real and that this black and white ribbon is on my uniform. I kissed the cross ... and yet I did nothing more than my duty...'[49]

The Battle of the Aisne

The evening's award ceremony capped a good day for Generaloberst von Bülow. Earlier that day, German forces had withdrawn across the Aisne river to higher ground, to dig in, in order to withstand the British Expeditionary Force and French troop concentrations that followed them. Called the First Battle of the Aisne, this action resulted in a German 'line of defence which ran along the heights from east of Compiègne to north of Reims ... [in which there would be] dogged fighting with attacks and counter-attacks, but [with] little or no real progress [being made]'.[50] Ultimately, these attacks 'did not cease until the opposing armies raged along a line of trenches stretching from the Swiss frontier to the coast of Belgium'.[51]

Bad weather in mid-September restricted flying until the 20th, as Berthold noted:

'Finally the weather again improved somewhat. Quickly, an aeroplane was sent off ... The gap between the 1st and 2nd Armies had still not been closed, despite the shifts in position. The troops advancing from Maubeuge were engaged in heavy fighting south of Laon; our flank near Berry-au-Bac was in great danger and therefore we headed there. To the northeast, I saw strong troop concentrations – about a division – moving eastward, with much artillery. Friend or foe?

'I ordered my pilot to circle continuously. Then it became clear that they could only be masses of enemy troops. But in order to be quite sure, I had my pilot go down low. Suddenly I felt a hit against my back and I turned around: a French bullet was sticking out of my seat, thereby confirming my hunch. The Army High Command had no idea that so many enemy soldiers were marching here.

'In an instant we were in an aerial combat with a Frenchman. So ... we had to shake off this fellow and then, as quickly as possible, make our report. I had a pistol fitted to a rifle stock,[52] while the Frenchman had a machine gun in his aeroplane ... I aimed as carefully as I would at a firing range, until I saw the whites of the opponent's eyes, then I fired. Suddenly, the enemy machine tilted up and fell away. We did not bother with him further and flew directly toward our lines.

'From afar I saw a long, dark column heading for Fère-en-Tardenois and Soissons. The mystery was solved: the French had pulled troops from their frontlines to roll up our flank. I completed my sketches quite calmly and then we flew back. It was not fast enough for me. After we landed, I jumped out of the aeroplane and into a waiting car and was off to the Army High Command headquarters ... Based on my report, that night, one of our guards divisions was called out. The opposition was apprehended and struck!'[53]

As effective as Berthold and his pilot were, without in-air radio equipment they could not use their aeroplane's full potential for aerial reconnaissance. That failure was influenced by sceptical early German aviators, who saw only disadvantages to carrying heavy, cumbersome electronics gear aboard their frail, underpowered aircraft and were slow to adapt the application of existing technology to newer and better aeroplanes.[54]

Berthold received an advantage of sorts on Monday, 21 September, when FFA 23 was moved closer to the frontlines to reconnoitre the Allied armies. The abteilung was assigned to an airfield at Bazancourt,[55] less than ten kilometres northeast of Reims. Toward the end of the month, the weather turned cold and rainy with blankets of fog, all of which conspired to dissuade even the most devoted flyer. But at least the airmen did not have to dig trenches and build living quarters around them. Rather, they dispossessed residents of civilian houses near their airfield and made themselves much more comfortable than they had been while living in tents. The aircrews at FFA 23 had experienced many long, gruelling flights and were glad for the comfortable rest. That level of personal comfort was enjoyed by most airmen – on both sides – due to the static nature of war that began in 1914. As one historian noted: 'The line established in November 1914 did not move as much as ten miles in either direction until February-April 1917 …'[56]

Never one to stay idle, Rudolf Berthold soon found work to keep himself busy. His aeroplane's engine was now completely worn out and he worked with FFA 23 mechanics on another aircraft to make it airworthy. While in the midst of those labours on Sunday, 4 October, he and Oblt Vogel von Falckenstein were summoned to the Army High Command headquarters. Berthold thought they would be assigned a new mission. He was irritated that the aeroplane was not yet ready to fly.

At the headquarters, and in the presence of officers on his staff, Generaloberst von Bülow presented Berthold with the Iron Cross 1st Class. The young pilot wrote in his diary in the manner of a man who has just had a dream come true:

> 'It was the most beautiful moment in my life so far! I wept for joy that again my chest would be decorated – was it really happening or only a dream? Again, as in the previous instance, I was, after General von Bülow, the first man in our [2nd] army to receive this high award!
>
> 'I am overjoyed …The Iron Cross 1st Class, and for what? That I … was always ready to fly, even when the weather was bad? That I brought back the decisive report about the Marne and Reims? That I never returned from a flight without results and that all my findings were correct and important? I only did my duty …'[57]

A crash at Bazancourt airfield a few days later had the unintended consequence of enabling Rudolf Berthold to return to Germany. Following the accidental death of Unteroffizier [Corporal] Friedrich Ostermann on Thursday, 8 October,[58] Berthold's pilot, Otto Marschalck von Bachtenbrock, refused to fly in any of the abteilung's DFW B.I aeroplanes. Berthold noted that Ostermann 'crashed to his death due to uncertain causes. He flew a new bird, the same type and series that we have. My pilot could not be induced to fly in it further. He wanted to obtain a new bird from the factory. Then we would fly it from Frankfurt or Cologne directly to our airfield …'[59]

On Saturday, 10 October, FFA 23 was ordered to move westward to a new airfield outside St. Quentin in the Picardy section of northern France. The following day, whether due to the current bad weather or Marschalck von Bachtenbrock's impassioned plea, he and Berthold were authorised to head off by train for the DFW factory in the Lindenthal suburb of Leipzig.

Berthold's writings offer no details about his month-long absence from FFA 23, but we can assume that he and Marschalck von Bachtenbrock could have devoted a few days' time to be with their respective families. Then, of course, they could select a new aeroplane that inspired their confidence and arrange to fly it back to the battlefront.

With the strengthening of German 2nd Army positions in the Picardy region, the city of St. Quentin became ever more crowded with military units. Hence, while Berthold and Marschalck von Bachtenbrock were in Germany, on Thursday, 29 October, FFA 23 was relocated to the grounds of Château Roupy, some ten kilometres southwest of St. Quentin.[60]

Events after their return suggest that Berthold took a more than usual interest in the DFW Flying School, also at Lindenthal, which was affiliated with the regional military aviation facility at Grossenhain.[61] For, upon returning to the abteilung, Berthold convinced his superior, newly-promoted Hauptmann [Captain] Otto Vogel von Falckenstein,[62] to release him to the nearby Etappen-Flugzeug-Park 2 [Advanced Area Aeroplane Depot 2] at Château de Grand Priel – subject to immediate recall, as needed – so he could resume his pilot training. Berthold presented a plan that would benefit the abteilung, as he subsequently wrote in his diary:

'Before the war broke out, I had already undertaken a certain amount of training as a pilot ... My activity as an observer during the time of mobile warfare made enormous demands on me. But now, as November brought on bad weather and ...for weeks flying was cancelled, the longing to complete my training as a pilot took hold.

'I went to the aeroplane depot, as I declined to go to a flying school in Germany. I told my Abteilungsführer that I would like to continue to serve as an observer with the abteilung; for, I would want to immediately return as such if I should become only an average pilot. He agreed to that.'[63]

Berthold's request was approved and he was off to EFP 2, which was located on the grounds of a larger and more elegant château, less than fifteen kilometres away.

CHAPTER FOUR
PISTOLS TO MACHINE GUNS

'I view the aeroplane ... as a living thing that must be as one with me. Only he who handles his the way a rider handles his horse would have such ... a bond with his bird that he would never feel so close to it as he does when he leaves the ground and roars over the countryside.'[1]

RUDOLF BERTHOLD

In October 1914, the area around Etappen-Flugzeug-Park 2 was an island of relative tranquillity amidst the war raging at the frontlines. The men at EFP 2 felt secure behind a barrier of fortifications, artillery and ground troops – and under the leadership of an outstanding pre-war military aviator, Hauptmann Normand Knackfuss.[2] To the men at the park, the thunder of artillery fire some twenty-five kilometres to the west was a minor distraction to the activities of their daily lives. Thus, Rudolf Berthold was able to complete his pilot training quickly and uninterrupted. An entry in his diary reflected the positive developments:

> 'Fortunately, I was assigned to be instructed by one of our earliest peacetime flyers, Ernst Schlegel.[3] His greatest quality was that he ... tried to get into the innermost thoughts of his pupils in the aeroplane ... I have Schlegel to thank that I view the aeroplane not as an unfeeling, dead heap; but, rather, at all times as a living thing that must be as one with me.
>
> 'Only he who handles his aeroplane the way a rider handles his horse would have such ... a bond with his bird that he would never feel so close to it as he does when he leaves the ground and roars over the countryside. He who works the control column with a rough hand will never fully be in the soul of the aeroplane and trust it. That is really the first prerequisite for a good flyer.'[4]

While at EFP 2, Rudolf Berthold became friends with twenty-four-year-old Leutnant der Reserve [Second Lieutenant, Reserve] Hans Joachim Buddecke, who had learned to fly in the USA and returned to Germany after the war began. Buddecke[5] had been commissioned in the Leibgarde-Infanterie-Regiment (1. Grossherzoglich Hessisches) Nr. 115 – one of the oldest regiments in the German army[6] – but, rather than return to that unit, he was qualifying as a military pilot. He confided to Berthold that he had 'problems' with his commanding officer, Hptm Alfred Keller[7] of Feldflieger-Abteilung 27.

Keller forbade Buddecke from practicing tight turns and other aggressive air combat manoeuvres, and refused his request to fly a monoplane fighter aircraft.[8] Hence, Buddecke asked Berthold to urge Hptm Vogel von Falckenstein to request him for FFA 23. Berthold

Staff and student pilots at Etappen-Flugzeug-Park 2 enjoyed the amenities at Château de Grand Priel. Attendees at a pleasant weekend outing were, in the top row, Hptm Normand Knackfuss (fourth from left) and Ltn Rudolf Berthold (sitting on the banister). In the lower row, Ltn.d.Res Hans Joachim Buddecke (far right) and (second from right) an unidentified observer from FFA 32. (Tobias Weber)

did not have to work hard to persuade his superior to accept such an experienced pilot as Buddecke.

Berthold wrote in his diary:

'Of all the comrades [at EFP 2], Buddecke is the closest to me. Loyal and sincere, he is a daredevil to the point of recklessness; tenacious and with no consideration for himself, yet he is also full of empathy and is so modest. We have at all times stuck together and will remain good friends in the future.'[9]

Just as friendship bonded Berthold to Buddecke, admiration linked him to his civilian flight instructor Ernst Schlegel, about whom he wrote:

'Only a few ... flights with Schlegel were enough to inspire me with trust for my aeroplane. One day I just flew alone. It was so obvious that I did not feel any insecurity for even a moment; on the contrary, I was never so proud and happy as I was on the day of my first solo flight. After the first smooth landing, I would have preferred to continue flying if Schlegel, exercising his authority, had not stopped me ...

'In rapid succession ... I flew all of the aircraft types that were then in use at the frontlines. In early January 1915, I reported to my abteilung that from this time forward I would like to be deployed as a pilot.

'Shortly before my return to the abteilung, Schlegel became ill and I had to take over for him in performing acceptance flight tests of new machines [arriving at EFP 2]. How proud I was that such trust was placed in my flying skill ... furthermore, test flying the machines offered the great advantage of further improving my training. By dismantling new machines one may encounter one or two little flaws that would otherwise hardly be noticed ... If one overlooks the smallest flaws, then the aeroplane will crash. For me, these testing flights were the best way to probe the airworthiness of the aeroplane ...'[10]

Pre-war pilot Ernst Schlegel (left) presented this signed photo to Rudolf Berthold (right) as a memento of their flying experiences at EFP 2. (Greg VanWyngarden)

Berthold was anxious to return to his unit, but he departed from EFP 2 with conflicted feelings about the war. He confided to his diary:

'Yes, it was a beautiful time ... at the Flugpark! No discord ever disturbed our being together; our comrades were all happy, yet serious-minded... [and] we passed many carefree hours together. How cosy it was to sit by the big officers' mess window after lunch ...

'During the evenings, from time to time, we took a little stroll to St. Quentin; we also wanted to see people again. Here and there in passing one caught a fiery glance – mostly filled with hatred – from a pretty little French woman … And, evidently, that is how we were viewed by some of the inhabitants, as nothing more than feared "barbarians" …

'There we were joyously happy for the moment. Perhaps one would be dead in the morning. That was the emotional relationship between seriousness and joy, between duty and freedom; both righteous, both understanding.'[11]

A Leader Falls

Sunday, 10 January, 1915 started out as a marvellous day for Rudolf Berthold. He had fulfilled his qualifications at Château de Grand Priel and headed back to FFA 23 to complete a few final requirements for the Militär-Flugzeugführer-Abzeichen [military pilot's badge],[12] which would be a proud addition to his uniform. But, as he wrote, the day turned out to be dreadful:

'How I looked forward to rejoining my old abteilung. Instead, the return was one of the hardest days of my life. For, our leader, Hptm Vogel von Falckenstein, to whom I was loyally devoted, had not returned from a combat mission on the day I arrived … After that, it always seemed to me that I had to search for him. My only thought was how to wipe his loss out of my mind. I flew and worked until I was so tired that I collapsed, and then struggled to my feet again with one thought always in mind: "He did not return from a combat mission."'[13]

Upon Rudolf Berthold's return from EFP 2 he learned that Hptm Otto Freiherr Vogel von Falckenstein had been forced down and killed in this aircraft, Rumpler B.I 483/14. (Heinz J. Nowarra)

Fierce ground fighting had taken place that morning as German forces defended their positions at La Boisselle, northeast of Albert,[14] in the Somme sector. FFA 23 was ordered to provide aerial reconnaissance of the area. Serving as observer this time, Hptm Vogel von Falckenstein undertook the mission in a new biplane, Rumpler B.I 483/14. His pilot was a man new to the abteilung, Oblt Franz Keller.[15]

The German flyers' mission took them over French territory, west of Albert, where they were spotted by the crew of a two-seat French Morane-Saulnier Type L high-wing monoplane. The two aircraft were evenly matched in terms of firepower – the Rumpler's observer was armed with a rifle[16] and his French counterpart with a carbine[17], but the latter had an advantage: the pilot, Sergent Eugène Gilbert,[18] was a seasoned pre-war flyer who, by this time, had already participated in downing two German aircraft.

Gilbert and his observer, Lieutenant Alphonse Bros de Puechredon, closed in to do battle. Gilbert manoeuvred into a favourable position and his observer fired shots that forced their adversaries to land at Rainneville, southeast of Villers-Bocage. The German pilot was wounded and taken prisoner; his observer had been killed.[19]

FFA 23's Hptm Vogel von Falckenstein and Oblt Franz Keller were brought down by a Morane-Saulnier Type L monoplane of the kind seen here. (Volker Koos)

A French account of the 10 January aerial combat, filed by the Reuters news agency, appeared later in the month in Germany:

'No doubt with the intention of ramming his adversary, the German flyer turned his aeroplane and fired in a direct line at the Frenchmen. A sharp turn saved the latter from the, apparently inevitable, catastrophe. The French observer now fired four well-aimed shots.

'The first bullet hit the German observer Captain von Falckenstein in the heart, the second smashed the upper arm of the pilot, the third wounded him in the neck and the fourth penetrated the radiator of the engine. Despite his severe wounds, the pilot succeeded in bringing his machine to the ground intact. The landing of both machines occurred within French lines ...

'And what happened next was a scene that made an unforgettable impression on the men looking on: slowly the German pilot climbed out of his machine, approached and offered his uninjured hand to the French observer and said in flawless French: "Although the battle turned out to be not in our favour, I am still proud to have duelled with so worthy an adversary."'[20]

While the German pilot's gallant tribute to the French crew may have been true, it was among a number of early World War I aviation-related anecdotes that gave rise to a myth that combat airmen on both sides were members of an élite flying fraternity that was bound by a chivalric code of honour. In fact, most combat flyers, including Rudolf Berthold, understood warfare and were intent on destroying their enemies.

Vogel von Falckenstein was succeeded in command of FFA 23 by thirty-one-year-old Hptm Karl Seber,[21] who had reported to the unit in October 1914, while Rudolf Berthold was back in Germany, taking delivery of a new aeroplane. Seber quickly established himself as a tenacious aerial combatant. During one mission, he and his pilot, Oblt Gottfried Glaeser, dropped bombs on the rail yard at Amiens and apparently shot down a French two-seater. Although they may not have been victorious, as there was no corresponding French casualty,[22] the following July, Seber and Glaeser were honoured for their actions during that fight.

They received the Kingdom of Saxony's *Ritterkreuz des Militär-St.-Heinrichs-Orden* [Knight's Cross of the Military St. Henry Order], the first of four steps in a series of

Hptm Karl Seber, an observer and FFA 23's second commanding officer, later helped to found the Finnish Air Force. (Heinz J. Nowarra)

honours that comprised the highest Saxon bravery award (which was also the oldest military order of all the German states).[23] Seber's citation for the award makes an interesting, but inaccurate, Saxon claim to the unit:

'Leader of the Royal Saxon Feldflieger-Abteilung 23 ... Hptm Seber performed heroically as an observer on many occasions. He carried out an especially gallant act on 18 November 1914, when, with Oblt Glaeser, he forced down a superior French aeroplane with shots from a pistol on their return from Amiens.'[24]

A Pilot at Last

Meanwhile, on Monday, 18 January 1915, Rudolf Berthold completed his flying qualifications, which included a flight over the frontlines. Once again, his personal sense of mission prevailed when he described that accomplishment:

'I am a pilot! Yesterday, I passed the final test. As of today I wear the Militär-Flugzeugführer-Abzeichen! Finally, I have attained what I had strived for in peacetime. Now I am a fully-qualified flyer, independent of the will of another person in the aeroplane. There are good reasons why I pressed on to become a pilot … Over the course of time my activities as an observer did not completely satisfy me. It was just as if I were only flying for fun. Also, my pilot did not suit me at all … Now it has turned out well: I feel like a victor, so inwardly liberated!'[25]

Now in control – rather than in charge – of the aeroplane, Berthold could be more aggressive during combat flights and perhaps even use his hand-held sidearm to help bring down an opponent. FFA 23's old aeroplanes had been replaced by much better Rumpler B.I and Albatros B.II biplanes. Berthold was familiar with the latter, having flown them with his flight instructor, Ernst Schlegel, and he was happy to have been assigned one. To further improve the situation, in mid-February, Berthold was paired with an eager and energetic observer, Ltn Josef Grüner.

After the French report of Hptm Vogel von Falckenstein's death became public knowledge, Berthold was certain that he had seen the French pilot responsible. He meant to avenge his former commanding officer, as he noted in his diary:

'A French monoplane often crosses over Amiens. I know the fellow well, as my Abteilungsführer was his victim. Woe unto him if he comes in front of my pistol!

FFA 23 airmen posed for this view with a new aeroplane. Standing are (from left): Ltn Trentepohl, pilot; Ltn Hans-Joachim Freiherr von Seydlitz-Gerstenberg, pilot; Oblt Franz André Paul Souchay, observer; Hptm Karl Seber, abteilung leader; unknown; Hptm Eberhard Bohnstedt, observer; Oblt Fritz Böhmer; Ltn.d.R Anton Hirsemann, observer; Oblt Friedrich Schueler van Krieken, observer; and Ltn.d.Res Erwin Tütschulte, pilot. Seated are (from left): Ltn Walter Gnamm, observer, and Ltn Rudolf Berthold, pilot – others unknown. (Heinz J. Nowarra)

I challenge him almost daily. He always appears quite suddenly, soon sits behind me or close above my aeroplane so that I cannot see his face.

'As we still do not have machine guns in our aeroplanes – only rifles and pistols have been issued – I prefer to rely on making aerial manoeuvres until I have him at a disadvantage. One time I succeeded in flying right above him. I shouted to my observer: "Shoot him!" The shot thundered. The other observer threw his hands into the air and the French machine went straight down. But, as it turned out, we had not hit the aeroplane.'[26]

Following the French and British counter-attack along the Marne in September 1914 and the advent of static trench warfare, German forces concentrated on outflanking the Allies' northern wing. Thus, there was heavier fighting in Flanders, much to Berthold's disappointment, as seen in his comments about lighter activity in April and May 1915:

'In recent months the frontlines have been, and are still, fairly quiet. The flyers' reports are almost always the same. Opposite Paris, nothing had changed. We photographed much of the area. Often, I flew over enemy territory, with the area around Amiens as my target. I tried to go as far as possible behind enemy lines; for, only in that way does one gain a clear view of the opposition ... Only a few of our aeroplanes have succeeded in crossing over all the way to Amiens. I am proud that on every flight I made at least some turns over Amiens. Moreover, I never flew without bombs. The target was always Amiens ...'[27]

In response to these attacks, grouped French bomber units flew over German-held territory and targeted airfields. In turn, on Wednesday, 26 May, German 2nd Army headquarters ordered its sector's Feldflieger-Abteilungen to bomb French airfields and aviation depots.[28]

Aside from the light combat activity, Berthold was content with his success and certainly with the quality of the men with whom he served. In June, he reflected:

'I succeeded in having Buddecke transferred to my abteilung. Now we have all splendid fellows, such as: Oblt Fritz Böhmer; Leutnant der Reserve Anton Hirsemann; Ltn.d.Res Erwin Tütschulte; Rittmeister [Cavalry Captain] Friedrich Schueler van Krieken[29] and Ltn Josef Grüner – all forceful officers of the good, old style, firm as iron in performing their duties and in service overall.

'In terms of distances flown and numbers of combat missions, each crew seeks to surpass the others. True flying spirit. All for one and one for all! Moreover, we have the splendid ... Hptm Karl Seber [commanding officer] and Hptm Eberhard Bohnstedt[30] [executive officer] at the head of the abteilung. Both constantly strive to keep us all out of trouble, the emphasis and attitude is always refreshing and the same spirit is raised among the non-flying mechanics and non-rated men. They do not have it easy, but they do the job.

'Ltn Hans-Joachim von Seydlitz-Gerstenberg[31] – or, as I call him "Seidenspitz"[32] – is, to be sure, the most superb of them all. Although severely wounded in an air fight and not yet completely healed, he fled from the military hospital and tried desperately to be able to continue to fly; to do that, he had to be lifted into the aeroplane.'[33]

Berthold knew that it took more than iron will to prevail during defensive or offensive aerial combat. When FFA 23 received the weapons it needed, he wrote in his diary:

'At last ... our reconnaissance aeroplanes are being equipped with machine guns. The French already had them even in peacetime ... Machine guns for our aeroplanes came only sporadically. Now, a year after the war began, many aeroplanes still have only pistols. We cry out for machines that attack – we do not want aircraft that retreat.'[34]

The delay in equipping German aircraft with machine guns is inexplicable. In 1920, the pre-war aviation organiser and chronicler Major Georg Paul Neumann[35] wrote:

'Even before the war, thought had been given to using the capability of the air-cooled machine gun as the best suited ... weapon for aerial combats, which, admittedly, were hardly anticipated. But testing was not completed, despite several recommendations, including having the fixed machine gun controlled by the engine [i.e., able to fire through the propeller arc], patents for which existed before the war...

'Above all, the aeroplane was seen as a strategic means of long-range reconnaissance flights, and aerial combats were not considered ... Thus, it was [not until] the spring of 1915 that the air-cooled Parabellum machine gun was installed, initially for the observer, for defensive purposes ...'[36]

Berthold's observer had an opportunity to use his new swivel-mounted machine gun on Tuesday, 8 June, when French forces attacked the German 52nd Infantry Division on the Somme sector. In response, Feldflieger-Abteilungen 23, 27 and 32, supported by the Bavarian FFA 1b,[37] were out in force, photographing French positions and engaging enemy aircraft. But Berthold garnered no individual glory that day, which may have frustrated him. He was a rather highly-strung individual and had a pressing need to be in action continually. A short time later, the otherwise robust Berthold collapsed, perhaps due to anxiety, about which he wrote:

'As to my nervous system, I have not changed much; I am still the same old fellow, I feel as fresh as before. My collapse in June was probably of a serious nature, but soon resolved. Only my stomach nerves are not holding up. At first, the doctor thought it was dysentery, but after two weeks I was back to my old self.'[38]

Fighters and Bombers Arrive

Further, Berthold may have been comforted by news about a new German machine gun development. Forward-firing and synchronised to fire through the propeller arc, the gun was installed on the new Fokker Eindecker [monoplane] fighter in May 1915[39] and such guns could be fitted to two-seaters used by units such as FFA 23.

Meanwhile, the abteilung had begun using AEG G.II two-engine bomber aircraft and Rudolf Berthold had been sent to the factory at Hennigsdorf, near Berlin, to take delivery of one. It was among Germany's largest aircraft: with a wingspan of 52 feet and 6 inches, length of 29 feet and 10 inches and a loaded weight of 5,434 lbs.[40]

AEG G.II 21/15 seen shortly after Berthold delivered it to FFA 23. (Heinz J. Nowarra)

In August 1915, Berthold wrote in his diary:

'For months we have flown the Grosskampfflugzeug, which we call the "Big Barge". It has two engines that together produce 300 horsepower. It has places for two to three observers, two machine guns and can carry a bomb-load of 200 kilograms. I have flown it in combat and it is well suited ...'[41]

At about the same time, Berthold contended that he 'passed' on the opportunity to fly one of the nimble little single-seat Fokker fighters. He stated: 'In July, I was supposed to receive a Fokker Eindecker. I gave it up in favour of Buddecke, who asked me to do so. He was familiar with the type from his time in America ...'[42]

But there is more to the story. In the summer of 1915, the synchronised machine-gun-armed Fokker was unique to aerial warfare and, while German commanders were pleased by its success, they also feared its capture. A German 3rd Army air commander spoke for his peers in other army groups when he reported: 'These aeroplanes go up only to repel [enemy] aircraft that have broken through [our defences]; they have orders to not cross the lines under any circumstances.'[43]

Most likely, that restriction caused the ever-aggressive Berthold to have second thoughts about flying FFA 23's first Fokker Eindecker. As he wrote in his diary:[44]

'I do not want a Fokker yet, as one may not fly over the frontlines ... and I do not want to be a rear-area flyer. The little bird is indeed good in attacking, but it is flown too little at the Front; it would be ideal if I had both [my AEG and the Fokker] and could fly each as needed. It is unfortunate that one cannot attack with the G-type, but it is too unwielding for that purpose. Controlling the long wings, which are like arcs, takes a great effort in terms of flying.'

Hinting at the real reason he received the new fighter aircraft, Hans Joachim Buddecke wrote: '... finally I got my Fokker, which scarcely anyone else wanted'.[45]

Buddecke was not bothered by constraints, as he knew British and French aircraft would venture over German-held territory. And Berthold was happy, for the moment, that he could attack Germany's adversaries within their own lines.

Consequently, it was supposed to be a routine event when, on Wednesday, 15 September 1915, Rudolf Berthold took off in AEG G.II 21/15 on a bomb-dropping mission over French lines. The sudden appearance of heavy storm clouds, however, compelled him to cancel the flight and return urgently to his airfield at Roupy. But no sooner had the big bomber touched down

Dutch-born aircraft manufacturer Anthony H.G. Fokker and an early unarmed model of the monoplane that, when equipped with a synchronised machine gun, gave Germany an advantage in early aerial combats. (Volker Koos)

when it nosed over. The long wings and double landing gear, one under each engine, made landing the AEG G.II difficult at times and this type of accident was not uncommon. In any case, neither Berthold nor any of his crew had been injured, but the aeroplane was badly damaged and had to be dismantled and sent back to Germany by rail.[46]

Berthold could only return to flying two-seat reconnaissance aeroplanes.

CHAPTER FIVE
THE FIGHTER ACE ERA BEGINS

'Berthold always had big plans, so he was never at a loss for words.
His thoughts were already far ahead, on the first gust of wind,
the first shot of anti-aircraft fire over the lines... he could already
envision ... how to manoeuvre the approach.'[1]

HANS JOACHIM BUDDECKE

While Rudolf Berthold carried out reconnaissance flights from Roupy, reports began to circulate within the Fliegertruppe of two Fokker Eindecker pilots from Feldflieger-Abteilung 62 who were gaining success and recognition by individually shooting down hostile aeroplanes. By this time, FFA 62's Leutnant Oswald Boelcke had scored two aerial victories while flying one of the diminutive and deadly Fokkers[2] and his comrade Ltn Max Immelmann had two confirmed 'kills' and claimed two others[3] with his Fokker. Then, on Sunday, 19 September 1915, Berthold's best friend in FFA 23, Ltn.d.Res Hans Joachim Buddecke successfully brought down a British two-seater for his first air combat triumph[4] – also while flying a Fokker Eindecker.

Berthold celebrated an achievement of another sort when, on 21 September, he was promoted to Oberleutnant.[5] A few days after that, he was off to Germany to take delivery of FFA 23's replacement bomber, AEG G.II 26/15.[6] Given the short time he was away from the unit, Berthold must have flown – or been flown – about 800 kilometres to the AEG factory and then returned in the new aeroplane. At a normal cruising speed of about 100 kilometres per hour, the journey by air would have taken a day and a half, with re-fuelling stops; the journey by rail could have taken from several days, including stops and train changes.

Due to intermittent bad weather at the end of September 1915,[7] Berthold first flew AEG G.II 26/15 in combat on Friday, 1 October. The mission was a flight of over 100 kilometres each way from Roupy, west of St. Quentin, to a major British barracks complex at Abbeville and back. Capable of a maximum speed of just over 145 kph[8] and including time to circle over the target, the AEG could make the entire flight in just over two hours – longer if there were strong head winds. Berthold was accompanied by his favourite observer/gunners, Leutnants Josef Grüner and Walter Gnamm.

Returning from Abbeville during favourable weather the following day, Berthold and his crew were attacked by a Vickers F.B.5,[9] and eluded it. The crew made almost daily bombing and reconnaissance flights over hostile territory – on 4 October, for example, they dropped 200 kilograms of high explosives on the Abbeville barracks.[10] But Berthold surely regarded the abwehr [air defence] missions they flew on 15, 18 and 22 October as highly desirable.[11] During those sorties, their AEG served as a well-armed gunship, ready

The château at Roupy was expropriated for housing and its spacious grounds became an airfield for FFA 23 in 1915.

to deal with hostile aircraft. In that capacity, they bolstered flights ordinarily assigned to FFA 23's Fokker Eindeckers.

Royal Visitors

Berthold and his crew reported no aerial combat during those flights, but they had a harrowing experience on Saturday, 23 October. That afternoon, FFA 23 prepared for an inspection visit by high ranking officers and dignitaries on a battlefield tour to boost troop morale. This group included Prince August Wilhelm of Prussia, the twenty-seven-year-old fourth son of the kaiser, and Duke Ernst August of Braunschweig. Berthold was scheduled for a flight to Abbeville, after which he would be on hand to welcome the visitors.

On the way out to his aeroplane, Berthold encountered Hans Joachim Buddecke, who recalled:

'Berthold always had big plans, so he was never at a loss for words. His thoughts were already far ahead, on the first gust of wind, the first shot of anti-aircraft fire over the lines; even before the hours that would bring him over Amiens to the coast, he could already envision the encampment at the mouth of the Somme river and how to manoeuvre the approach. He was angry ... as he always was up to the moment of success. In the meantime, his nervous tension proclaimed itself in exquisite expletives, which he discharged too easily at his two observers – even during the most difficult moments in the air ...

'[Before take-off] you look at every flyer – you will always find something ... even the bravest person has his own little superstition. Usually it manifests itself in the clothing, but often in other actions, such as before each flight when a comrade urges his observer to rub the propeller for luck.

'Whether it was a superstition with Berthold or something else ... first he put on his regimental uniform jacket, which was actually worn out, even though he had it only since 1914 ... Over the jacket Berthold wore a fur coat, then a scarf, horn-rimmed glasses on his face and a large pair of flying goggles over them, then a thick wool balaclava helmet around the head and ... the crown in the form of an oily brown leather beach hat.[His orderly] Bart had washed this talisman – in hot water, of course – and it shrank and was no longer any sort of head covering. That did not matter. The hat had to be there when Berthold flew...'[12]

The bomber took off and other members of FFA 23 went about preparing for the inspection. The distinguished guests were scheduled to arrive at Roupy airfield at 2:00 p.m. But suddenly, at 1:45, Buddecke was dispatched to nearby St. Quentin to intercept a hostile aircraft heading their way. Soon thereafter he was joined by Ltn.d.Res Ernst Freiherr von Althaus in a second Fokker Eindecker. Just after the fighter pilots left, Berthold returned in the AEG – somewhat the worse for wear, according to Buddecke:

'Many shreds of fabric hung out from the rear observer's seat. Following the attack on Abbeville, a piece of shrapnel from a big shell had passed between the observer's legs without hitting anything. It was a glorious event that the brave lads had survived ...'[13]

Oblt Rudolf Berthold's AEG G.II 26/15 was the focal point of visitors viewing an aerial combat overhead, as during the event on 23 October 1915. (Tobias Weber)

Buddecke pursued his quarry, a British B.E.2c two-seat bomber, down to 100 metres' altitude, within sight of Roupy. The newly-arrived guests joined others at the airfield, watching as the hapless two-seater continued downward. Then, its tail reared up and the biplane plunged to the ground, just short of the airfield.[14]

German soldiers soon arrived at the crash site and removed the bodies of the twenty-seven-year-old pilot, Captain Cecil Hoffnung Marks, and his observer, Second-Lieutenant William George Lawrence, age twenty-five. The observer was a younger brother of Captain (later Lieutenant-Colonel) T.E. Lawrence, best known as Lawrence of Arabia. Subsequently, both British airmen were buried at St. Souplet, northeast of St. Quentin.[15]

The afternoon's display of flying skill and bravery must have impressed Duke Ernst August of Braunschweig, as he took a moment to express his appreciation. A few words to his aide-de-camp produced the necessary tokens of gratitude. At the end of the day's events, Buddecke wrote:

'As the highnesses climbed into their cars and gave all of us good, sincere handshakes, the duke presented three of his crosses with their beautiful blue and yellow ribbons. It was truly splendid.'[16]

Ernst August bestowed a trio of his Duchy's third-highest military decoration, the *Kriegsverdienstkreuz* [War Merit Cross], an honour that he had authorised a year to the day earlier.[17] They went to Buddecke and Althaus for 'protecting a high personage from an enemy bombing attack'.[18] As a noted German World War I aviation awards expert, the late Neal W. O'Connor, wrote: 'protocol would [have] required the duke to recognize [FFA] 23's leader [Hptm Karl Seber, by also] handing out the cross [to him] on this occasion.'[19] Having already received high honours, Rudolf Berthold could appreciate what a fine moment it was, but he probably wondered when his time of glory would come again.

A Deadly Encounter

Berthold and his comrades returned to routine bombing raids until Wednesday, 3 November, when they again shared abwehr duties with FFA 23's two Fokker Eindeckers.[20] The AEG crew returned to Roupy with no success for their efforts, but, three days later, their luck changed when they spotted a Vickers F.B.5 over enemy-held territory and went after it. A Royal Flying Corps communiqué reported: 'When north of Péronne, the [F.B.5 crew] were attacked by a Fokker [*sic*] biplane with passenger and machine gun. Unperceived till within 150 yards, the Fokker dived from 200 feet above them and opened fire at 100 yards.'[21]

The British crew misidentified their opponent but, through skilful flying and proficient aerial gunnery, they drove off their attacker. Again citing the RFC communiqué: 'The ... [F.B.5 crew] are convinced that the observer of this [German] machine was put out of action and other serious damage was done.'[22]

In fact, the British gunner, 2/Lt Edward Robinson of 11 Squadron, RFC, had mortally wounded his German counterpart, Ltn Josef Grüner. Despite Berthold breaking away from the fight to rush his friend to medical facilities at the nearby air depot at Château de Grand Priel, Grüner could not be saved. He died the next day.

Berthold sunk into a deep melancholy over Grüner's death. Perhaps recalling Berthold's delicate emotional state in June, Hptm Seber granted the pilot a few weeks of home leave to recuperate. Seber knew that, when in top form, Berthold was a courageous and valuable member of FFA 23 and now his fragile emotional state needed to heal.

During his time away from the unit, Berthold apparently recovered from this episode of what in today's parlance would be called post traumatic stress disorder. He returned to FFA 23 in a better frame of mind, but now – more than ever – he felt compelled to become a fighter pilot.

A Fokker E.II with a 100-hp engine[23] arrived in October, but Berthold was still on leave and so the aircraft was assigned to Buddecke. Oblt.d.Res Ernst Freiherr von Althaus, a newer pilot, but senior to Berthold in date of rank,[24] flew Buddecke's relatively 'old' Fokker to a nearby aviation facility and received a newer Eindecker.

Berthold understood how he missed that opportunity to be assigned an Eindecker and continued to fly the AEG G.II without complaining. But the lingering memory of Grüner's death inspired in him an even more resolute sense of his duties. He wrote in his diary: 'Now I insist on flying a single-seat aeroplane. I want to be alone. And I will get a single-seater. It will be an older machine, but that is all the same to me. I want only to fly ... alone!'[25]

Until Berthold's wish could be fulfilled, he and other AEG crews had significant roles in taking defensive actions against British and French aircraft over the Somme sector, which would become so important in 1916. Joint flights by FFA 23's AEG and its two Fokkers[26] gave the unit's Eindecker pilots time to refine their skills. Royal Air Force historian H.A. Jones commented on Eindecker tactics during the autumn and winter of 1915:

'The tactical use of fighters was still obscure, and the Fokkers were undoubtedly robbed of their full effectiveness by being allotted in small numbers to various flying units ... to take on what came their way. Their method of attack drew inspiration from the hawk. The Fokker pilot would cruise at great heights ... and await the passing of suitable victims. He would then swoop down from behind, coming when possible out of the sun so that his opponent might have no warning before he was startled by the rattle of a machine gun. One long burst of fire came from the Fokker as it dived past ... If the British [or French] aeroplane was not shot down and persisted in its work, the German pilot would climb again and repeat his swift diving attack ...'[27]

Hans Joachim Buddecke was a successful practitioner of the swift-diving tactic. He shot down three enemy aeroplanes from September through November.[28] Early in December, however, Buddecke was transferred from FFA 23 to an air unit in Turkey to demonstrate his air-fighting skills for Germany's allies in the Ottoman Empire.[29] With that development, Berthold's luck changed. By virtue of his experience, Freiherr von Althaus received a newer Fokker and Berthold was assigned an older machine. He still had to learn how to master the nimble little monoplane, but at last he was a flying alone in a true fighter aeroplane.

Initially, Berthold remained scoreless and his promise to Grüner was unfulfilled. When Althaus shot down British two-seaters on 5 and 28 December,[30] however, Berthold flew with him,[31] continuing to gain valuable operational experience in a Fokker Eindecker.

Birth of a Fighter Unit

In late 1915, various German army group headquarters began to deploy monoplane fighters as operational sub-units to protect reconnaissance and bombing aircraft. Thus, a system of Kampfeinsitzer Kommandos [single-seat fighter detachments] – abbreviated KEKs – was established on the Western Front.32 As part of that effort, on Tuesday, 11 January 1916, a KEK was formed at an auxiliary airfield at Vaux-en-Vermandois,33 a short distance from FFA 23's main airfield at Roupy. As he had more overall flying experience than other pilots in the unit, Rudolf Berthold was designated as officer in charge of the temporarily-assembled KEK Vaux, as the detachment became known. He and Althaus represented FFA 23 and, after more Fokker Eindeckers arrived, they were joined by pilots from other Feldflieger-Abteilungen to form a dedicated fighter unit.

Berthold was pleased with his new circumstances, now that he had the means to aggressively attack enemy aircraft, and he wrote in his diary about his work at Vaux:

'Located about a half hour away from our Feldflieger-Abteilung base, Château Vaux reposes in a big, old park, far away from the main traffic route. When I received my AEG aeroplane last August and I needed space for a big hangar, I decided to use the grounds in the vicinity of the château as an airfield, with the château itself to be our living quarters ... A big barn was converted immediately to house my bird. The fields in front of the barn were transformed into a landing field.

'The whole place was ideal for our purpose, only thirty paces away from where we would stay. We formed a small Kommando [detachment] of six officers and thirty men. We were independent and yet at all times linked to the respective abteilungen.

KEK Vaux took its name from another expropriated château at Vaux-en-Vermandois where German flyers were housed. The adjacent flat landscape made an ideal airfield. (Heinz J. Nowarra)

'Gradually the G-type aeroplanes disappeared from all of the combat aircraft units [whose members made up KEK Vaux] and thus the observers were also reassigned. It became lonely at our place for a short time, but I endured it. When more single-seat fighter aeroplanes came to the [2nd] Army, I assembled my Fokker Kommando. Thus, now we had five single-seaters and, as we flew daily, we held back the French flyers ...

'Single-seaters can be at the Front continuously only, to some extent, during favourable weather, so in January the ... [opposition] was somewhat restrained. The month ... was difficult, and it almost demoralised me. I flew and flew, but did not have an opportunity to fire my guns. I built a dummy aeroplane on the ground and attacked and shot at it diligently. It helped me feel more secure about myself and my ability.'[34]

The new, overly cautious approach to single, and double, aircraft flights over the lines, which had been so successful for Allied airmen, can be attributed to the increasing 'kill' scores recorded by Fokker Eindecker pilots. Reacting to that situation, RFC headquarters ordered on 14 January:

'Until the Royal Flying Corps are in possession of a machine as good as or better than the German Fokker [monoplane] ... a change in the tactics employed becomes necessary ... In the meantime, it must be laid down as a hard and fast rule that a machine proceeding on reconnaissance must be escorted by at least three other fighting machines ... From recent experience ... the Germans are now employing their aeroplanes in groups of three or four, and these numbers are frequently encountered by our aeroplanes. Flying in close formation must be practised by all pilots.'[35]

After the most successful Fokker Eindecker pilots, Oswald Boelcke and Max Immelmann, had each shot down eight aeroplanes, on 13 January 1916 they were presented with the *Orden Pour le Mérite*.[36] Officially the highest bravery award of the Kingdom of Prussia, the decoration became, *de facto*, the German Empire's highest military honour. Attaining it also became keenly desired by most German airmen.

On Wednesday, 2 February, medals were not on Rudolf Berthold's mind as much as the weather: intermittent rain and low clouds

Rudolf Berthold and his ground crew posed uneasily by his Fokker E.III 411/15 at KEK Vaux. (Greg VanWyngarden)

did not offer much hope for aerial combat. While other KEK Vaux pilots were out looking for targets, Rudolf Berthold and Ernst von Althaus were inside the château at Vaux, warmed with mugs of coffee. But a telephone call at about 3 p.m. sent them running for their aeroplanes. An enemy aircraft had been spotted over Péronne, a short distance away.

It began to rain again as they took off, but after attaining 2,000 metres' altitude, they found a hole in the clouds. Within that space they saw a pair of French two-seat reconnaissance aeroplanes and headed for them. A short fight ensued and Berthold shot down his opponent, a Voisin LA biplane.[37] Later, he was officially credited with his first aerial victory. His quarry came down intact in a field in Chaulnes, some thirty-five kilometres west of St. Quentin. The French pilot, twenty-nine-year-old Caporal [Corporal] Arthur Jacquin,[38] was unharmed and taken prisoner; the observer, Sous-lieutenant [Second-Lieutenant] Pierre Ségaud,[39] age thirty-seven, was killed during the fight. Later, Berthold said he felt he had avenged the death of his observer/gunner, Ltn Josef Grüner[40] – 'an eye for an eye' ...

Freiherr von Althaus pursued a Nieuport two-seat biplane and set it on fire with his incendiary ammunition. It crashed and burned near Biaches, a few kilometres outside of Péronne.[41] Both crewmen were killed. Althaus was credited with his third confirmed aerial victory.

Berthold's Second Victory

The following Saturday, 5 February, Berthold wrote:

> 'Today I brought down my second opponent, this time an Englishman. Over Bapaume, I took him out from a formation of five aeroplanes. It did not take long; he was all done after the first shot.'[42]

Berthold's account overly simplifies his actions in forcing B.E.2c 4091 of 13 Squadron, RFC, to land between Grévillers and Irles. As was commonly done, an examination of the aircraft by a German ground unit determined that the two-seater sustained numerous ground-fired hits. Nevertheless, a 2nd Army Senior Command report concluded: 'The aeroplane ... was shot down by a Fokker of Feldflieger-Abteilung 23, [piloted by] Leutnant Berthold.'[43]

The British pilot, 2/Lt Leonard John Pearson, was unwounded and taken prisoner. His observer, 2/Lt Edmund Heathfield Elliott Joe Alexander, suffered a 'shot in the right forearm and hand'[44] and was taken to a first-aid station before being turned over to the German Feldgendarmerie [field police] for transport to the rear area and processing as a prisoner of war.

Berthold Shot Down

Berthold thought he had his third victory in his gun-sight when he and another Fokker pilot dived on three B.E.2c aircraft – one serving as a reconnaissance machine and the other two as escorts – on the morning of Thursday, 10 February. One RFC source noted that the first 'single-seater Fokker ... opened fire at seventy-five yards, gradually closing to twenty yards, and [his] tracer bullets were seen to hit the [British] machine. The German dived and at the same time a second Fokker attacked.'[45] 2/Lts C. Faber and R.A. Way in B.E.2c 4132 of 9 Squadron, RFC,[46] were hit, but 'Lt Faber recovered, righted the machine, climbed to 3,000 feet, and landed ... safely on the [squadron's] aerodrome.'[47]

The other two British aircraft concentrated on Berthold in the second Fokker. Lt R. Egerton and his observer 2/Lt B.H. Cox opened fire 'and clearly saw tracer bullets enter the cowl of the Fokker, which dived steeply and landed safely in a field south of Roisel.'[48] 2/Lts V.A.H. Robeson and T.E.G Scaife 'in the reconnaissance machine also fired at this Fokker and saw him dive to the ground'.[49]

The observer's flexible machine gun on a Royal Aircraft Factory B.E.2c, the type that sent Berthold down on 10 February 1916. (Volker Koos)

Berthold was lucky to survive that fight. As it was, he received 'numerous hits, including two in the fuel tank ... [and] was forced to land near Bernes, west of Hervilly; he slightly injured his left hand'.[50] There is no doubt that Berthold tangled with the trio of 9 Squadron B.E.2c aircraft, as he landed near Bernes, a few kilometres from Roisel, where the British airmen last saw him.

In any event, Berthold's injury was of little importance – or, at least, he did not let it affect his flying – as he flew one of FFA 23's two-seat biplanes during a night-time bombing raid. On the evening of 20/21 February, Berthold dropped some 230 kilograms of high explosives and incendiaries on railway stations and other military objectives in Amiens and, farther east, in Lamotte-en-Santerre.[51]

Also on the morning of Monday, 21 February, a massive German artillery bombardment of fortifications at Verdun[52] in north-eastern France opened one of that war's most horrific battles. Rudolf Berthold was far removed from that fighting, but would become involved in another carnage-laden onslaught: the Battle of the Somme.

Berthold's courage and perseverance were recognised on leap year day, 29 February 1916, when he was honoured by his Bavarian homeland. He was presented with the *Militär-Verdienst-Orden 4. Klasse mit Schwertern* [Military Merit Order 4th Class with Swords]. Berthold became one of only twelve aviation recipients of the 4th Class award throughout the war. And, as medals became the acknowledged currency of bravery and honour recognition, Berthold could take pride in knowing that he joined such illustrious company as Oswald Boelcke and Max Immelmann.[53] Berthold was the sole FFA 23 recipient of this decoration.

FFA 23's fighter detachment began to enjoy the success of the Fokker supremacy, as Berthold and two other KEK Vaux aircraft proved on Monday, 13 March, when they dived on a reconnaissance flight from 8 Squadron, RFC. According to a British report:

'The 3rd Army reconnaissance [flight] was attacked by three Fokkers … At Moeuvres two … Fokkers attacked from behind, opening fire at about 200 yards. Almost immediately one of the escort machines (2/Lt Orde[54] and 1/AM Shaw [in] B.E.2c 4151) turned and began to spiral down. The Fokkers were engaged by all of the remaining machines of the reconnaissance [flight] and eventually driven off.'[55]

Orde's aeroplane came down at Bourlon. It was confirmed as Berthold's third victory.[56]

Berthold's Fourth Victory

Berthold's next air combat claim, on Saturday, 1 April 1916, is not as easy to prove. And confirming aerial victories was (and still is) important for fighter pilots; for, in addition to fulfilling patriotic duty, combat pilots understood that higher 'kill' scores generally resulted in greater rewards. In tracking these combats as completely as possible, historians seek to assemble reports and other accounts to reasonably propose which airmen were involved in which air fight – essentially, who shot down whom. With that research interest in mind, throughout this book the author will propose names and information about Allied airmen who Rudolf Berthold very likely opposed in air combats.

In the case of the 1 April 1916 air battle, Berthold contended that he shot down a Farman two-seat biplane near Lihons, just over thirty-five kilometres west of St. Quentin. The aircraft is said to have 'plunged to the ground burning, part on our side of the lines, part over enemy lines'.[57]

Based on existing historical evidence, the best match among French losses that day was a Farman F.40 reconnaissance aircraft from Escadrille MF 54, crewed by Sgt Louis Paoli[58] and his observer, Lt Alfred Braut. As MF 54's airfield at Savy-Berlette[59] was less than sixty kilometres north of Lihons, it is reasonable to assume that Paoli could have flown that distance and fought with Berthold. However, a contemporary French magazine reported that, while ranging artillery fire, Paoli's aeroplane 'took a direct hit, killing the observer, [and leaving] Paoli … badly wounded. Nevertheless he was able to bring his aeroplane back to our lines, but died a few hours after landing.'[60]

As a practical matter, if Paoli's wood-frame, linen fabric-covered aeroplane had taken 'a direct hit' by an artillery shell, it would have been turned into confetti. On the other hand, 'a direct hit' by Berthold's machine gun could have left the Farman F.40 damaged, but reasonably able to return to its airfield. In any case, available evidence convinced Berthold's superiors that he had attained a fourth aerial victory.

Exactly two weeks later, on 15 April, Rudolf Berthold received his highest military honour thus far when the Kingdom of Saxony presented him with its *Ritterkreuz des Militär-St.-Heinrichs-Orden* [Knight's

The fuselage of a Farman F.40, a type that Berthold claimed on 1 April 1916, shows the gunner's access hatch and his single Colt-Browning 0.30-calibre machine gun. (Kilduff Collection)

Cross of the Military St. Henry Order].[61] The award citation noted: 'During the campaign, Ltn Berthold was one of the most successful fighter pilots. In the period 5 February to 13 March 1916, he was one of the first to fly the new Fokker machine and won several air battles as a member of Royal Saxon Feldflieger-Abteilung 23.'[62] In addition to the handsome medal, Berthold received a conferral document signed by King Friedrich August III.[63]

Berthold's Fifth Victory

As if to further validate the award, the next day, 16 April, Berthold shot down a British two-seater that was directing artillery batteries against German forces east of Albert. He was so determined to halt this source of deadly messages to his enemies that he braved his own anti-aircraft fire while attacking his target. In the informal tradition that arose spontaneously among aviators on both sides of the lines, after attaining a fifth victory Berthold became acknowledged as a 'fighter ace', an honour that earned him high respect among his peers and people at home looking for heroes. This latest victory was soon confirmed, as Berthold's shots hit the pilot, whose aeroplane – B.E.2c 2097 of 9 Squadron, RFC – came down within German lines south of Maurepas. According to a British report:

'2/Lt W.S. Earle[64] (pilot) and 2/Lt C.W.P. Selby[65] (observer) were bought down in the German lines east of Maricourt as the result of a fight in the air. The machine was apparently on fire. Lt Earle was killed and his observer severely wounded.'[66]

Rudolf Berthold became an ace when he received confirmation for his fifth aerial victory, B.E.2c 2097, seen here after it crashed. (Rainer Absmeier)

No doubt due to the severity of his wounds, Selby was later repatriated to Britain, where he recounted his fateful encounter on 16 April 1916:

'Our machine was attacked by a Fokker at 10:05 a.m. while the [German] AA guns were still firing ... My pilot was killed by the first ... [bullet] fired, but the machine remained in control long enough to allow me to fire a drum [of ammunition], luckily hitting the attacking pilot in the leg. This I learnt when I was in the same hospital as him at St. Quentin.

'When the machine began to [lose] control, I climbed back to the pilot's seat and endeavoured to regain control, but found the rudder wires shot away. The machine then fell, controlled only by the elevators. I luckily managed to get clear, falling about fifty feet from the machine, thus escaping any fatal injuries.'[67]

Selby was lucky to have survived such a fall at a time when aeroplane crews were not equipped with parachutes. While he may have fired a machine gun at Berthold, he did not hit the German ace and send him to the hospital. Rather, within a fortnight Berthold was brought down by something as prosaic as engine failure over his airfield. But he ended up in the main military hospital in St. Quentin, where the patient in the next room was 2/Lt Selby. It would be the first of several hospital stays for Berthold and, in this case, would keep him out of action for the next four months.

CHAPTER SIX
EARLY AIR COMBAT SUCCESS

'We were standing there on the airfield, when a rumbling sound filled the air around us. An aeroplane came spiralling down through the mist and landed ... we rushed toward it. "What? Did you think I was dead?" Berthold asked ...Then he told us about his fight.'[1]

HANS JOACHIM BUDDECKE

Under a canopy of 'bright and fine' skies,[2] Tuesday, 25 April 1916 promised favourable flying along both sides of the battle lines in France. But it turned out to be a better day for British airmen than for their German counterparts. First, a reconnaissance flight by a two-seat B.E.2c of 15 Squadron, Royal Flying Corps, protected by seven other aircraft, gathered important information about German construction of 'new and formidable defences behind the Somme front'[3] to impede an Allied advance. Second, one of the British defenders that day was a new Airco D.H.2 single-seat rear-engine fighter, a type that challenged Germany's vaunted Fokker Eindeckers with growing success.

In this instance, it was reported that D.H.2s of 24 Squadron, RFC, were able to 'outmanoeuvre the [German] aeroplanes and beat off the attacks. One Fokker was driven down'.[4] The stricken Fokker was most likely flown by Oberleutnant Rudolf Berthold, who was uninjured, but suffered a consequential misfortune.

Part of his engine had been shot off during that fight, requiring him to make an emergency landing. The only available replacement machine was a Pfalz Eindecker (E.IV 803/15). Built by the Pfalz Flugzeugwerke, Berthold's new aeroplane bore a superficial resemblance to his Fokker – both were rotary engine-powered mid-wing monoplanes – but the Pfalz was significantly inferior to the Fokker. It was a license-built version of the pre-war French Morane-Saulnier Type H[5] and had been adapted to carry the same synchronised machine gun as the slightly longer, lighter and more manoeuvrable Fokker Eindecker.[6] Berthold recorded in his diary:

'Because the Pfalz was universally disliked, I thought I should look at it thoroughly. But when it was disassembled, it was clear that something was wrong, and the bad reputation of the factory was well deserved...

'I started out, lifted off from the ground and, at that moment, the engine quit. I was at about 100 metres. In a flash the bird went down. I heard the aeroplane splintering, felt a blow to my head, suddenly I was in agony and then can remember nothing more.

'Another intense pain brought me back to my senses and caused me to burst into a violent torrent of words. I ... thought that I was done for and was just being pulled out from under the wreckage. There was a thundering "Hurrah!" and I could hear voices:

The wreckage of Pfalz Eindecker E.IV 803/15 after Oblt Rudolf Berthold's crash at KEK Vaux on 25 April 1916. (Greg VanWyngarden)

"He is swearing again – he is alive!" Then everything went black again.

'When I regained consciousness, I heard: "He may yet pull through, but he will be blind." That is when I cried out for the *coup de grâce*. I tried desperately to open my eyes, but I saw nothing. Good Lord, not that! Then I was once again cloaked in blessed sleep.'[7]

After the crash, Berthold was taken to Kriegslazarett 7 [Military Hospital 7] in St. Quentin.[8] He regained his eyesight, but did not become fully conscious until two days later. He recalled:

'I pondered my situation ... I had crashed, but at the last moment I threw the aeroplane over onto its left wing and somewhat lessened the impact of the crash. The aeroplane was completely shattered. I had a complicated leg break, my upper jaw [maxilla] and nasal bone were broken, and there was damage to my optic nerves. The worst thing for me was the thought that I would have to lie in bed for weeks, perhaps even months.

'In the next room lay the badly wounded observer from the British aeroplane that I had shot down ... earlier.'[9]

The British airman, eighteen-year-old Second-Lieutenant Cuthbert W.P. Selby, had been severely shot up during his fight with Berthold on 16 April. Selby later stated that he had met and spoken with Berthold.[10] If so, they may have used French to communicate, as there is no record of Berthold's having learned English.

Death and Despair

Chatting with a wounded former adversary would have been of little interest to Rudolf Berthold in view of the war news he received next. On Saturday, 29 April, his brother Wolfram was killed three days after his twenty-fourth birthday. An Offiziersaspirant [officer candidate] with the Bavarian 9th Infantry Regiment, Wolfram was in the front lines south-west of Lille during a German-launched chlorine gas attack. Suddenly, the wind changed direction and blew the poisonous vapours back over the German positions.[11] Wolfram Berthold, a theology student at Erlangen University before the war,[12] was among 132 German soldiers killed in that incident; all were buried the following day in the military cemetery at Pont-à-Vendin.[13]

Confined to his bed, Rudolf Berthold noted that the 'good fellows from the units come as often as their duties allow'.[14] But his comrades from Feldflieger-Abteilung 23 and Kampfeinsitzer-Kommando Vaux also added to his frustration by relating unvarnished accounts of the course of the war.

In this manner Berthold learned that, on 20 May, Leutnant der Reserve Max Emil Bernward Gross, a new arrival to FFA 23, was on his first flight over the lines when his LVG B.I two-seater was shot down northwest of Péronne. Gross and his observer, Ltn Karl Musset,[15] who Berthold knew, perished. Berthold had heard that LVG B.I developmental problems meant the design had to be re-worked several times.[16] And he recalled his late and much-lamented friend Josef Grüner's gallows-humour reference to the manufacturer's name, LVG – the abbreviation for Luft-Verkehrs-Gesellschaft [air transport company] – as also standing for 'Leichen-Vertriebs-Gesellschaft' [cadavers distribution company].[17] The worst part of the account was that Gross and Musset had been downed by new British D.H.2 fighter biplanes.[18]

The Airco D.H.2 effectively seized the lead in fighter operations previously enjoyed by the Fokker Eindecker series. (Volker Koos)

Even though he was in hospital, Berthold had not been replaced as KEK Vaux leader. Consequently, he received copies of German 2nd Army message traffic and would have seen the 22 May 1916 report that assessed the Fokker monoplane's fall from grace. Classified as 'secret' to emphasise the report's maximum candour, it stated:

'The Fokker Eindecker, which for a long time maintained [air combat] superiority, no longer has that dominance ... [over] the new British aeroplanes. The most recent British aircraft are better in their abilities to climb to altitudes above 3,000 metres and are only slightly slower than [the Eindecker]. The small British fighter aeroplanes surpass the Fokker in all flight characteristics ...'[19]

Berthold also could not dispute the report's other findings and outlook for the near-term:

'The opposition is ever more successful in using aerial observers to direct their guns with precision against our artillery batteries. Their flyers fire ... machine guns constantly at our reinforced trenches. Up to now, our defensive fire can do little against them ... When our Fokkers attack, the enemy pulls back, only to quickly reappear as soon as they have gone. We are seldom in a position to use combat aircraft to make it secure for [two-seater] aeroplanes to reconnoitre or direct artillery fire.'[20]

By this time, Oberstleutnant [Lieutenant Colonel] Hermann von der Lieth-Thomsen, the Chef der Feldflugwesens [chief of field aviation] in Berlin, was already reviewing proposals from German aeroplane manufacturers – including Dutch-born Anthony Fokker's company in Schwerin – to develop single-seat fighter biplanes for frontline service. But, until the new aeroplanes arrived, Berthold and other air unit leaders had to rely on aircraft at hand and their own skill.

A harsh blow for German fighter pilots came on the afternoon of Sunday, 18 June 1916, when the highly successful Eindecker pilot Oblt Max Immelmann was killed in combat while flying a Fokker E.III. To keep German combat pilot morale high, and naturally for propaganda reasons, in order to prevent the loss of another top pilot, Germany's highest-scoring ace, Hauptmann Oswald Boelcke, was removed from flight status on orders from German Crown Prince Wilhelm,[21] Commander of the 3rd Army. Boelcke was sent to Vienna, Budapest, Belgrade, Constantinople and other eastern points on an 'inspection tour' of German units and their local allies.

Battle of the Somme

British and French forces launched an ill-conceived offensive against the German 2nd Army on Saturday, 1 July. First day British casualties of 57,450 men[22] presaged the carnage to come. Rudolf Berthold felt the force of the battle's early operations when the once calm and orderly hospital in St. Quentin was suddenly overwhelmed with newly wounded men. He wrote in his diary at the time:

'With the beginning of the Somme offensive the war as we knew it ended ... it was the beginning of hell ... insane numbers of casualties ...with frightful wounds! The hospitals were completely overfilled. Doctors and nurses worked … without a rest. Day and night the wounded were brought in, and we heard the screams of those who were badly hit.'[23]

In response to the Allied offensive, on 5 July 1916, the German 2nd Army strengthened its air units by reorganising them into four groupings.[24] FFA 23 and KEK Vaux were joined with two other units assigned to an army group commanded by General der Infanterie [Lieutenant General] Ferdinand von Quast and deployed in coordinated multi-unit flights.

But even that arrangement did nothing to halt the flow of German casualties. By the end of July, Berthold and other wounded and injured men were being prepared for transport back to Germany to make room for more severe battlefield casualties. With his usual stubbornness, Berthold decided that he would not leave the frontline area. In his diary he noted his solution to giving up his much-needed hospital bed while making progress in his recuperation:

'The unit sent a car one morning and I "disappeared". A short time later I was back at Feldflieger-Abteilung 23 [and KEK Vaux]. When I saw everything again – my dear friends, my mechanics – I screamed for joy! Ten days later, I still could not walk by myself, but I could sit in an aeroplane again …

'My left leg still did not work right; it was shorter and weak and stiff; but it had to function – my will required it! Stiffness in the knee joint was soon remedied. My orderly braced himself beneath the leg, while I leaned over the bed post and pressed my thigh down onto him. Resolving a swelling in the knee joint was the first success and I could move the leg better day by day. The eyes still gave me difficulties, but they improved with time. I was happy that at least I could see …'[25]

Once Berthold began to regain his mobility, he was faced with other, grimmer realities:

'A pitiable weakness in morale grips the people at home. This terrible agitation has already begun to take hold out here … it has sneaked up to the frontlines with new replacement soldiers and men returning from leave. Our newer officers are also not worth much … Those who come now are raw recruits and, unfortunately, also very arrogant and not yet fully trained …

'There is no longer any real rest and recreation time. We are using up flyers at an enormous rate. For many long weeks the opposition has dominated the air without dispute …'[26]

Buddecke Returns

German Chief of Field Aviation von der Lieth-Thomsen put to good use the lessons learned from deploying KEKs and other single-seat fighter detachments to two-seater units. He expanded the scope of single-seat fighter operations by establishing larger Jagdstaffeln [literally 'hunting flights' or fighter squadrons] that would attack enemy aircraft throughout their respective army corps sectors. On Friday, 11 August 1916, he cabled Hptm Oswald Boelcke, cancelling the inspection tour and ordering the top-scoring fighter pilot to return to France to establish and take command of the first such unit, Jagdstaffel 2,[27] in the 2nd Army sector.

A week later, Oblt.d.Res Hans Joachim Buddecke was ordered back from Turkey, to proceed to the 2nd Army sector, where he would command Jasta 4. While Buddecke was en route to his new assignment, Berthold proved, if only to himself, that he was as bold a combat pilot as ever.

Sixth Victory and a High Honour

On Thursday, 24 August, he made his first combat flight in a single-seat biplane fighter, which photographic evidence suggests was a Halberstadt D.II, a type then entering frontline service.[28] Berthold needed to be helped into the aeroplane, but, once strapped in, he was ready to fight. According to his unit's daily records, Berthold 'shot down his sixth [enemy] aeroplane, north of Péronne. In addition, at 7 p.m. he forced down a Nieuport. It cannot yet be determined whether this [second] aeroplane landed within our lines.'[29]

Oberstleutnant Hermann von der Lieth-Thomsen, the Chief of Field Aviation, assigned early German military air commanders. (Kilduff Collection)

Rudolf Berthold most likely flew a Halberstadt D.II when he attained his sixth confirmed aerial victory. (Heinz J. Nowarra)

During the day's first air combat, Berthold most likely shot down Caporal Henri Dangueuger[30] of Escadrille N 37,[31] who flew a new Nieuport XVII fitted with a single 7.7-mm Vickers machine gun[32] that was synchronised to shoot through the propeller arc. But the Frenchman may not have been able to fire his gun; at this point, Berthold still employed a hawk-like attack, diving down with the sun behind him, a tactic that brought so much success to the Fokker Eindeckers.

Berthold's victim on 24 August 1916 was a Nieuport XVII, a type seen here in the markings of Escadrille N 76. (Kilduff Collection)

But there was little doubt that Rudolf Berthold was working his way toward an eighth confirmed victory that would result in his being presented with the *Pour le Mérite*. Indeed, he was subsequently notified that, on 27 August, he was to receive Prussia's second-highest bravery award: the *Ritterkreuz des Königlichen Hausordens von Hohenzollern mit Schwertern* [Knight's Cross of the Royal Order of the House of Hohenzollern with Swords].[33] He had already received both grades of Prussia's Iron Cross awards and the Hohenzollern House Order was, 'the customary intermediate award for officers between the Iron Cross 1st Class and the *Orden Pour le Mérite*'.[34]

Jagdstaffel 4 Established

Jagdstaffel 4 was officially established on 25 August 1916 at Flieger-Ersatz-Abteilung 9[35] in Darmstadt. While new aircraft were being sent to Vaux from FEA 9, Berthold drew the new unit's personnel locally, as noted in his diary:

'At the beginning of September ... I assembled the new Jagdstaffel 4 for Buddecke. My Abteilungsführer [Hptm Hermann Palmer] provided personnel, as he could spare them.

They were good, sound people, who I knew and could rely upon. Our airfield was again at our old Vaux, which, for us, invoked many beautiful memories. The old spirit of FFA 23 was carried over to Staffel 4.'[36]

Due to Berthold's injuries, his superiors thought he could not yet resume active command – but he could still achieve objectives by exercising the power of his iron will. Oblt.d.Res Hans Joachim Buddecke recalled returning to Vaux:

'Then I again met with ... "the incomparable Franconian", as we called Berthold. He had been through a lot ... and after he returned to Roupy, he had himself hoisted into his aeroplane and resumed his duties.

'He had prepared everything for me and brought together the most capable pilots ... We pitched our tents again at Vaux, to house over a dozen aeroplanes ... Now we could all work together to wrest air superiority from the enemy.'[37]

Berthold's Seventh Victory

On Sunday, 17 September, Rudolf Berthold claimed victory over a single-seat Martinsyde G.100 bomber on its way to hit targets in Valenciennes. However, the nineteen-year-old British pilot, Lieutenant William Hugh Stobart Chance,[38] later said that engine failure caused him to land near Cambrai, some thirty kilometres short of his target:

'... I realised that a forced landing was inevitable (I had already dropped my bombs on a wood). We had just been issued with tracer bullets for our Lewis [machine] guns and were warned that the *Boches* were claiming that they were explosive and contrary to the Hague Convention [of 1899]; so before landing I fired off both machine guns and threw out the spare ammunition drums. Picking a likely looking stubble field, I landed without difficulty and, clutching the incendiary torch with which we were equipped in case of a forced landing, jumped out – set the torch alight and poked it into the canvas of the main [wings] ... There was a great gush of flame and I ran headlong to clear myself of the burning [aeroplane] ...'[39]

Lt Chance was uninjured and taken prisoner. Seen by witnesses as following and firing at his quarry, Oblt Rudolf Berthold was confirmed as having downed the Martinsyde, which was credited as his seventh victory.[40]

Berthold was not so fortunate two days later. He and two other Jasta 4 pilots attacked a flight of B.E.12s – the single-seat fighter variant of the B.E.2 reconnaissance aircraft[41] – and each claimed to have shot down his target, but none was credited with a victory. There is no doubt that air combats took place, as Captain Ian H.D. Henderson, a B.E.12 pilot with 19 Squadron, RFC, reported that at about 11:15 a.m. on 22 September:

'When leading an offensive patrol over Fins, Havrincourt and Bapaume, I was attacked from behind by a Fokker biplane [sic]. I fired my Lewis [gun] at him and turned to the right [to the] B.E.12, who flattened out and followed me. I thought he was all right, but on looking back three or four minutes later, I saw him spiralling down very low with

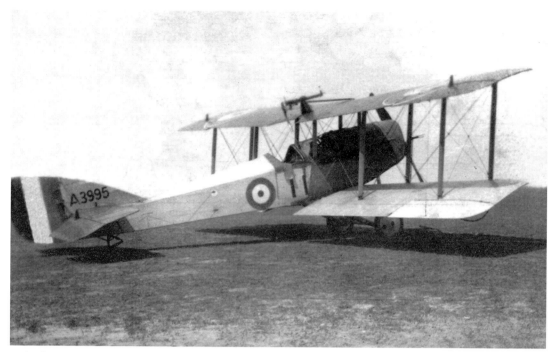

A single-seat Martinsyde bomber similar to this one was claimed by Berthold on 17 September 1916. (Trevor Henshaw)

German intelligence officers seen inspecting a captured B.E.12 single-seat fighter/bomber, a type Berthold encountered on 22 September. (Volker Koos)

two hostile machines on his tail. I ... followed down to help the B.E.12. On reaching 5,000 ft., I saw he was very low – about 1,000 ft. and still diving, so I stopped to watch. All three machines disappeared under a cloud and I lost sight of them ...'[42]

That day's RFC casualty summary reported two 19 Squadron aircraft 'believed to have been brought down near Bapaume' and the pilots 'reported to have died whilst prisoner[s] of war'[43]: B.E.12 6561, piloted by twenty-three-year-old Second-Lieutenant Robert Douglas Herman[44] and B.E.12 6591, flown by 2/Lt Reginald Howard Edwards.[45] Despite the physical evidence that must have existed about these two B.E.12s and their pilots behind German lines, none of the Jasta 4 claims was confirmed.

Buddecke was in charge of a late morning offensive patrol two days later, but when Berthold spotted a target, he simply dived on it. Buddecke described the incident:

'We crossed over the lines ... and ten minutes later, far below me, Berthold went after a small Nieuport. We all ... dashed down to get close to the scene. But the Nieuport fell into all sorts of somersaults and disappeared into a cloud. One by one each of us returned to our formation and regained altitude ... But Berthold was so far below me that I could barely keep an eye on him ... when he dived down again.'[46]

Berthold's target was a Nieuport XVII – accompanied by a second. According to a contemporary French aviation magazine account, Berthold was saved by his opponents' eagerness to finish him off. The article about the 24 September attack by Sergent André Steuer[47] and Sergent François Roman[48] of Escadrille N 103 noted that 'in the ardour of the fight, the two French aeroplanes collided with each other. One of Steuer's wings broke off and both aviators plunged to the ground.'[49]

Oblt Buddecke related the rest of the story:

'... one of our men came back from the flight and reported, out of breath, that he had seen Berthold diving down. We did not know what to say, standing there and talking about it on the airfield, when a rumbling sound filled the air around us. An aeroplane came spiralling down through the mist and landed. Thank God – we rushed toward it. "What? Did you think I was dead?" Berthold asked. "That is just not so." Then he told us about his fight. Two Nieuports had attacked him from behind during the dive ... they had rammed into each other and, without wings, had fallen down by him.'[50]

Berthold claimed victory over one of the Nieuports, both of which came down near Rancourt,[51] southeast of Bapaume. Once again, however, his claim for the elusive eighth victory – and the high honour that would come with it – was not confirmed.

That situation changed two days later, on the 'fine but hazy'[52] afternoon of Tuesday, 26 September 1916, when Berthold claimed a B.E. near Bertincourt,[53] east of Bapaume. The only aircraft of that type downed that day was B.E.2c 7079 of 9 Squadron, RFC, which was on a contact patrol over the area around Lesboeufs, southwest of Bertincourt. A British report stated that the two-seat biplane was 'brought down by [a] direct hit by A.A.' fire[54];

the crewmen – Lt Bernard Tarrant Coller, age twenty-two,[55] and 2/Lt Thomas Earle Gordon Scaife, age twenty-four[56] – were killed. Whatever the cause of their demise, the credit for it was awarded to Rudolf Berthold as his eighth 'kill'.

Pour le Mérite Awarded

After what must have been an interminable wait of almost three weeks, the much-anticipated news from Berlin arrived at Jasta 4. Buddecke described the occasion:

'Then came a beautiful but yet sad day for the staffel. We received telegrams stating that His Majesty [the kaiser] had awarded Berthold the *Pour le Mérite* and that he was also being transferring to command a Jagdstaffel in Alsace.'[57]

Kaiser Wilhelm II signed the bestowal document for Rudolf Berthold's award on 12 October 1916.[58] Before Berthold left to report to Jagdstaffel 14 in Armee-Abteilung A[59]

Attendees at Jasta 4's party honouring Berthold's award of the *Pour le Mérite*, held in the stately Château Vaux, included four other recipients of Prussia's highest bravery decoration. Sitting second from left was Ltn Walter Höhndorf and beginning with fifth from left: Oblt Rudolf Berthold (with the ribbon of the newly presented award visible around his neck), Oblt.d.Res Hans Joachim Buddecke, Ltn.d.Res Wilhelm Frankl and Oblt.d.Res Ernst Freiherr von Althaus. Third from right in the third row was Oblt Fritz Otto Bernert, who received the award in October 1917. Often mischievous, the flyers posed a white uniformed dummy behind and between Berthold and Buddecke. (Tobias Weber)

[Army Detachment A] sector four days later, a celebration was held in his honour at Château Vaux. He was the tenth aviation recipient of the award and, in addition to himself, five of the other seven living *Träger* [award holders] attended: Oblt.d.Res Ernst Freiherr von Althaus; Oblt.d.Res Hans Joachim Buddecke; Ltn.d.Res Wilhelm Frankl; Ltn.d.Res Walter Höhndorf and Ltn Kurt Wintgens. The only *Pour le Mérite* fighter ace not there was Oblt Oswald Boelcke, who was busy training his new unit, Jasta 2.

The following day, Berthold received a grand send off. Adding to well-wishers on the ground, Buddecke arranged an aerial salute, so that 'at twelve noon, two of our aeroplanes circled over the railway station at St. Quentin, from which a train carried away our faithful companion to new duties'.[60]

On the train, Berthold had time to read his assignment orders from the chief of field aviation, which also noted the array of aircraft he would lead: seven Fokker D.II fighter biplanes, a Halberstadt D.II fighter biplane and two Fokker Eindeckers.[61] Berthold had mixed feelings, leaving for a much less active sector while the Battle of the Somme was still raging, but he resolved to fight as hard as ever. He wrote in his diary:

'When I left my old unit on 10 October in order to head east to a new unit in Alsace, the day was foggy, damp and cold; my mood was dismal and melancholy. All of my comrades, who were very close to me, saw me off on the train. Many furtive tears were wiped away. From time to time Buddecke shook my hand. Above us was the sound of aeroplane engines – a farewell gesture. The train was ready to pull out. Quick handshakes from my faithful comrades in arms and then I no longer looked back. I headed out on a dark journey.

'My destination was Saarburg [now Sarrebourg, France] ... It was raining when I arrived at my new duty station. The really hearty greeting I received from the gentlemen of my new staffel soon dispersed the dark cloud that weighed on my soul like a bad dream.'[62]

Commanding Jagdstaffel 14

Surely, the men of Jasta 14 were thrilled to have a 'star' of the magnitude of Rudolf Berthold leading them into combat from the airfield at Bühl [now Buhl-Lorraine, France]. The staffel had been founded as the Fokker-Kampfstaffel Falkenhausen, in honour of the sector commander, General der Infanterie Ludwig von Falkenhausen, on 9 February 1916[63], but had recorded no successes to date. Its first leader, Hptm Krieg, presided over the transition to Jasta 14 on 28 September,[64] after which he was transferred to make way for Berthold.

Jasta 14 then underwent quick changes, as Berthold noted in his diary:

'The staffel was thoroughly prepared within a short time and was flying at a high level of proficiency. Whatever the weather, they practiced: turning, attacking, defending and primarily shooting ...On this point I was adamantly strict.

'My gentlemen cursed me more than a little. When I sharply criticized one of them for a failure, the pilots strongly protested again and again. But here, too, I remained true to my conviction: "Accomplishment is born only out of inner joy."'[65]

Upon Berthold's arrival at Bühl Airfield, he was greeted by a field of Jasta 14's Halberstadt D.II single-seaters. They were soon replaced by newer Albatros fighters. (Heinz J. Nowarra)

The pilots worked hard, but Berthold also gave them incentives:

> 'One of my first jobs was to have the *Kasino* [pilots' mess] reconditioned. Within a few days it was so nicely fitted out that everyone could feel good about it. Nothing elevates the joy of service as much as the refreshing feeling of wellbeing and relaxing in a space in which you must spend hours every day.'[66]

Jasta 14's Fokker D.II biplanes turned out to be disappointing. Hence, the arrival of Albatros D.I and D.II aircraft further boosted morale at Jasta 14. The Albatroses' water-cooled Mercedes 160-hp stationary engines made them faster and more manoeuvrable than the Fokkers and 120-hp-engined Halberstadt D-Types then in service.[67] The Albatroses were small, agile and fast single-seat biplanes. They were also equipped with two 7.92-mm synchronised 'Spandau machine guns and 700 rounds of ammunition for each gun ... [to enable them to] maintain performance parity with Allied fighters'.[68]

The value of Jasta 14's relentless training, strict discipline and attention to duty became apparent on Saturday, 28 October, when Germany's most successful fighter pilot, the 40-victory ace Oswald Boelcke, was killed in aerial combat. He had not been felled by enemy bullets, but by the action of a subordinate who momentarily flew too close to him and accidentally hit his top wing, which came loose and – in the absence of parachutes in aeroplanes at the time – sent the ace plunging to his death.

Also on that day, Berthold received a fitness report from Hptm Bruno Volkmann, Armee-Abt A's Stabsoffizier der Flieger [staff officer for aviation]. Volkmann expressed his appreciation of Berthold's accomplishments in such a short time, noting:

> '[Berthold] is extraordinarily energetic, has great will-power and does not think about his own needs. He has taken his Jagdstaffel well in hand within the shortest time.

75

Jasta 14's first Albatros D.II (number 1717/16) went to Oblt Berthold, seen here in the cockpit. (Greg VanWyngarden)

Looking from the cockpit of Albatros D.II 1717/16, an older Halberstadt D.II is seen off to the left. (Greg VanWyngarden)

'Through his personality and his shining example, he forcefully leads his officers and non-commissioned officers forward and will surely attain the best results. In peacetime, Oblt Berthold would be first rank as an organiser, aviation technical expert, pilot and machine-gun expert and could provide valuable services for the Fliegertruppe. He will do well in any other position for them.'[69]

Even though Armee-Abt A occupied a relatively quiet sector of the Western Front, Berthold maintained Jasta 14's rigorous training schedule. The training paid off when, on 11 November 1916, Vizefeldwebel Schuhmann shot down a French aeroplane over Champenoux, about fifteen kilometres northeast of Nancy, one of the major cities in eastern France. Details of the encounter are lacking, but Schuhmann[70] and Jasta 14 were credited with a first victory.

As a consequence of the morale-building first victory, the staffel was in top form when, in mid-December, Kaiser Wilhelm II made an inspection tour of the troops and facilities in the area. The kaiser was joined by his oldest son, Crown Prince Wilhelm, and Rudolf Berthold was introduced to both royal personages, who congratulated him on attaining the *Pour le Mérite*. Speaking with the new air hero privately, the kaiser said that he had been personally touched by Boelcke's death. Reportedly with deep regret in his voice, the supreme war lord, as he was also known, said to Berthold: 'I wanted to prohibit him from continuing to fly, but he would not stop.'[71]

Berthold's first appearance in the popular Sanke postcard series was rushed into production so quickly that the publisher used an older photo of him and had an artist paint in the flyer's recently awarded *Pour le Mérite*. (Kilduff Collection)

Many more combat airmen would be needed in the year ahead, as Germany and the Allies struggled for air superiority over each other's trenches and rear areas. No doubt, the kaiser would play his role as father of the nation and, in personal meetings, profess to worry about the loss of highly-accomplished airmen – while his ranking officers continued to send more of them into combat. The coming battles would offer national leaders many opportunities for such political theatre.

Kaiser Wilhelm II (centre) led the way when his entourage inspected troop formations. The second officer behind him (with the death-head hussar's hat) was his oldest son, Crown Prince Wilhelm. (Kilduff Collection)

For Rudolf Berthold, however, the future offered opportunities for more achievements that would advance his career even further than it had come in the past twenty-nine months. Even though still feeling some pain from his crash injuries, Berthold was glad to be able to maintain a full duty schedule – and to be in command of his own staffel, at that.

CHAPTER SEVEN
LEADERSHIP IN THE AIR

'There were no pilots in the staffel who would have hesitated to shoot down an opponent in aerial combat. This was not my doing; I had merely trained and properly led them against the opposition...'[1]

RUDOLF BERTHOLD

Failures in the Battle of Verdun led to major changes within the German military structure. On 29 August 1916, General der Infanterie Erich von Falkenhayn, chief of the general staff and proponent of the Verdun offensive, was relieved of command and later retired. He was succeeded by Generalfeldmarschall [Field Marshal] Paul von Beneckendorff und von Hindenburg, the renowned Eastern Front commander. The shift at the highest level benefitted the Fliegertruppe, as Oberstleutnant [Lieutenant Colonel] Hermann von der Lieth-Thomsen, the chief of field aviation, was a protégé of Hindenburg's chief of staff, General der Infanterie Erich Ludendorff.

With Ludendorff's support, von der Lieth-Thomsen (generally called Thomsen) was able to alter and improve the deployment of German aircraft and units. His efforts came to formal fruition on 8 October, when Kaiser Wilhelm II proclaimed that: 'the growing importance of the air war requires uniting the entire air combat and air defence capabilities of the army, in the field and on the home front, into one entity.'[2]

The Luftstreitkräfte Emerges

With that action, the Fliegertruppe was transformed from a loose organisational structure into a unified command. Generalleutnant Ernst von Hoeppner, a thirty-seven-year-old military veteran and non-flyer,[3] was appointed Kommandierende General der Luftstreitkräfte [commanding general of the air force] or Kogenluft in abbreviated form. To assure that the Luftstreitkräfte was included in major war developments, Hoeppner reported directly to Hindenburg at the Oberste Heeresleitung [Supreme High Command].

Oberleutnant Rudolf Berthold enthusiastically embraced the new Luftstreitkräfte's evolution, but he saw a greater need for massed German efforts to stop enemy aircraft. He recorded in his diary:

'My ambition was to concentrate the air units into larger entities, which ... would be guided by one hand. I proposed the use of Geschwaders [large formations or air wings] ... as a collective opposition.'[4]

As part of the reorganisation that led to development of the Luftstreitkräfte, individual

Armee Stabsoffiziere der Flieger [army aviation staff officers] were elevated to Armee Kommandeure der Flieger [army commanders of aviation] – abbreviated Kofl – and given greater responsibilities.[5] Hence, in January 1917, Berthold met with Hauptmann Bruno Volkmann, the Kofl for Armee-Abteilung A, and in great detail proposed broader use of massed air units. His discussions with Volkmann were in vain, but, as Berthold noted in his diary:

'... In spite of all failures, I continued to fight for my idea and, later, found support and understanding for my efforts from Hptm Wilhelm Haehnelt [5th Army Kofl], a far-sighted and forward-striving old flyer. But even he could not get through to a higher authority. Nevertheless, completely independent of other armies, he introduced this kind of organisation within his unit.'[6]

Jasta 14 Early Victories

On Saturday, 3 February 1917, Berthold received satisfaction from his work with Jasta 14 when the unit recorded its second aerial victory. Leutnant der Reserve Adolf Kuen shot down a two-engine Caudron G.4 bomber near Emberménil, less than

When Generalleutnant Ernst von Hoeppner was appointed to command the Luftstreitkräfte his highest award was Prussia's Order of the Red Eagle 2nd Class with Swords, worn at the neck. Later he received the *Pour le Mérite*. (Kilduff Collection)

twenty kilometres from its own airfield at Lunéville.[7] The two French crewmen were killed and credit for the victory was awarded to Kuen.[8] Berthold was gratified that the bomber had been stopped before it got too far into German-held territory.

Jasta 14's third victory occurred on Sunday 11 February, when Oblt Berthold and Offizierstellvertreter [Warrant Officer] Hüttner patrolled over Parroy forest. Again, they were not far from the French airfield at Lunéville when they attacked five Nieuport XVII single-seat fighters. Despite the odds, the staffel record shows: 'Hüttner forced one of the Nieuports to land ... The [enemy] aeroplane came down within German territory and was later repaired by the staffel. Berthold held off the other four and chased them away.'[9] Hüttner was credited with his first victory,[10] and the pilot of downed Nieuport XVIIbis No. 2405, Brigadier [Corporal] Lambert of Escadrille N 506, was taken prisoner.[11]

Four days later, Berthold received a distinctive honour from the chief of field aviation: a one-litre silver goblet known as the *Ehrenbecher* [cup of honour].[12] Bearing the

Oblt Rudolf Berthold was a constant presence at Jasta 14's airfield at Bühl, assuring that his men understood the high standards he had set for the unit. (Greg VanWyngarden)

Berthold is seen climbing out of Nieuport XVIIbis No. 2405, which was captured after a fight in which he participated. (Lance J. Bronnenkant)

inscription *'Dem Sieger im Luftkampf'* [To the Victor in Aerial Combat], the goblets were presented to combat flyers who shot down enemy aeroplanes; the first recipients were Oswald Boelcke and Max Immelmann, who had six and seven victories, respectively, when they were honoured on Christmas Eve 1915.[13] The 20-cm tall goblets were produced by Godet, an exclusive jeweller in Berlin.[14] Berthold received his *Ehrenbecher* after his eighth victory, but, in coming months, he and other air unit leaders would present the goblets to officers and enlisted men alike after they had scored their first air combat successes.

Jasta 14's Albatros D.I and D.II aircraft were soon replaced by the improved D.III model. The type's sleek appearance – with its pointed nose and streamlined, plywood-covered semi-monocoque fuselage – led to its being nick-named the *haifisch* [shark]. Fitted with a new high-compression engine[15] and twin machine guns, the sleek fighter had speed and killing power, just like its voracious namesake.

An example of the *Ehrenbecher* that Berthold received from the Chief of Field Aviation. (Kilduff Collection)

Plans to transfer Jasta 14 in February raised hopes that the unit would leave the relative quiet of Alsace for greater challenges to the west. However, as Berthold wrote in his diary:

> '...the move meant we were only half satisfied [as] we did not go to face the British in Flanders; [rather] we went to Laon in the Aisne sector. I found ... such sad conditions there that I would not have considered them possible. We did not find suitable living quarters in any of the communities ...
>
> 'Luckily, I had flown ahead by myself and left orders that the staffel should be prepared to relocate only after it received my orders by telegram. For two weeks I worked alone with the people responsible for providing quarters. I constantly received orders that my staffel had to move, but I always sent one answer: First, there must be quarters for my staffel and not before. Finally, the move went forward ...'[16]

Berthold did not know of high-level German plans to capitalize on the inhospitable environment he complained about. As the Royal Air Force historian H.A. Jones pointed out: 'On the 3rd of March the Germans captured an important staff memorandum of [Général Robert Georges] Nivelle which fully revealed the French commander-in-chief's strategy'[17] for the coming French offensive in the Aisne sector. Thus, as another historian

Berthold test-fired the guns in the newly-arrived Albatros D.III 2182/16. This aircraft is believed to be the first fighter on which his personal emblem was applied to the natural wood finish of the fuselage. Appropriately, he chose the winged sword of an avenging angel. (Greg VanWyngarden)

After Jasta 14 settled into its facilities at Marchais, Berthold's Albatros D.III 2182/16 (centre) received final attention before he flew it in combat. (Greg VanWyngarden)

noted: '... the Germans had ample time to convert ... natural barriers into a veritable fortress.'[18] German planners carried out a strategic withdrawal to what they called the Siegfried Line, named after the legendary Germanic hero who had been popularised in Wagnerian operas.

Move to the Aisne Sector

In mid-March Berthold felt that Jasta 14's new facilities were ready for the unit and he ordered a caravan of lorries to journey over 200 kilometres southwest from Alsace to the Aisne. The new airfield was at Marchais, a town outside Laon and about forty kilometres from Berthold's old airfield at Roupy. He recorded in his diary:

'Within twenty-four hours of its arrival at the new airfield my Jasta was completely ready for combat ... There was a magnificent spirit in the staffel! Fourteen aeroplanes had been off-loaded from transport vehicles, assembled, test-flown and had their gun sights checked. Workshop, carpentry shop, office and quarters set up with the help of only 125 men – it was a masterly achievement...'[19]

On the staffel's first full day at Marchais, Saturday, 17 March, it recorded its third victory. An Albatros 'haifisch' flown by Vizefeldwebel Otto Gerbig shot down a two-engine Caudron outside of Paissy. Demonstrating the close proximity of the aerial adversaries' operating areas, the French bomber went down in a field less than twenty kilometres south of Jasta 14's new airfield. The bomber was Gerbig's first 'kill'.[20]

A factory-fresh and unmarked Farman F-1, 40b-Type 61 two-seater, a type that Berthold claimed on 24 March 1917. (Christophe Cony)

A week later – on 24 March, Rudolf Berthold's twenty-sixth birthday – he scored the unit's fourth victory. With Ltn.d.Res Georg Michaelis flying cover, to assure his leader was not surprised from behind, Berthold attacked a Farman Type 61 two-seater between Aizy and Vailly-sur-Aisne. The French aeroplane was no match for the fast and manoeuvrable Albatros, which sent it down onto Folemprix Farm, southeast of Ostel. The Farman was 'completely smashed to pieces … [and] both crewmen[21] were dead'.[22] Kogenluft records listed this downed aircraft as Berthold's ninth victory.[23]

Berthold's Tenth Victory

Even before Général Nivelle's offensive began, the east-west road from Laon to Soissons attracted the interest of French reconnaissance aircraft. On Thursday, 6 April, Berthold spotted a big two-engine Caudron R.4 near the road and shot it down over La Malval Farm in the town of Braye-en-Laonnois. The staffel reported that 'two [of the French] crewmen were killed and one [most likely, the pilot] was wounded'.[24] The downed aeroplane was confirmed as Berthold's tenth aerial victory.[25] It also had intelligence value, as noted in a Kogenluft report:

'Oblt Berthold of Jasta 14 shot down a two-engine … Caudron on 6 April 1917. The pilot's seat has 8-mm thick galvanised iron armour in the shape of an armchair, [behind it] a carapace-like protective shield three-quarters of a metre high, a shield beneath the [pilot's] derrière, and a shield on each side of the [pilot's] thighs. According to the account of a French prisoner, this type of aeroplane is called … Caudron "Cuirasse" [body armour]. The observer and the aerial gunner, however, are not protected by armour. The engines are also not armour-plated. The aircraft are said to be used for long-range flights.

'After an aerial combat with a … Caudron, a Jasta 14 pilot [Berthold] saw that the aerial machine gunner sitting in the rear was slumped lifeless over the gun-mount, while the aeroplane flew on undisturbed. According to Jasta 14, only attacks from the front or hits to the engines have a chance of disabling [the aircraft]. The subsequent firing tests against the armour of the captured Caudron, however, revealed that tracer bullets penetrate the armour at 150 metres, and SMK [steel-cored pointed bullet] ammunition at 155 to 300 metres.'[26]

Rudolf Berthold commanded Jasta 14 at the time the second Sanke card (No. 423) was issued. This time, he was depicted wearing his actual *Pour le Mérite*. (Kilduff Collection)

On 11 April, the hard-driving Berthold fought with an equally determined French pilot southeast of Laon, where he and Off.Stv Hüttner encountered a pair of single-seat SPAD S.VII fighters. After an extended fight, Berthold slipped behind his opponent and sent him down south of Corbeny.[27] But then Berthold had to land at nearby St. Paul Ferme due to engine problems,[28] possibly damage inflicted by his recent adversary. In any event, he was credited with his eleventh aerial victory.[29]

Beginning at about 11:30 a.m. on Saturday, 14 April, Berthold and three comrades patrolled near the main road southeast of Laon and initiated several air combats. First to attack was a twenty-two-year-old Berthold protégé, Ltn.d.Res Josef Veltjens, who went on to become a leading German World War I fighter ace. Over Craonne, Veltjens shot down a SPAD S.VII, the first of his eventual thirty-five confirmed aerial victories.[30]

A short distance away, Berthold pursued a Sopwith 1A2 (French-built version of a British two-seat) reconnaissance and bomber aircraft; he sent it down over Beau Marais Wood. The downed aircraft, attached to Escadrille N 15,[31] was confirmed as Berthold's twelfth victory.[32]

The two-seat Sopwith 1½ Strutter was built under license in France and designated the 1A2. Berthold claimed a 1A2 as his 12th victory. (Volker Koos)

On the ground, German combat engineers facilitated the withdrawal prior to the Nivelle offensive. According to H.A. Jones: 'With a ruthlessness that exceeded their military needs, the [German armies] laid waste the countryside as they went. They fell back on defensive systems from which they could, at their wish, develop a counter-stroke at any moment.'[33]

While wrecking their former facilities, German forces destroyed the living quarters that Berthold and his comrades used a year earlier. The elegant châteaus at Roupy[34] and Vaux were levelled. This destruction created an emotional conflict for Berthold. After flying over the area, he confided to his diary:

'Below us we saw the abandoned territory. It looked terrible; a vast wasteland. Also our dear old Vaux had to be seen to be believed. The beautiful piece of land that we had tended so well became a heap of rubble. We [flyers] did not smash it to pieces, destroying other people's property; we sought to protect it, even though the necessity of war disconnected our emotions to it ...'[35]

Berthold Wounded Again

The German air casualty report of Tuesday, 24 April 1917 reported that 'one officer [was] killed, three severely wounded and two injured in emergency landings'.[36] Among airmen wounded that day was Oblt Rudolf Berthold, who 'had a fierce dogfight with a Caudron R.9. During the attack, Berthold was shot ... in the right lower shin and had to break off firing at the enemy, who then went back over the lines in a dive.'[37]

The incident occurred a day short of the anniversary of Berthold's bad crash in a Pfalz Eindecker. Yet, with typical bravado, he wrote about the latest incident in his diary: '... luckily, it was a clean shot that passed right through [my shinbone]. Actually, it is quite remarkable, as my first wound was to my left leg and now [one to] the right leg; I have not yet been hit in the right arm – but I do not even want to think about that.'[38] The wound was serious and, after Berthold left the field hospital, he was sent home on recuperative leave from 23 May to 15 June.[39]

Initially, Oblt Rudolf Berthold remained with Jasta 14 after he was wounded on 14 April. This photo, taken a month later, following the staffel's move to La Neuville, also shows Vfw Gerbig (second from right), Vfw Bredow (behind Berthold) and Ltn.d.Res Veltjens (behind Bredow). (Lance J. Bronnenkant)

By the time Berthold left France, the overall conflict – known as the Second Battle of the Aisne – had come to a horrific end with high casualties on both sides. French losses were 'augmented by the destruction of ... morale in widespread mutinies ...'[40]

Despite the ground war pause during Berthold's absence, Jasta 14 found targets in the air and accounted for eight enemy aircraft.[41] Upon his return, Berthold was initially pleased with those results and wrote: 'My staffel works very well, it lacks only enemy flight operations to attack. It is quite something else with the British up in Flanders ...'[42]

Then, inexplicably, Berthold's mercurial mood flipped from buoyant to sour and he saw his men in a negative light: 'Gradually the joy of flying began to wane; I felt more and more that ... the attitude of the staffel was becoming lukewarm. The ambitious ones remained only because they did not want to abandon me.'[43]

To Berthold, the solution was obvious: he could not lead his men from the ground; he had to return to flight status and lead his men in the air. The first days of August 1917 offered no promise of victories for Jasta 14, so Berthold took the only action he could. Perhaps under the guise of going home on leave, he returned to Germany and found a sympathetic physician at the aviation replacement unit, Flieger-Ersatz-Abteilung 6, in Grossenhain, the same facility from whence he had gone to war three years earlier. There, he was pronounced fit to fly, even though the notice did not come through until 18 August 1917.[44]

Transferred to Jagdstaffel 18

The journey back to Saxony had been unnecessary, as the Luftstreitkräfte bureaucracy finally responded to his earlier requests to become more actively involved in the air war. During Berthold's time away from Jasta 14, orders arrived, transferring him to command Jasta 18, which was assigned to Army Group Wytschaete with the 4th Army in Flanders.[45] He took up his new post on Sunday, 12 August, and later wrote in his diary:

'As so much was going on in Flanders, I requested to be transferred there. Up to the last moment I had hoped that the entire Staffel 14 would be allowed to go with me, but then came the order that I was to be the leader of Jasta 18 ... and so with a heavy heart I departed from my people and once again headed out alone toward an unknown destination.'[46]

Despite his emotionally-dramatic note, Berthold did not travel by himself. His arrival at Jasta 18's airfield in Harlebeke, Belgium was recorded in another diary, that of twenty-three-year-old Ltn.d.Res Paul Strähle: 'Oblt Berthold ... takes over the staffel and brings several pilots and mechanics with him.'[47] The seasoned pilots accompanying Berthold were: Ltn.d.Res Josef Veltjens and Vfw Otto Gerbig, a civilian flyer before the war,[48] and Vfw Hermann Margot, another former FFA 23 comrade. In return, a like number of Jasta 18 pilots[49] and mechanics were sent to Jasta 14.[50]

Oblt Rudolf Berthold succeeded Rittmeister [Cavalry Captain] Karl Heino Grieffenhagen in command of Jasta 18. Grieffenhagen, commissioned into Dragoner-Regiment von Wedel (Pommersches) Nr. 11[51] before the war began, later served with two-seat and single-seat fighter units and led Jasta 18 since it was formed on 30 October 1916.[52] After being injured in a forced landing with Jasta 18, Grieffenhagen left frontline service to lead the Kampfeinsitzerschule [Single-Seat Fighter School] in Paderborn, Germany.[53]

Following their failed Aisne offensive, Allied planners shifted their efforts to the British Front in Flanders.[54] Thus, Berthold arrived at Jasta 18 at a critical time, during the Third Battle of Ypres, in which British forces advanced steadily eastward. Although the staffel was an already-experienced and battle-trained unit, Berthold wanted to lead it his way.

He wrote in his diary: 'In Flanders the British dominated the air; good fighter pilots were needed there. First I had to make my new staffel thoroughly prepared to fly. During the [rest] of August, we flew only practice flights ...'[55] The last sentence is a misstatement, however, as Paul Strähle's diary records daily air combats in good and bad weather during the early days of Berthold's command of Jasta 18.

One element of flight that might be considered as training occurred on Thursday, 16 August, when Berthold insisted that all of the aircraft in the early afternoon flight take off in formation. Strähle commented that the simultaneous take-off was 'a wonderful sight, but a little dangerous'.[56] Following a minor lull, ground 'fighting at Ypres re-intensified'[57] and, overhead, Jasta 18 logged its first victory under Berthold. Off.Stv Johannes Klein, who had arrived at the staffel a few days before Berthold, drove down a SPAD near Passchendaele, northeast of Ypres; he received credit for his first victory.[58]

After Rudolf Berthold's first meeting with his immediate superior, Hptm Helmuth Wilberg, the 4th Army's Kommandeur der Flieger, he wrote in his diary:

'I have found a new ally for my idea in Kommandeur [Wilberg]. At my recommendation, four staffeln were combined into so-called Jagdgruppen [groups] and each of these units was placed under the leadership of an old reliable officer who was also a proven fighter pilot. We still lacked them in even higher command positions over these gruppen, but we have taken a big step closer to the goal. We still do not have such excellent aircraft as our opponents have, so we will have to fight to win air superiority and we will do that only when a unified spirit reigns.'[59]

Grouping fighter units was not a new development. Four Jagdstaffeln had been combined to form Jagdgeschwader 1 [Fighter Wing 1] on 23 June 1917,[60] also in the 4th Army sector. That assembly of Jastas 4, 6, 10 and 11 – each led by a noted fighter pilot – was commanded by Germany's highest-scoring fighter ace, Rittmeister Manfred Freiherr von Richthofen, and it capitalised on his prestige as the Red Baron. But, as noted by Luftstreitkräfte Commanding General Ernst von Hoeppner, lesser known groupings of newly-emerged Jagdstaffeln had already taken place in the 5th Army sector[61] after Berthold brought his ideas to that army's Kommandeur der Flieger, Hptm Wilhelm Haehnelt. So it was fitting that, when the 4th Army announced a 'formation of Jagdgruppen by combining Jagdstaffeln', Berthold was assigned to command one of them, Jagdgruppe 7, comprising Jastas 18, 24, 31 and 36.[62]

For all of the success that Berthold then enjoyed, another aerial victory seemed to elude him. During an early evening flight on 17 August, he led the charge against a formation of British artillery spotters and their fighter escorts, but all he had to show for it was 'several bullet holes' in his aeroplane.[63]

During the kaiser's review of forces at Courtrai, Rittmeister Manfred Freiherr von Richthofen (centre) headed the aviation contingent. The first row behind him included three other *Pour le Mérite* airmen, from left: Oblt Paul Freiherr von Pechmann, Oblt Eduard Ritter von Dostler and Oblt Rudolf Berthold. (Lance J. Bronnenkant)

Berthold's fortunes improved on 20 August, when he was invited to participate in Kaiser Wilhelm II's troop review of 4th Army units at nearby Courtrai.[64] He was in good company with Rittmeister Manfred Freiherr von Richthofen and other *Pour le Mérite* flyers. Returning to Harlebeke, Berthold found he had received a photo and personal note from Prince Eitel Friedrich of Prussia, the kaiser's second son and a commander in the 1st Guards Infantry Division. During the war, the monarch's six sons were in uniform and most sent such mementoes to high-performing military officers to reinforce their mutual interests in service to the nation. In this case, Berthold had met the prince a few weeks earlier at a Sunday lunch near the 7th Army frontlines and found him to be 'a basic and unaffected man with a stern view of things'[65] – the same values Berthold considered himself to possess.

Berthold's Thirteenth Victory

The following morning was also a fine occasion for Berthold, as he added to his aerial victory score. At 7:25 a.m., he led five of his men on a patrol over the Ypres salient and up to Roulers and Thourhout. Paul Strähle's diary notes that, just over half an hour later: 'A SPAD two-seater passed above us. Berthold attacked him. I followed and also attacked; finally, Berthold shot him down near Diksmuide ...'[66]

Once again, the heat of battle led to some confusion about the type of aerial adversaries encountered. Strähle identified Berthold's target, later credited as his thirteenth victory,[67] as a big French two-seater – in an area of all-British operations. Most likely, Berthold shot down a big British two-seater, Airco D.H.4 A.7577 of 57 Squadron, Royal Flying Corps, which was then conducting aerial reconnaissance between Menin and Roulers, southwest of Diksmuide. Later, a German aeroplane dropped a message within British lines stating

Berthold's thirteenth victory was most likely an Airco D.H.4 two-seat reconnaissance aircraft, the type seen here. (Volker Koos)

that the downed aeroplane's pilot, twenty-year-old Lieutenant Cecil Barry[68] and Second-Lieutenant Frederick Ewan Baldwin Falkiner, MC,[69] age twenty-two, were both dead.[70]

Berthold's First Double Victory

Despite making daily flights, it was almost two weeks before Berthold scored again. During an early morning patrol over Ypres on Tuesday, 4 September 1917, he attacked a lumbering R.E.8 two-seat artillery spotter. Considered to be 'an easy mark for enemy fighters',[71] under the force of Berthold's bullets it went crashing down on the northern edge of the city. A British source claimed the aeroplane was hit by German anti-aircraft fire, but no flak [anti-aircraft] units claimed a victory that day.[72] Hence, it is reasonable to conclude that R.E.8 B.3411 from 7 Squadron, RFC, was counted as Berthold's fourteenth victory.[73] Both of its crewmen – nineteen-year-old 2/Lt Thomas Ernest Wray[74] and his observer, 2/Lt Wilfred Stuart Lane Payne,[75] age twenty-four – were killed in the fight.

At about 5 p.m. that day, Berthold was with two other Albatros D.IIIs when he dived on an R.E.8 over St. Jean, a few kilometres north of Ypres. According to a British report, the aeroplane was 'attacked and shot down' and the pilot, 2/Lt G.N. Moore of 9 Squadron, RFC, was wounded.[76] However, Moore managed to return to British-held territory with his observer, who was uninjured.[77] Apparently, Berthold's fifteenth victory was confirmed on the basis of Germans who saw the badly stricken R.E.8 going down, although within its own lines.[78]

The following afternoon, Berthold and his comrades were patrolling near Roulers when they attacked British two-seaters approaching nearby Gitsberg. One of the two-seaters eluded the German fighters, but Berthold caught another, Airco D.H.4 A.7530 of 55 Squadron. After an eastward chase of less than twenty kilometres, he sent it down near Thielt. The crewmen – Lt John William Fraser Neill and 2/Lt Thomas Milligan Webster[79] – were wounded and taken prisoner.[80] The aircraft was credited as Berthold's sixteenth victory.[81]

Jasta 18's victory score continued to rise and on the afternoon of Saturday, 15 September, Berthold added to it by shooting down a British reconnaissance aircraft near Zillebeke lake, southeast of Ypres. There is no question that he prevailed over a two-seater in this area and it was confirmed as his seventeenth victory, but the *Nachrichtenblatt* [Kogenluft's weekly intelligence summary] listed the British aeroplane as a 'Sopwith',[82] while the 4th

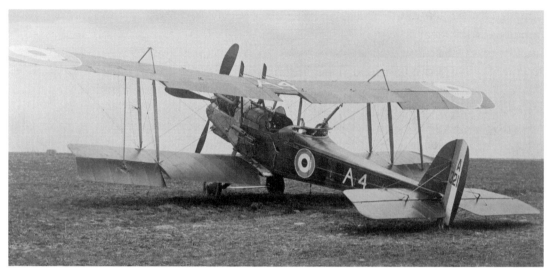

Of Rudolf Berthold's 44 confirmed aerial victories, five were Royal Aircraft Factory R.E.8 two-seaters like the one seen here. (Volker Koos)

Ltn.d.Res Paul Strähle posed alongside 1 Squadron, RFC Nieuport 17 A.6678, which he brought down on 25 May 1917. (Greg VanWyngarden)

Army's weekly operational report has it as an R.E.8. More likely, Berthold's opponent that day was Airco D.H.4 A.2130 of 55 Squadron, RFC. The crewmen – Lieutenants Eric Edward Foster Loyd and Thomas G. Deason – were uninjured and taken prisoner.[83]

Berthold's Second Double Victory

The next day, Berthold shot down a pair of R.E.8s. At about 6:00 p.m., he and his patrol – including Oberleutnants Harald Auffarth and Ernst Wilhelm Turck, and Ltn.d.Res Josef Veltjens – were near Ypres when, to the east, Berthold went after R.E.8 A.4693 of 6 Squadron, RFC. Following a short fight, he sent it down over Glengorse wood near Becelaere, killing both crewmen, 2/Lt Herbert Haslam[84] and Lance Corporal Alfred John Linay.[85 86] Some twenty minutes later, Berthold and his comrades split up and each singled out a two-seater in the area to attack. Berthold's target was another R.E.8 – A. 4728 of 4 Squadron, RFC – which he shot down northwest of Becelaere. His shots hit the crewmen, Second-Lieutenants Leslie Glendower Humphries[87] and Frederick Laurie Steben, killing the former and wounding the latter.[88] In addition to Berthold's nineteenth victory, each of his comrades was credited with an aerial victory that day.[89]

By this time, and no doubt following the example of Manfred von Richthofen and his gaudily-painted aircraft, Rudolf Berthold ordered his staffel's aircraft to be painted dark blue on the fuselages and wings, and bright red on the engine areas. These unit markings were a tribute to his roots in the infantry, which for parade dress 'wore red collars on their dark blue tunics'.[90] As he wrote in his diary:

'... in September ... the British knew the blue birds with red noses of Jasta 18 – my old Jasta in improved circumstances ... There were no pilots in the staffel who would have hesitated to shoot down an opponent in aerial combat. This was not my doing; I had

Berthold's Albatros D.III (left) in his new blue and red colour scheme with his flying sword insignia. The third aircraft from left, with the white arrow marking, was flown by his protégé, Ltn.d.Res Josef Veltjens. (Greg VanWyngarden)

merely trained and properly led them against the opposition. Their splendid performance showed what a ... spirit there was in the entire unit and in each individual pilot ...'[91]

At about 10:00 a.m. on the morning of Wednesday, 19 September, Oblt Rudolf Berthold attacked an R.E.8 on a photo reconnaissance flight east of Ypres and sent the two-seater down over German-held Becelaere. He was credited with his twentieth aerial victory.[92] Only one R.E.8 – B.3427 of 4 Squadron, RFC[93] – went down in that area; the crewmen were nineteen-year-old 2/Lt John Syers Walthew, whose body was not recovered, and Lt Michael Charles Hartnett, age twenty-one, who was buried near Jasta 18's airfield at Harlebeke,[94] a few kilometres north of Courtrai.

Even though he was, at last, flying and fighting in the active combat environment he seemed to crave, Berthold remained dissatisfied. He wrote in his diary:

'As it was a year earlier, during the Somme offensive, once again we had to go into battle [in Flanders] with an inferior fighter aeroplane. The British and French continually improved theirs. They had already brought to the frontlines the third improved versions of their aircraft, however, our pilots are far better.'[95]

When the author visited Paul Strähle in May 1967, the former Jasta 18 pilot noted that his staffel leader was often given to wide-ranging mood swings. Strähle related:

"Berthold would fly into a towering rage over some small point and then, in an instant, be overjoyed with everything. Later, we learned that medical personnel were providing him with a narcotic for the pains he continued to suffer from his crash over a year earlier and the leg wound he received after that. At the time, such drug use was accepted, as we did not realise the effects of addiction caused by them."

Fifty years later, when discussing Rudolf Berthold with this author, Oberst der Reserve a.D. Paul Strähle still had the Nieuport's rudder as a souvenir of his fifth victory. (Kilduff Collection)

Ever since Rudolf Berthold's bad crash in April 1916, he had complained of chronic pain. Suffering a gunshot wound a year later aggravated the condition and that is when he probably began to seek pain relief. World War I historian and physician Dr. M. Geoffrey Miller cited the 1915 *Encyclopaedia of Medical Treatment* when he told the author:

'Three painkillers or narcotics were given at this time. These were morphine, given by mouth or injection; codeine, which is methyl morphine, given by mouth or injection; and opium, given by mouth. Morphine was used frequently and, of course, was addictive ... It was the main painkiller during the war ... but habituation and addiction to morphine cause constant somnolence [drowsiness]. The latter suggests Berthold used cocaine, which is likely to give mood swings and agitation. It causes increased activity and keeps one awake.'

Seven More Victories

During the successful days of September, Jasta 18's older Albatros D.III fighters were replaced or augmented by improved Albatros D.Vs and new Pfalz D.IIIs.[96] Irrespective of Berthold's mood, during the next ten days of relentless effort, he increased his personal score.

On Friday, 20 September, during 'low clouds, strong wind and rain',[97] at about 9:50 a.m.

Line-up of Jasta 18 pilots, from left: Ltn Hugo Schäfer, Ltn Richard Runge, Oblt Ernst Wilhelm Turck, Ltn Walter Dingel, Ltn.d.Res Josef Veltjens, Oblt Rudolf Berthold, Oblt Harald Auffarth, Ltn.d.Res Arthur Rahn, Ltn.d.Res Paul Strähle and Ltn Otto Schober. (Paul Strähle)

German time (8:50 a.m. Allied time), while flying southeast of Ypres, Berthold attacked a single-seat fighter and shot it down between Wervicq and Menin. Due to the weather, the adversary was initially identified as a SPAD single-seater, but it may have been a similar Airco D.H.5. (A.9179) that was lost in that area. The aeroplane, from 32 Squadron, RFC, was described in a British report as 'last seen about 9 a.m. when [the] machine was apparently hit by a shell from the ground[98] and fell into our barrage ... pilot [2/Lt William Oliver Cornish,[99] was] killed in action or died of wounds ...'[100] Most likely, Cornish was Berthold's twenty-first victim.[101]

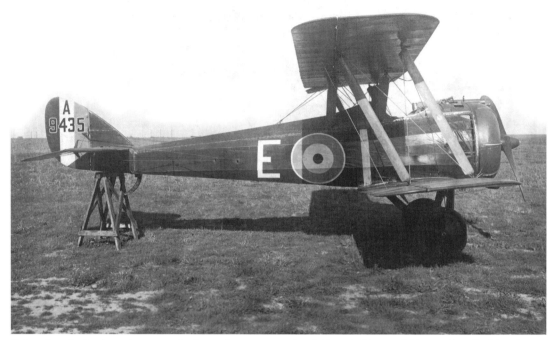

Other than its backward staggered wings, the rotary-engined Airco D.H.5 could be confused with other Allied fighter aircraft. (Volker Koos)

The weather improved throughout the following morning and Berthold was flying west of Menin when he encountered and shot down SPAD 7 B.3533 of 19 Squadron, RFC, and killed twenty-four-year-old 2/Lt Frederick William Kirby. At first, the victory was listed as 'noch nicht entschieden' [not yet determined],[102] but after several weeks of reviewing numerous German victory claims, Kogenluft staff awarded Berthold official confirmation for it.[103] As British airmen later recorded, their 'high' formation of six SPADs and two S.E.5s 'suddenly encountered many [enemy] scouts ... [and] a general fight ensued ... Lieut. [Norman] McLeod ... thinks he saw fifteen enemy aircraft altogether in this fight.'[104]

On the morning of 22 September, Berthold and his patrol were over Ypres when they spotted British two-seaters in the area. Berthold went after one, a Bristol Fighter, an aircraft with a reputation for being 'strong, fast and manoeuvrable'.[105] Berthold avoided the pilot's forward-firing gun and, after a short duel with the observer and his flexible machine gun, he shot down Bristol F.2B A.7205 of 22 Squadron, RFC, east of Zillebeke lake. Both crewmen – 2/Lts Elvis Albert Bell and Roger Emmett Nowell – were killed in the fight.[106] It was his twenty-third victory.

During an early-evening patrol near Ypres on 25 September, a British fighter was making a dangerous low-level ground patrol east of the city. Amazingly, the aeroplane was unescorted – and vulnerable. Berthold dived on the single-seater and sent it down near Gheluvelt along the road from Ypres to Menin and thereby scored his twenty-fourth victory. His target, SPAD 7 B.3520 of 19 Squadron, RFC, was flown by nineteen-year-old Lt Bernard Alexander Powers,[107] who paid the ultimate price for his devotion to duty. A

The French-built SPAD S.7, seen here in RFC markings, was used successfully by 19 Squadron and other British fighter units that Berthold encountered. (Volker Koos)

squadron report stated: 'A message was received that [German] troops were massing for an attack on the [British] 10th Corps front. Lt Powers, after studying the position on a map ... jumped into his machine (which had been made ready for him) and left the ground a ... few minutes after the message was received in order to fly over the sector of [German] lines in question and to try to bring back information. He did not return.'[108]

While British forces continued to advance east of Ypres on the morning of 26 September, a patrol of five Sopwith Camels from 70 Squadron set out on a low-level trench-strafing mission. 2/Lt C.G.V. Runnels-Moss later reported that 'after firing [their] ammunition off, the machines returned toward our lines as fast as they could, but the formation was rather split up, and at one point [Runnels-Moss] turned to the north while most of the others went towards the south ... It is very difficult to make out what happened – in fact, we have no idea. It is possible that some enemy machines saw our patrol flying low and attacked it after its ammunition was all spent. At that height, a single shot in a vital part of any of the machines could force [it] to land in enemy territory.'[109] 2/Lt Runnels-Moss and Lt G.R. Wilson[110] made it back to their airfield; the other three Camel pilots were reported as missing.[111] One of the aircraft – B.2358 piloted by a twenty-four-year-old Canadian, Lt Walter Harvey Russell Gould[112] – most likely was shot down and killed by Rudolf Berthold near Becelaere. It was his twenty-fifth victory.

At mid-day on 28 September, eight two-seat Bristol Fighters of 20 Squadron, RFC were sent on a photo reconnaissance flight over Menin, which was less than fifteen kilometres

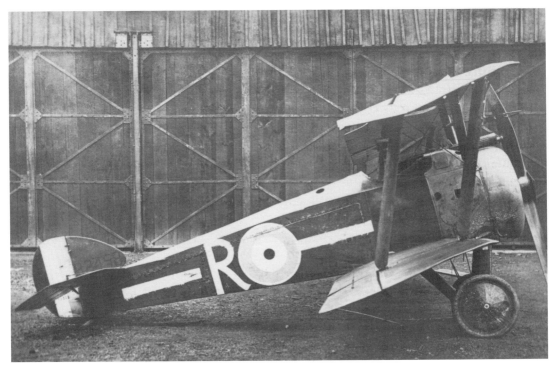

Rudolf Berthold claimed to have shot down only one Sopwith 1F.1 Camel, of which a captured example is seen here. (Volker Koos)

There was a brief celebration and Berthold's Albatros D.III was decorated with a wreath to commemorate his 25th victory. (Greg VanWyngarden)

from Jasta 18's airfield at Harlebeke. The British airmen reported encountering 'about 25 Albatros scouts',[113] which included units of Berthold's Jagdgruppe 7. Bristol Fighter crews claimed to have shot down two Albatroses, but Berthold's men came through unscathed. In fact, three Jasta 18 pilots each claimed a two-seater. But 20 Squadron reported only two losses: Bristol F.2B A.7210 and the crew of Capt John Santiago Campbell and Private G. Tester;[114] and F.2B A.7241 crewed by 2/Lts Harry Francis Tomlin and Harold Taylor Noble,[115] all of whom were killed. Berthold claimed his victim south of Zillebeke lake, over British lines; Oblt Harald Auffarth gave a location of south of Wervicq, within German lines; and Ltn.d.Res Josef Veltjens stated east of Hollebeke, over British territory. None of these victories was announced in the regular September listing; rather, they appeared in an August-September supplement, issued five weeks later. All three Jasta 18 pilots were credited with a victory, Berthold with a Martinsyde (none of which were lost that day[116]), for his twenty-sixth victory, and his comrades each with a vaguely-defined 'British two-seater.'[117]

Just before noon on 30 September, Berthold led a patrol that arrived over the lines in time to save a German two-seat reconnaissance aircraft under attack by a flight of Sopwith Pup single-seat fighters. An account of the fight appears in British records:

> 'A patrol of 66 Squadron pursued a hostile two-seater when they were dived at by a [German] formation. The [British] pilots, though taken at a disadvantage, fought well and one of the enemy machines was destroyed by Captain [Tone Hippolyte Paul] Bayetto, while another was driven down out of control by Lieutenant [Walbanke Ashby] Pritt. Two of our machines were lost on the other side and two were forced to land in our territory, while several of the other machines were shot about, one coming back with a cylinder completely shattered.'[118]

German fighter units reported no casualties that day,[119] but Jasta 18 likely accounted for the loss of the two 66 Squadron Sopwith Pups: B.2185 piloted by 2/Lt Joseph Gordon Warter,[120] who was reported 'coming down in a spin just south of Geluwe' and was killed, and B.1768, flown by Lt J.W. Boumphrey, who was also last seen descending over Geluwe and was later reported taken prisoner.[121]

Once again, these two victories were not confirmed in the regular bimonthly *Nachrichtenblatt* listing and appeared in an updated accounting weeks later. When the Jasta 18 combat reports were sorted out, victory credit for shooting down 'Sopwith single-seaters' was granted to three pilots at different locations: Oblt Berthold at Deûlémont, his twenty-seventh victory; Oblt Auffarth at Wambeke and Ltn.d.Res Veltjens at Ploegsteert wood.[122] The three crash locations are between ten and eighteen kilometres away from Geluwe, where the two British Sopwith Pups were last sighted. Present-day historians can only wonder how Kogenluft staff arrived at these determinations, awarding credit where due, and offering leeway to some pilots but not others.

Jasta 18's September successes – all attained with no casualties to the unit – may have been so invigorating that they slightly inflated Berthold's ego. On the last day of the month, Berthold's diary entry gives a glowing account which is not supported by existing documentation:

The Sopwith Pup downed by Berthold on 30 September 1917 may have been repaired and ended up like the trophy seen here. Admiring this Pup was Oblt Fritz Otto Bernert, a Berthold comrade from their KEK Vaux days. (Volker Koos)

'End of September 1917. Today is the fourth time that Jasta 18 has cleaned up in the unassailable force of the British bombing squadrons. My three Jastas brought down seventy-three enemy aeroplanes in September.'[123]

The *Nachrichtenblatt* report for that day showed relatively light British casualties claimed overall. Further, September victories for Berthold's Jagdgruppe 7 tally only fifty-five aircraft and no captive observation balloons, as follows: Jasta 18 – thirty aircraft, Jasta 24 – ten aircraft, Jasta 31 – five aircraft, and Jasta 36 – ten aircraft.[124]

The flurry – to say nothing of the fury – of his six weeks at Jasta 18 may have taken their toll on Rudolf Berthold. He would never have admitted to such an unavoidable personal failing and continued to act as if his body were as iron as his will and totally invulnerable.

CHAPTER EIGHT

STORMY TIMES

'Under Hauptmann Berthold's excellent leadership,
and energised by his personal daring and skill,
Jasta 18 has won eighteen... aerial victories over enemy aeroplanes.'[1]

GENERALLEUTNANT KARL DIEFFENBACH

Blustery, rainy autumn weather hampered air operations over Flanders in late September 1917. So, when low-hanging clouds dispersed on Tuesday, 2 October 1917, Allied and German aircrews were out in force. The *Nachrichtenblatt* weekly summary of air operations for that day noted 'brisk activity on both sides. In the 4th Army sector, [British] bombers and reconnaissance formations thrust far into our rear areas; Jagdstaffel 18 led by Oberleutnant Rudolf Berthold shot down three of five aeroplanes in a bomber formation.'[2]

The other side of the German claim was reported in the day's Royal Flying Corps War Diary entry:

'When returning from a bomb raid on Abeele aerodrome, five De Havilland 4s of 57 Squadron were attacked by about fifteen Albatros Scouts. In the combat that followed, 2/Lt. F.A. Martin and Lt. J. O'Neill were attacked by three of the scouts and the observer shot one down in flames. Capt. D. Hall and 2/Lt. E. Hartigan engaged a number of the Scouts. One attacked from the side and then turned and flew parallel with the D.H.4, the observer fired about ninety rounds and the struts were seen to be shot away on one side and the main [wings] came together. The machine broke up and fell out of control.

'Another [German] machine passed in front of the D.H.4 and the pilot [fired] fifty rounds into it [whereupon] it immediately dived, broke into flames and crashed. The pilot then fired into another Scout, which went completely over and fell out of control.

'One Albatros Scout continued to follow the D.H.4, firing at long range, so when getting nearer the lines the D.H.4 throttled down and allowed the Albatros Scout to approach. When [it was] within 200 yards, the D.H.4 [pilot, Capt. Hall] turned his machine and the observer fired a burst into the E.A. [enemy aircraft], which turned over and over and fell out of control.'[3]

One of the German pilots shot down in that fight, Jasta 18's Leutnant Walther Kleffel, was 'wounded in the calf',[4] but was also credited with shooting down an Airco D.H.4 two-seat bomber[5] for his first victory. Oblt Berthold was credited with shooting down another bomber from 57 Squadron, RFC. It crashed near Roulers and was confirmed as his twenty-eighth aerial victory.[6] His opponents were Second-Lieutenant Colin Geen Orr

MacAndrew, age twenty, and his twenty-four-year-old observer, Leicester Philip Sidney,[7] in Airco D.H.4 A.7581; both men were killed in the fight.[8] Berthold's staffel-mate Ltn Richard Runge forced a third D.H.4 to land near Roulers[9] and thereby scored his eighth victory.

The Jasta 18 War Diary month-end entry made a reference to Berthold that could be taken two ways: 'His aeroplane was known by friend and foe only as *"der feuerspeiende Berg"'*[10] – literally the 'fire-spewing mountain' – with machine-gun fire pouring forth. On another level, the phrase could also have meant 'volcano', reflecting Berthold's fiery and ever more erratic temperament. The pilot wounded in the most recent fight, Ltn Walther Kleffel, recalled:

> 'Berthold was a strange person, one time charming, another time not so. I did not get on well with him. That was probably because, upon returning to Jasta 18 after being wounded, I often crash landed, as I always had to fly in the highest position – mostly over 6,000 metres – without any of the aids [such as oxygen] that were available later for [flying at] this altitude. Thus, I became extremely nervous due to overexertion, which was explainable by the high altitude.'[11]

The pilot of S.E.5a B.507 of 60 Squadron, RFC inadvertently landed at Harlebeke Airfield, then home to Oblt Rudolf Berthold's Jagdstaffel 18. (Greg VanWyngarden)

The return of stormy weather on 3 October led to greatly diminished flying activity over the Flanders sector for a week. Heavy mist caused nineteen-year-old Second-Lieutenant John Joseph Fitzgerald of 60 Squadron, RFC, who started out on the morning of Friday, 5 October, to inadvertently land his S.E.5a fighter (B.507) on the German airfield at Harlebeke. Jasta 18 was based at that facility and one of its pilots, Ltn.d.Res Paul Strähle, noted the lucky acquisition of a new British fighter aircraft in his diary: 'Early this morning a disoriented Englishman in an S.E.5 with [a] 200-hp Hispano-Suiza engine landed on our airfield. Great excitement!'[12] The aircraft was turned over to the Inspekteur der Flieger [inspectorate of aviation] for examination and testing and the Irish-born pilot became a prisoner of war.[13]

Berthold Shot Down Again

Wednesday, 10 October seemed to offer a break in the steady rain. German weather staff reported: 'Low-hanging clouds and rain … detrimental to flying activity; in the afternoon, it cleared up temporarily, allowing reasonable visibility in the 4th and 5th Armies' sectors.'[14] A British communiqué noted: 'Little flying was possible, except in the early morning and the evening, owing to rain and wind.'[15]

Eager to get back in the air, despite unsettled skies, Berthold led eight other Jasta 18 aeroplanes[16] to the area over Roulers, north and east of Ypres. The Albatroses departed Harlebeke at about 4:45 p.m. (German time). Two flights of S.E.5s from 56 Squadron, RFC, one of the highest-scoring British fighter squadrons of the war, also took advantage of the weather that afternoon and headed for the same area.[17] The leader of 'A' Flight, Capt Gerald C. Maxwell, MC, then a twenty-victory ace, later wrote in his combat report:

'Crossed lines at 14,000 feet and patrolled area. At about 5 p.m. [I] saw and attacked about twelve E.A. Scouts, east of Ypres. Dived on several and fired a drum of Lewis [machine-gun ammunition] and about 100 rounds of Vickers [ammunition] at very close range. E.A. went down very steeply and I lost sight of him. At 5:10 p.m. I saw a machine go down in pieces about over Gheluvelt; whether it was an E.A. or one of our machines, I do not know.'[18]

Captain (later Major) Gerald Joseph Constable Maxwell, MC led 'A' Flight of 56 Squadron, RFC into combat with Jasta 18 on 10 October 1917 and very likely shot down Oblt Rudolf Berthold. (Alex Revell)

Although Maxwell was not credited with a victory that day, he most likely shot down Berthold's Albatros. Ltn.d.Res Paul Strähle later wrote in his diary that the Jasta 18 flight had 'aerial combats with several formations of S.E.5s, D.H.4s and [Sopwith] triplanes. Oblt Berthold was severely wounded in the right upper arm (bone shattered) … Other Albatros flights joined in the battle. They shot down two Englishmen. One of them broke up in the air. Oblt Berthold landed smoothly at our airfield, despite having half-severed ailerons and heavy bleeding from his wound.'[19]

There is some thought among aviation historians that Berthold was flying Pfalz D.III 4004/17, seen here, when he was shot down during Jasta 18's encounter with 56 Squadron, RFC. (Greg VanWyngarden)

The staffel leader lost consciousness immediately after landing[20] and was rushed to Kgl.Bayer.-Reserve-Feldlazarett 45[21] [Royal Bavarian Field Hospital 45] in Courtrai, some five kilometres from Jasta 18's airfield. An examination of Berthold's aeroplane revealed that the bullet that did so much damage to him had ricocheted off part of his cockpit and entered his upper arm at an odd angle, causing a comminuted fracture of the humerus. It was exactly a year to the day since Berthold had arrived at Jasta 14, mostly recovered from earlier injuries. Now he was in hospital once again.

There would be no way to conceal the sudden and probably long-term absence from frontline service of a major, highly-decorated fighter ace such as Rudolf Berthold. Consequently, just over two weeks after he was hospitalised, the *Nachrichtenblatt* announced to the Luftstreitkräfte:

'During a hotly-contested air battle over Zonnebeke on the evening of 10th October, Oberleutnant Berthold was severely wounded by a shot in the right upper arm, but was able to land his aeroplane smoothly on his home airfield.'[22]

Any chance for a speedy recovery was dashed when it became apparent that treating and helping such a complicated injury to heal was beyond the scope of a field hospital. After Berthold was deemed to be in a stable condition, on Wednesday, 31 October, he was transferred to the St. Vincenzstift Hospital in Hannover.[23]

While Berthold was on the way back to Germany, his Jasta 18 comrades wired news of the transfer to his sister Franziska in Berlin, where she was a nursing supervisor in the Viktoria-Lazarett[24] [Victoria Hospital], which was affiliated with the Charité University Hospital in the German capital. She prevailed in her request to have her brother transported to Berlin for treatment by Dr. August Bier, one of Europe's foremost bone specialists and the hospital's chief instructor for physicians training to become military surgeons.[25] Clearly, Rudolf Berthold was to receive the best possible medical attention available at the time.

Return to Berlin

He arrived at Dr. Bier's well-known clinic in the Ziegelstrasse on 2 November 1917[26] and began a four-month course of treatment. Bier's priority was to avoid amputation of the arm and then to determine what mobility Berthold might have with it.

Two days later, Rudolf Berthold began to receive the tributes of a nation and army grateful for his sacrifices in battle. The first came from Generalleutnant Ernst von Hoeppner, Commanding General of the Luftstreitkräfte, who wrote:

'His Majesty the *Kaiser und König* [Emperor and King], in recognition of your outstanding achievements as a fighter pilot and leader, has been moved to promote you to Hauptmann [captain]. With sincere congratulations on this example of recognition by your supreme warlord, I join in the wish that full recovery allows you to, once again, participate and succeed in the struggle for German supremacy in the air.'[27]

Next, Generalleutnant Karl Dieffenbach, Commander of the 9th Reserve Corps and Army Group Wytschaete, wrote:

'With deep regret I have received the news about your serious injury. I am moved to express my heartfelt thanks to you for the excellent and meritorious deeds you have accomplished during your affiliation with Gruppe Wytschaete.

'In an admirable, vigorously aggressive spirit and the most relentless use of your own person, you have succeeded, often against a numerically superior enemy, with no regard for the circumstances under which you found him, to still challenge him and in the short time of six weeks to have personally shot down sixteen aeroplanes.

'Under your excellent ... leadership, and energised by your personal daring and skill, Jasta 18 has won eighteen – and the Jagdgruppe has eighty-four – aerial victories over enemy aeroplanes ... I hereby acknowledge, on behalf of all of the troops in the Gruppe, your splendid achievements and contributions, and express to you my warmest thanks for them.

'I wish you for the course of your recovery all the best from the heart and hope to see you refreshed and robust back among us.'[28]

And, from Hptm Helmuth Wilberg, Commander of Aviation for the 4th Army:

'To my joy, I hear that you are feeling better and you are under the attentive care of Professor Bier. I am sure the course of your recovery will be successful.

'With all my heart but I would like to ask you to not come back too early! If you did, you would not give the best service to yourself or the Fatherland. We will need you in the spring, but not in the winter! This way … you will help to harden your weakened body for the heavy tasks that await us.

'We are all fine. Wytschaete is slowly but surely becoming a quiet sector. Your worthy men are working as gallantly as ever.

'Once again, all best wishes and sincere thanks for what you have achieved for the 4th Army through your tireless zeal and selfless application of your talents.'[29]

Berthold's superiors were military men and had no real sense of the extent of his injuries. At this point, entries in Berthold's *Persönliches Kriegstagebuch* [personal war diary] took on a new tone. Written in the third person, most likely by his sister Franziska, who devoted herself almost entirely to her brother's care, the diary entries offered insight into Rudolf Berthold's true condition, as noted early in his convalescence:

> 'A long, difficult ordeal began, made tolerable only by countless examples of recognition and respect from the widest circles. It was due to Herr [Doktor] August Bier that the arm was saved; it healed slowly, but remained paralysed.'[30]

Exercising the same strong will-power as her brother, 33-year-old Franziska Berthold took charge of matters relating to his hospitalisation in Berlin. (Heinz J. Nowarra)

A Difficult Convalescence

Berthold was officially on medical leave. Thus, four days after he was hospitalised, temporary commands of Jasta 18 and Jagdgruppe 7 (now comprising Jastas 18, 24, 33 and 36) were assigned to Oblt Ernst Wilhelm Turck,[31] a senior regular army officer and fighter pilot. Even though Berthold was severely wounded, he focused on eventually returning to his frontline commands. An undated diary entry recorded a potential stumbling block – and his determination to overcome it:

'Berthold's return to flying was, in the judgment of the doctors, ruled out. But Berthold did not let himself be discouraged. He learned to write with his left hand and said: "If I can write, I can fly!"'[32]

Berthold was kept informed of wartime developments. Hence, to him, the Bolshevik Revolution, the subsequent collapse of the Russian army and the peace talks at Brest-Litovsk that began in December 1917 related only to their effect on the Western Front. Within this view, German troops and air units freed from duty on the Eastern Front would aid the spring 1918 offensive against British and French forces.[33]

Exciting days lay ahead and Rudolf Berthold was eager – and impatient, as usual – to be back in the air. His attending physician, Dr. Bier, was also a pioneer in the development and use of spinal anaesthesia, achieved by injecting cocaine into the spinal column.

In view of Bier's successful use of the cocaine for surgery and its acceptance at the time by Dr. Sigmund Freud and others to treat melancholy (clinical depression), it is easy to see how that drug would have been prescribed for Berthold's chronic pain. But, as World War I historian and physician Dr. M. Geoffrey Miller told the author: 'Bad temper and aggressiveness are common features of cocaine ... Cocaine only relieves pain when given locally by injection; taking it by mouth or intravenously ... [only] gives the patient a feeling of euphoria when first given and that is why cocaine users continue the drug, ignoring the irritability and aggression [that accompany it]. Using cocaine by intravenous injection ... would suggest psychological addiction.' Those points make Berthold's subsequent actions more understandable.

When the boredom of a hospital room in Berlin and its treatment programs became more than Berthold could bear, a drug-inspired impetuosity triumphed over his sense of reason. As an entry in Berthold's diary noted: 'In mid-February [1918], scarcely eight days out of bed, he reported to the Feldflugchef [chief of field aviation] and stated that he wanted to ... resume command of [Jagdgruppe 7].'[34]

Given his stature in the German military aviation establishment, Berthold would have had access to the Feldflugchef, Oberstleutnant [Lieutenant Colonel] Hermann von der Lieth-Thomsen, and he would have been allowed to present his case for reinstatement at such a high level. He must have been persuasive, as his diary ghost-writer continued: 'Berthold ... would no longer let himself be stopped, although the arm [wound] still festered badly and his body was still weakened. With sorrow and grief in their hearts, those who cared for him watched him depart [from Berlin].'[35]

On Friday, 1 March 1918, Berthold reported to the medical office at the aviation replacement unit Flieger-Ersatz-Abteilung 5 in Hannover. He was examined and allowed to proceed back to Jasta 18, but restricted from flying.[36] While he was convalescing in Berlin, his staffel had benefitted from the successful German counter-attack at the conclusion of the Battle of Cambrai in November 1917. Jasta 18 moved south from the 4th Army sector in Belgium to an airfield in Avelin, France, just outside of Lille, in the 6th Army sector.

The airfield was new to Rudolf Berthold, but many of his old comrades were still there and he received a warm welcome from them on 6 March.[37] Just the sight of their staffel leader was inspiring. And, in terms of air combat success, a recent issue of the weekly

Luftwaffe [Air Weapon] magazine listed him as Germany's third highest-scoring living fighter ace at the time.[38]

As he could not yet lead them in the air, however, he found the ideal pilot who could: Hptm.d.Res Hans Joachim Buddecke. Berthold's oldest and best friend had returned from his second tour of duty with the Turkish air arm, but no command in France was available for him. Consequently, when Berthold requested that his friend join him at Jasta 18, Buddecke was able to leave his post at Jasta 30 and, on 8 March, the long-time comrades were reunited at Avelin.

It was a joyous occasion when Hptm.d.Res Hans Joachim Buddecke arrived at Jasta 18 to help his old friend. Seen at the reception at Avelin Airfield were, from bottom left: Vfw Hermann Margot, Ltn Hugo Schäfer, Ltn Hans von Buttlar, Ltn.d.Res Josef Veltjens, Berthold (with his arm in a sling) talking to Buddecke, Ltn Johannes Klein, Ltn Oliver Freiherr von Beaulieu-Marconnay and Ltn.d.Res Arthur Rahn. Top row from left: Ltn Georg von Hantelmann, Ltn Paul Lohmann, Oblt Ernst Wilhelm Turck, Ltn Walter Dingel, Ltn Walter Kleffel and Vfw Theodor Weischer. (Arthur Rahn Album via NMUSAF)

A Hero's Death in the Air

The co-leadership arrangement seemed to be ideal: Berthold motivated the pilots on the ground and Buddecke, a master air fighter, led them to targets in the sky. Jasta 18 had become almost scoreless and needed much inspiration. Shortly after noon on Sunday, 10 March, the weather was good, but visibility was poor[39] and Buddecke led a patrol of red and blue Albatroses southeast, towards Lens.

At about 1:00 p.m., east of Lens, the German patrol was surprised by a flight of Sopwith 1F.1 Camels from 'C' Flight of 3 Squadron, Royal Naval Air Service. The fast and nimble little fighters, fitted with twin Vickers .303-calibre machine guns, were formidable opponents. In the hands of a veteran pilot such as twenty-four-year-old Flight Lieutenant Arthur Treloar Whealy (in B.7220) the Camel was deadly. As Whealy's flight dived on the Albatroses, he singled out one and, as he reported:

'I immediately dived on his tail and opened fire at about 100 yards, firing a burst of about forty rounds from each gun. The E.A. turned half over on its back and went down in a series of stalls and spins. I watched till it was about 3-4,000 feet above the ground and then lost sight of it on account of the haze ...'[40]

JG 2 commander Hptm Adolf Ritter von Tutschek earned the highest bravery awards of the Kingdoms of Prussia (*Pour le Mérite*) and Bavaria (Knight's Cross of the Military Max-Joseph Order). The latter was presented before he became a pilot. (Greg VanWyngarden)

Ritter von Tutschek seen preparing to take off in Fokker Dr.I 404/17, the aircraft in which he was killed. (Greg VanWyngarden)

Before the 'staffel-swap,' Jasta 15 used markings such as those seen on Off.Stv Richard Schleichardt's Albatros D.V 2226/17. (Volker Koos)

Hans Joachim Buddecke, fell and crashed within German lines at Harnes, northeast of Lens – dead at age twenty-seven. He was credited as Whealy's tenth 'kill.'[41] Once again, Berthold was stunned by a great personal loss, as if he expected his closest friend to be invincible.

Berthold had no time to dwell on Buddecke's death, however; the initial attack of the *Kaiserschlacht* [Kaiser's Battle], the German term for the spring offensive, bolstered by fresh troops from the Eastern Front, was to be launched on 21 March. German units in the 17th, 2nd and 18th Armies – from Arras south to La Fère – prepared to separate French and British forces in the Somme sector before American troops could effectively be deployed.[42] Jasta 18, based close to the 17th Army sector, was ready to respond as needed.

But another event altered Berthold's role in the coming offensive. On Friday, 15 March, Hptm Adolf Ritter [Knight] von Tutschek – the commander of Jagdgeschwader 2 (JG 2), a twenty-seven-victory ace and a *Pour le Mérite* recipient – was killed in aerial combat.[43] The following day Berthold, who had twenty-eight victories, was appointed to succeed von Tutschek in commanding JG 2. Later that day he was driven some 140 kilometres south-southeast from Avelin to JG 2's airfield at Toulis in the 18th Army sector to meet his new comrades.[44]

Berthold Commands JG 2

Berthold had long advocated grouping four Jagdstaffeln into Jagdgeschwadern [fighter wings] led by experienced and combat-proven fighter pilots. Now, at last, his efforts had been recognised. Encouraged by the success of Jagdgeschwader 1, formed the previous June under the leadership of Rittmeister Manfred Freiherr von Richthofen in the 2nd Army sector, on 2 February 1918 the chief of the German general staff had authorised creation of two more fighter wings[45]: JG 2 commanded by Ritter von Tutschek, then a twenty-three-victory ace, and comprising Jastas 12, 13, 15 and 19 for the 7th Army sector; and JG 3 led by Hptm Bruno Loerzer, who also had twenty-three victories, and made up of Jastas 2, 26, 27 and 36 in the 4th Army sector.

Hardly settled into JG 2, which was about to change airfields[46] in preparation for the offensive, Berthold made an unprecedented request. He had strong personal ties to Jasta 18, which he felt had been much more proficient under his leadership. But, as his new Geschwader's units were permanently assigned to it, he could not add or replace a staffel. Berthold's request, or quietly-stated requirement, came at the worst possible time, four days before the offensive was to begin. Yet, he was accommodated, as noted in JG 2's war diary:

> 'Hauptmann Berthold wanted very much to exchange Jasta 15 for his old Jasta 18. He himself was generally grounded. Only when the Geschwader was deployed in its entirety would he be allowed to fly with it... Hauptmann Berthold saw his wish just about fulfilled; from Jasta 18 came a line of old friends, proven comrades-in-arms and reliable subordinates ...'[47]

The former Jasta 18 pilots and ground crewmen, now re-named as Jasta 15, brought with them the red-nosed blue aeroplanes that had had become synonymous with Rudolf Berthold's success. The 'new' Jasta 18 adopted a white and red colour scheme, and relocated to the 17th Army sector.[48] On the eve of the first offensive, Berthold exercised an air of entitlement that had always worked for him. He was granted a brief leave to attend Hans Joachim Buddecke's funeral in Berlin. Given the frequency of air traffic from the battlefield to the homeland, it would have been easy for flights to be arranged to transport Berthold to the German capital and back within a short time.

Buddecke was a native of Berlin and, appropriately, his body was to be buried with great honour and pageantry in the Invalidenfriedhof [Invalids' Cemetery]. Established in 1748 by King Friedrich II of Prussia (Frederick the Great), that cemetery became the burial ground for distinguished Prussian military personnel.[49]

On the day of the funeral, Friday, 22 March,[50] Rudolf Berthold was comforted by his sister, who, almost certainly, wrote the entry in his diary, noting that 'the friends were together barely five days ... Berthold was not weak, indeed, his eyes looked more determined than ever, although his voice trembled [during final remarks] at the grave of his friend. [He] found no one out there to replace Buddecke, his last friend.'[51]

Immediately following the funeral, Berthold returned to JG 2, but his absence may have hindered the Geschwader's role in the opening drive of the *Kaiserschlacht*, on 21 March. German 18th Army records for this period are sporadic, but it was not until three days later that Hptm Alfred Streccius, the commander of aviation, reported about activities on 23 March:

'The 113th and 28th Infantry Divisions complain about the strong dominance of enemy flyers. The troops have the impression that British flyers can do anything with impunity. Use of Jagd- or Schlachtstaffeln [close air support units] is strongly desired here. Jagdgeschwader 2 has received orders to deploy all available forces immediately.'[52]

JG 2's results in the air accompanied initial tactical success of the ground battle, which 'achieved an advance of about forty miles in eight days'.[53] But the opening stage of the offensive had failed to achieve its strategic objective: splitting French and British forces in the Somme sector. So a second drive was launched in April – yet another month during which Rudolf Berthold had to remain on the ground while his Geschwader comrades fought against ever-improving and ever-growing aerial opponents.

Also at this time, the post-war JG 2 history recorded, 'the slender Hauptmann, with his right arm in a sling, did not betray what he thought. A warm glow was not to be found in his big fiery eyes ... He said over and over, "And I will fly again ... even if they must carry me to the aeroplane!"'[54]

Until he could fly, Berthold devoted his personal energy, willpower and intellect to inspiring the men of his four Jagdstaffeln. One such occasion was during the ceremony after Jasta 12's Ltn Hermann Becker scored his ninth victory on 12 April. The thirty-year-old pilot was about to be presented with the *Ehrenbecher* [cup of honour] to mark the achievement when Berthold told him:

'As the war becomes more like iron every day, so this goblet is no longer made of silver, but, rather, of iron. The outward appearance of an award does not convey its value, but only indicates the achievement. Thus, a fighter pilot ... may find this type of *Ehrenbecher* to be more valuable than receiving one made of silver ...'[55]

As events would show, Berthold picked the right symbol to exemplify the hard times to come.

Chapter Nine
Beginning of the End

'I am pleased to express my appreciation and gratitude for your fortieth victory in aerial combat ... We hope for new successes that will accrue to the glory of you and your branch of service and to the salvation of the German Fatherland.'[1]

General der Infanterie Johannes von Eben

The German Luftstreitkräfte suffered a severe blow to its morale on Sunday, 21 April 1918. During a noontime aerial combat over the Somme sector, Germany's leading fighter pilot – the eighty-victory ace Rittmeister Manfred Freiherr von Richthofen – was shot down and killed behind British lines. Many tributes were written and Richthofen was buried with honours by his foes. But Hauptmann Rudolf Berthold took the death of this legendary German as a personal loss, one he, again, felt compelled to avenge, even in the face of overwhelming odds. Written in his diary was this self-challenge: 'Richthofen has fallen, comrades fall daily, the British have surpassed us; I must show young people that duty stands above all else.'[2]

Berthold willingly and eagerly tried to carry out that promise, even while continuing to suffer great pains from his most recent wounds. He described his misery, at times in great detail, in letters to his sister Franziska, to apprise her of his medical condition. Some years later she provided those texts to the German military writer Werner Schulze von Langsdorff,[3] whose early research is the source of a letter dated 25 April 1918, describing a medical treatment Berthold required:

> 'The evening of the [23 April], a bone splinter protruded from my lower wound. My very capable medical orderly came immediately with a pair of tweezers, and with much skill and force, he removed [it] ... by the light of day. I passed out during this violent procedure. The pains were horrific. But the lower wound is beginning to close. Only the upper wound still festers very heavily.
>
> 'When the bone splinter was being withdrawn it broke into pieces, as the opening was too small and the splinter was snagged in the flesh, and so he had to probe and extract each piece. Out here one cannot ask for too much and my medical orderly believes that if we do not find a wound specialist, it would be pointless to consult with other doctors – as the orderly knows as much as they do about this problem.'[4]

In the same letter, Rudolf also shared other concerns with Franziska – worries that hinted at his precarious mental state:

'I have so much worry and trouble, as I must let three staffel leaders go. It is a hard blow. Now that Richthofen is dead, I am the very last [Geschwader commander]. And instead of cooperation, one finds difficulties. It is ugly and wears one down. The staffel leaders had formed a sort of conspiracy to overthrow me. I will be ruthlessly hard. In the coming days, I want to fly again. The "boys" should be ashamed of themselves and I will get rid of these disruptive brothers. The death of Richthofen has been very depressing. Now I have to move on as one of the "old guard". Maybe I will also be killed.'[5]

That letter was another by-product of Berthold's increasingly black moods, which could have been caused by chronic cocaine usage. So it should be noted that, first, he was not the last (or only) air wing commander; Richthofen had designated a successor at Jagdgeschwader 1, Hptm Wilhelm Reinhard, to assure a smooth transition in the event of his death. Second, there is no evidence that Berthold's leadership was ever challenged by his subordinates. For the most part, his men admired and even idolised him, despite his outbursts of temper and fits of loud swearing. And, third, there was no mass exodus among JG 2's staffel leaders. Over the next three weeks, in the normal scheme of things, three of his four staffel commanding officers moved on to newer units that needed combat-experienced leaders.

Even though Rudolf Berthold did not fly during the first five months of 1918, he had a new Pfalz D.IIIa in readiness. Here, it is seen at right, at Balâtre Airfield in early April. (Greg VanWyngarden)

After learning of her brother's continual severe pains, Franziska Berthold understood that he needed the pain relief offered by drugs, if even at the frightful personal cost of a descent into paranoiac delusion. To quote an entry in the diary she maintained for him:

'Under his leadership, his Geschwader ... performed magnificently ... But his vigour was gone. The constant discharge from his wounds and the nerve pain wore down the body more and more. In order to work [in the air] and have inner peace again, he had to be given [drugs]. He would not relinquish his newly begun work, as he saw how every part of it was needed. His old faithful comrades were all dead or back home. The young ones no longer understood him and that, for him ... probably remained the greatest pain.'[6]

Not informed of his mental state, but very aware of his perverse desire to return to flying, Berthold's superiors increased his administrative duties to keep him busy. On 8 May he was appointed to coordinate all fighter aviation within the 18th Army sector.[7] But, when the second German drive (the Lys Offensive) also failed to achieve strategic success and was followed by a third drive (the Aisne Offensive), beginning on Monday, 27 May,[8] Berthold could no longer stay out of the fight.

His units had soldiered on with rapidly aging Albatros D.Va aircraft that experienced wing design difficulties and Fokker Dr.I triplanes plagued by production problems, but the rugged tubular steel construction of the new Fokker D.VII biplane fighter offered German airmen the best hope of protecting their skies. Indeed, Berthold was so anxious to fly the aeroplane – even though technically forbidden to fly at all – that he borrowed one from JG 1. He liked the aeroplane very much and noted that 'it flies very nicely. Above all, the control column is so light that I could work it even with my right arm.'[9]

More Berthold Victories

On the morning of 28 May, Berthold ordered his new Fokker D.VII rolled out at Le Mesnil (Nesle) Airfield for his first combat flight since leaving the hospital almost three months earlier. As he told his men during the pre-flight briefing: 'We are not here to carry out cavalier aerial combats at 500 metres' altitude. The infantry is out there in the mud, waiting for us, and we have to help them.'[10] He and a patrol of Jasta 15 fighters headed southeast, toward the most active lines.

At about 11:15 a.m., Berthold and his wingman, nineteen-year-old Ltn Oliver Freiherr von Beaulieu-Marconnay, dived on a pair of French SPAD XVI two-seaters that were attacking German positions near Crouy, northeast of Soissons. Berthold wrote in a letter:

'After a few shots, [my] opponent was finished ... The second was shot down by [von Beaulieu-Marconnay]. It is a ray of hope. Above all I have a better grip on my Geschwader and can tell the people at Kogenluft the truth [about my capabilities].'[11]

The two aircraft from Escadrille Sop 278[12] were counted as Berthold's twenty-ninth victory and his companion's first.[13]

Despite having to fly in a heavy mist the following evening,[14] JG 2's pilots must have felt that 'the old Berthold' was back in action. Beginning at about 6:30 p.m., he scored a double victory, hitting first a SPAD XIII single-seat fighter and then a two-seat Salmson 2A2 reconnaissance aircraft[15], which he described almost incidentally: 'I shot down my thirtieth and thirty-first within ten minutes, one of them over his own airfield. I almost

In late May, Berthold resumed combat flying in the first of several Fokker D.VII aircraft in markings that have since become iconic. (Helge K.-Werner Dittmann)

stayed over there ... as I shot up [my] propeller ...'[16] The mangled propeller caused his engine to run unevenly. Berthold turned it off, glided away from his falling second opponent and made an emergency landing within forward German lines south of Soissons.[17] He wrecked the Fokker D.VII, but suffered no injury to himself.

Berthold received a new Fokker D.VII a few days later and used it on the evening of Wednesday, 5 June. According to JG 2's war diary, he shot down an Airco D.H.9 two-seater in flames near St. Just-en-Chaussée,[18] less than twenty kilometres southwest of Montdidier. A British casualty report noted that a D.H.9 (C.6203 of 103 Squadron, RAF) was 'last seen going down in spirals, attacked by four [German aeroplanes] over the woods between Warsy and Lignières, apparently under control.'[19] After that sighting the aeroplane crashed and the crewmen, Capt Henry Turner and 2/Lt George Webb,[20] were found dead. The D.H.9 was recorded as Berthold's thirty-second victory. [21]

Even though very successful at this point, Rudolf Berthold relied on drugs to an obvious, but discreetly mentioned, extent. Nineteen-year-old Ltn Georg von Hantelmann of Jasta 15 mentioned it to his sister, Anna-Luise, who later wrote about Berthold:

'He had [the use of] only one arm, so his skill was all the more admirable; but he sought physical relief from pain through the use of morphine [more likely cocaine], which unfortunately often made personal dealings with him very difficult. So, despite the great respect that was accorded to him, he was not very popular in many instances.'[22]

Feindlicher Verluste
----
vom 23. bis einschliesslich 29.5.18.

fde. Nr.	Datum	Zeit	Sieger	Verband	Typ	Ort
1	23.5.18	11^{25} v.	Ltn. Thiede	Jasta 24	Gitterrumpf	in Gegend Avricourt
2	"	11^{25}-11^{45} n.	" "	" 24	Voisin-Git-terrumpf	b.Erchen diess. brennend abg.
3	"	11^{50} n.	" "	" 24	fdl.Flugzeug	bei Noyon zw. d.Linien
4	"	11^{45} v.	Ltn.Schneider	" 79	Bristol Fighter	bei Tricot
5	"	10^{30} v.	Ltn.d.L.Helber		Spad-Ein-sitzer	bei Remaugies
6.	"		Vzfw.Kunau	Fl.Abt.218		
7	28.5.18	11^{15} v.	Hptm.Berthold	Kdr.d.Jagdgn 2	frz.Ifl. Flgz.	nördl.Crouy, jens.
8	"	11^{15} v.	Ltn.v.Beaulieux-Marconnay	Jasta 15	A.R.Dopp. Sitz.	östl.Soissons jens.brend.ab
9	29.5.18	6^{30} n.	Hptm.Berthold	Kdr.des Jgd-gesch.2	Spad-Ein-sitzer	Südwestl.Sois-sons(bestät.
10	"	6^{40} n.	" "	"	frz.Dopp. Sitz.	Südöstl.Sois-sons(bestätigt)
11	"	6^{30} n.	Ltn.Veltjens	Jasta 15	Spad-Ein-sitzer	südl.Soissons (bestätigt)

- 16 -

Berthold's double victory of 29 May 1918 was included in the 18th Army Air Commander's weekly report. (Kilduff Collection)

An Airco D.H.9 in the markings of 103 Squadron, RAF, showing a crew that could have faced Rudolf Berthold on 5 June 1918. (*Cross & Cockade International*)

But the course of the war overrode all other considerations. As part of the fourth German drive (Noyon-Montdidier Offensive), on 9 June, General der Infanterie Oskar von Hutier's 18th Army 'attacked from the Noyon-Montdidier sector... [but] were soon stopped by French counter attacks'.[23] JG 2 aircraft were in the middle of this fierce battle and fought against a variety of Allied aircraft in hopes of helping to sustain the German advance. On Tuesday, 11 June, Berthold shot down a low-flying two-seater in the sector, while his comrades fought with British Sopwith 1.F1 Camels that were protecting the ground strafing aircraft. Confirmed as Berthold's thirty-third victory, in the heat of battle, it was identified only as a 'French infantry support aircraft'.[24] It was one of several brought down that day by Berthold's Geschwader.[25]

The following day, 12 June, German forces anticipated a French attack from Compiègne to their south and, while good weather held in the morning, JG 2 aircraft were out and scored three victories. A rainy afternoon curtailed flight operations and the airmen of Jasta 15 were confined to their *Kasino* at Mesnil-Bruntel Airfield. It was still raining at about 6:00 p.m., when Hptm Rudolf Berthold appeared in the doorway and announced:

'*Meine Herren* [gentlemen], get ready! The staffel takes off in ten minutes. I will lead. At the frontlines, northwest of Noyon, French bombers are pounding our artillery positions to smithereens and we are sitting here, drinking coffee. The weather is bad, so if the staffel becomes separated, each one of you will attack individually. I ... do not need to tell my flight that each of you will remain at the frontlines until the last drop of fuel [is expended]. The enemy advancing on the ground is also a worthy target'.[26]

Each pilot knew he had enough fuel for eighty minutes of flight time, according to Ltn Joachim von Ziegesar, a member of this flight.[27] Over the battlefield, there was a wild mêlée of German and French aeroplanes chasing each other through the mist. Berthold was seen attacking several adversaries.

After an hour into the flight and with only twenty minutes' of fuel remaining, the patrol formed up to return home. But then von Ziegesar saw Berthold go after another French aeroplane. The others waited briefly, but, with only ten minutes' of fuel left, they flew back to Mesnil-Bruntel. They landed with nearly dry fuel tanks. There was no sign of Berthold and an anxious time began, as von Ziegesar later wrote:

'We sat awake for a long time. Nobody thought of going to sleep without knowing, for certain, the fate of our leader. Finally a furiously angry telephone call comes in the early morning hours [of 13 June]. Hauptmann Berthold vanquished his opponent and, with an empty fuel tank and his machine all shot up, he landed within the lines of our forward infantry units'.[28]

The daring landing and the damaged aeroplane meant little to Berthold, who the following day wrote to his sister:

'Today, unfortunately, I cannot fly, as my engine was riddled with bullets in an aerial combat yesterday. The "boys" have plucked me clean in recent days. There were always too many of them. I shot down my thirty-third opponent … out of a [flight of a] hundred enemy aircraft …I have never seen so many opponents at one time …'[29]

Berthold's target was most likely a SPAD XIII of Escadrille Spa 96 flown by twenty-one-year-old Caporal [Corporal] Jacques Monod, who was badly wounded in the fight and died the following day.[30]

Vfw Albert Haussmann of JG 2's Jasta 13 posed with a French SPAD XIII of Escadrille Spa 89. (Volker Koos)

On Tuesday, 18 June, Berthold scored his fourth double victory, but it received brief mention in a letter to his sister a day later:

'Today we have rain. Thank God, for otherwise it would have been impossible for me to fly with [the Geschwader]. My arm has worsened. Beneath the still open wound it is … badly swollen and inflamed. I think the bone fragments are forcing their way out, as the cyst that formed is quite hard. The pains are just awful. Yesterday, during my aerial combat, in which I shot down two British single-seaters in flames, my thirty-fifth and thirty-sixth victories,[31] I screamed loudly in pain …'[32]

Capt John Steele Ralston, MC, an American pilot attached to 84 Squadron, RAF, was in that fight over Villers-Bretonneux. According to his combat report, at about 10:55 a.m.:

'I observed one formation of four E.A. approaching from the east a few hundred feet above, and one flight of about five E.A. at around 1,000 feet below. I concentrated on those above and when they dived I swung 'round, but was only able to drive off one of three which attacked Lieut. Nielsen, who was flying on my left rear...'[33]

Surely, Ralston saw Rudolf Berthold among the German fighter pilots attacking Lt Peter Nielsen in an S.E.5a (C.1923). It is likely that the JG 2 commander shot down Nielsen, who was last seen 'in combat with two E.A. northeast of Abancourt', as well as a second S.E.5a (D.259) flown by 2/Lt Robert Joss Fyfe, 'southeast of Abancourt',[34] and was credited with their destruction. Both men died.[35]

Following that victory, Berthold was out of action for over a week. He simply needed a rest. After nearly four years' work with battlefield casualties, his sister had gained great insight into combat-related wounds and she blamed the military establishment for her brother's continuing service as a fighter pilot. She wrote: '... when [his] name surfaced repeatedly, no army dispatch reported that in the victorious aircraft sat a sick man, who operated his aeroplane with his left hand, with his mouth and with his feet.'[36]

Clearly, Rudolf Berthold was not operating any part of a Fokker D.VII with his mouth but his sister's bitter hyperbole is understandable. She may have felt that he functioned as an aerial automaton, showing no emotion and reacting only to physical pain. But when he wrote to Franziska, he probably wanted to spare her grim details of combat and comment only on his medical condition, as seen in his letter of 28 June:

'Yesterday I flew again for the first time since shooting down my thirty-sixth opponent and have since shot down my thirty-seventh in flames. The arm is still not good. Since the lower wound has opened up again, the pain has subsided a bit and the swelling has gone down. I have screamed in pain, sometimes frantically. It seems to have been only a bone splinter ... I know that every pain hurts at least two or three times as much since I was wounded because I have not had time to get my body back to its old robustness. And ... of course, the war has greatly sapped my strength. But I must persevere, no matter what the cost. After the war, we can slowly bring the old bones back together again.'[37]

Berthold's thirty-seventh opponent was a Bristol F.2B (C.935), which he sent down out of a formation of two-seat fighters from 48 Squadron, RAF. The British patrol claimed destruction of several of the 'twenty Fokker biplanes'[38] that attacked it and observed that two of its own aeroplanes fell in flames during the fight. Berthold's victims were most likely twenty-eight-year-old Lt Edward Alec Foord and Sgt Leonard James, age twenty, both of whom were killed.[39] There were no JG 2 losses that day.

A Death in Berlin

Early July was a relatively quiet time for Jagdgeschwader 2 and Berthold was able to leave the frontlines to attend the latest Typenprüfungen [aircraft type tests] held at an airfield in Berlin and administered by the Flugzeugmeisterei [aircraft test establishment].[40] Beginning on Wednesday, 3 July, the tests enabled competing fighter aircraft manufacturers to have their new models test flown by some of Germany's best fighter pilots. Berthold was accompanied by Ltn Walter Dingel, a valued comrade from their days together in Feldflieger-Abteilung 23 and now JG 2's technical officer.

The tests got off to a bad start, however, when the Zeppelin-Lindau D.I prototype fighter[41] lost the top wing in a dive and crashed. The dead pilot, Hptm Wilhelm Reinhard, had succeeded Manfred von Richthofen as commander of JG 1.

While Berthold was in Berlin, Jagdgeschwader 2 was preparing for a brief move from the Somme sector to the Champagne sector. Berthold arrived at the new airfield at Leffincourt, northeast of Reims, in time to greet Luftstreitkräfte Commanding General Ernst von Hoeppner, who inspected area aviation units on 13 July. The following day, the 3rd Army's air commander, Hptm Hermann Palmer, Berthold's old boss in FFA 23, visited Leffincourt to discuss deployment of fighter aircraft[42] during the fifth German drive set to be launched on 18 July.[43] But the last German drive – also called the Aisne-Marne Offensive – came too late to stave off ultimate German defeat.

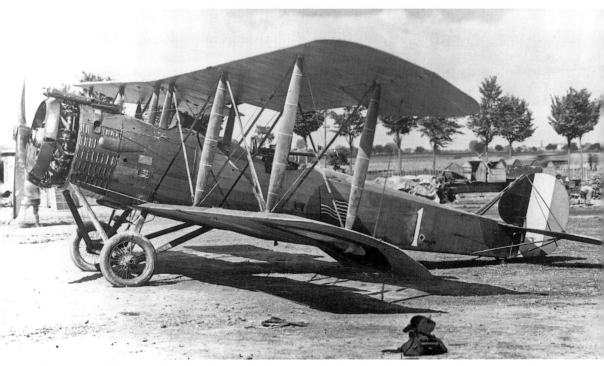

A Salmson 2A2 of the type shot down by Berthold on 19 July. The aircraft shown was from the American 1st Aero Squadron, which Berthold would subsequently engage. The unit marking, aft of the observer's station, was a US flag. (Colin Owers)

JG 2 had hardly arrived at the 3rd Army sector, when, on the second day of the offensive, half of its units, Jastas 15 and 19, were deployed westward to provide air cover for the 7th Army. Berthold's other two units, Jastas 12 and 13, covered the 1st Army.[44] German ground and air units had to re-deploy quickly in the face of a stiff American, French and Italian counter attack. Berthold flew with Jasta 15 and added to his victory score on 19 July, when he shot down a Salmson 2A2 two-seater from Escadrille Sal 40 over Soissons. He killed the pilot, Capitaine Henri Denis, but the observer, Lt Chappius, managed to land the aeroplane and survive.[45] Berthold was credited with his thirty-eighth victory.[46]

On Saturday, 20 July – amidst a record-making 100 combat flights carried out by JG 2 – Berthold scored his thirty-ninth victory; he shot down what was described as a 'SPAD two-seater southeast of Dormans (Marne).'[47] French records show no such SPAD casualty, although several other two-seaters were lost[48] and Berthold's victim may be among them. But victory came with a price that day. His aeroplane was badly shot up and he was forced to land at St. Gemme, north of Dormans, in the 7th Army sector. A newly-arrived subordinate, Vizefeldwebel Gustav Klaudat, was directed to fly his own Fokker D.VII to the stranded Geschwader commander, so the 'boss' could return to Leffincourt. But on landing back at his own airfield, Berthold flew into turbulence so strong that it flipped his aeroplane over and totally wrecked it. Luckily, Berthold emerged unhurt but another new Fokker D.VII was lost.[49]

Four days later JG 2 moved again, this time from the 3rd Army to Chéry-lès-Pouilly Airfield, north of Laon, in the sector of the newly reconstituted 9th Army.[50] As a parting gesture, the 3rd Army's commander-in-chief, Generaloberst Karl von Einem, issued a command-wide citation commending JG 2's role in the recent battles and noted, in particular, Berthold's most recent victory.[51]

A day later, unbeknownst to Rudolf Berthold, he was highlighted in the French weekly aviation magazine *La Guerre Aérienne Illustrée* as one of Germany's highest-scoring living fighter aces. It is a tribute to Allied intelligence gathering that the publication listed Berthold's score as thirty-eight confirmed victories,[52] a level he attained only six days before the magazine appeared in news kiosks.

The pilot of Berthold's likely 40th victory, 1st Lt William P. Erwin (right), poses with another observer, 1st Lt Arthur J. Coyle, by a Salmson 2A2 of the 1st Aero Squadron, USAS. Erwin was uninjured in the fight and made it back to Allied lines. (Clifford E. Andrews Collection via NMUSAF)

Berthold's Fortieth Victory

On the fourth anniversary of the beginning of World War I, Thursday, 1 August 1918, Hptm Rudolf Berthold achieved his fortieth aerial victory.[53] He had equalled the tally of his pre-war flying school comrade and the first aviation *Pour le Mérite* recipient Hptm Oswald Boelcke. It was JG 2's only victory that day and was listed as a 'French two-seater' that went down 'northeast of Château-Thierry, near Fère-en-Tardenois (on the other side of the lines).'[54] Most likely, Berthold's opponent was from the 1st Aero Squadron, US Air Service, which reported that one of its Salmson 2A2 photo reconnaissance aircraft flying in the area was involved in 'heavy combat with Fokker D.VIIs, [which was] shot up [and] forced to land.' Of the two American crewmen, First Lieutenant William P. Erwin was uninjured and First Lieutenant Earl B. Spencer was wounded in the fight.[55]

Two days later, General der Infanterie Johannes von Eben, commander-in-chief of the 9th Army issued a citation that surely validated Berthold's sacrifices and appealed to his innermost vanity:

> 'I am pleased to express my appreciation and gratitude for [your latest] and fortieth victory in aerial combat. The 9th Army views with pride the most capable combat flyer who at this time battles in its ranks and in its service. We hope for new victories that will accrue to the glory of you and your branch of service and to the salvation of the German Fatherland.'[56]

But it seemed that no amount of valour could forestall relentless Allied attacks on hard-won German gains. Eliminating or at least reducing three German salients improved: 'lateral railway communications along the Allied front and facilitated future operations.'[57] The attack on the last such salient, at Amiens, led to a 'great Allied victory [which] caused [German General Staff Chief Erich] Ludendorff to call 8 August 1918 the "black day" of the German army, since, for the first time, entire units collapsed.'[58]

Amidst reports of 'heavy clouds and mist along the entire [Western] Front' on 9 August, the daily *Nachrichtenblatt* heralded the role of Germany's leading fighter aces in responding to the jarring events of the previous day. That day's chronicle noted that, among others: 'Oblt Loewenhardt attained his fifty-second and fifty-third [victories], Hptm Berthold his forty-first and forty-second, Ltn Udet his forty-eighth and forty-ninth …'[59]

Flying with Jasta 15, at about 6:00 p.m., Berthold shot down an 'enemy two-seater' near Fricourt. It crashed south of Montdidier, which was a focal point of the French advance that day. Half an hour later, Berthold downed another two-seater near Beaucourt-en-Santerre, some twenty-five kilometres north of his previous triumph. His opponents were, most likely, a pair of SPAD XVI reconnaissance machines from Escadrille Spa 289, based at Poix-de-Picardie,[60] west of the second fight. The two crews perished.[61]

A German source reported that 'under varying cloudiness, [there was] heavy activity over and on the broad battlefield' on Saturday, 10 August.[62] Jastas 12, 13 and 15 took off for the frontlines and soon found a large and concerted British raid going on against 'the stations at Péronne and Equancourt on the Bapaume-Epéhy railway.'[63] The fifteen German aircraft were vastly outnumbered, facing twelve D.H.9 two-seat bombers from a combined force from 27 and 49 Squadrons, RAF. The bombers were escorted by a mix of S.E.5a single-seaters from 32 Squadron[64] and Bristol F.2B two-seaters from 62 Squadron, which were later joined by seven S.E.5as from 56 Squadron.

A pilot from 32 Squadron, 2/Lt John Owen Donaldson, referring to himself in the third person, reported that that he:

'... observed nine Fokker Biplanes, at 13,000 feet, over Péronne, at 11:30 a.m., dive on three S.E.5s. Pilot [Donaldson] came to their assistance, fired 150 rounds into first E.A. at close range, E.A. turned over on its back, and went down in a flat spin ...

'Pilot observed Lieut. Macfarlane fire at one E.A., and saw it fall side by side with the E.A. shot by pilot, [from] about 10,000 feet.'[65]

Lt Peter Macfarlane in S.E.5a C.8838 probably shot down one of three Fokker D.VIIs hit in that fight; all landed within German-held territory and suffered no loss of life. But then Lt Macfarlane was shot down, very likely by Rudolf Berthold, as his forty-third victory was confirmed as a 'British single-seater that went down in flames'.[66] It crashed near Licourt, south of Péronne but Macfarlane's aircraft was not recovered; consequently, he has no known grave.[67] The other S.E.5a lost in that fight, D.6921 piloted by Lt William Ernest Jackson,[68] went down southwest of Péronne, and was confirmed as the second victory of Ltn.d.Res Hans Joachim Borck of Jasta 15. According to British records, Lt Jackson survived his crash and was rescued, uninjured, by forward area French troops.[69]

Turning away from the falling S.E.5, Berthold spotted a D.H.9 bomber and went after it. The British two-seater crew resisted fiercely, but after ten minutes they were finished. The JG 2 history notes that Berthold's last glimpse of the bomber – his forty-fourth and final aerial victory[70] – was the dust cloud it kicked up as it hit the ground.[71]

Then, while surveying the hits to his own aircraft, Berthold was horrified to see how effective the British observer-gunner had been. One of the Englishman's shots had severed the Fokker's control column and, when Berthold tried to pull the aeroplane upward, he held only the top part of the now useless handle in his hand. He was at 800 metres' altitude and quickly heading for the ground.

For a split second it must have seemed like the end to Berthold. Then his basic, cool-headed military discipline prevailed. His aeroplane was equipped with a static line-activated parachute, but that life-saving device required two hands to operate and Berthold's paralysed right hand could not help him in this crisis. At 600 metres, he tried to level off using the controls that still worked. But he continued his downward rush. Then, a village came into view and momentum carried him just over the rooftop of one house – and straight into another house. The Fokker hit with such force that the engine tore loose from its mountings and plunged right down to the cellar.

Rudolf Berthold had come down in Ablaincourt, close to where the D.H.9 had crashed. Nearby German soldiers pulled him out of the rubble. Like his last opponents – 2/Lt H. Hartley and Sgt O.D. Beetham of 49 Squadron, RAF[72] – Berthold was still alive, but wounded.[73] Then he fell into unconsciousness.

He awoke at Feldlazarett 10 in the 2nd Army sector. Army doctors were amazed that he survived. But his, still unhealed, upper right arm bone was broken again and at the

Berthold's 44th and final aerial victory was an Airco D.H.9, the type seen here. (Volker Koos)

old fracture site. No one in the field hospital had the courage to tell Berthold that his air combat days were over.

As it turned out, 10 August 1918 was a disastrous day for German fighter aviation. In addition to Rudolf Berthold's injuries, the Luftstreitkräfte marked the loss of the fifty-four-victory ace and Jasta 10 leader, Oblt Erich Loewenhardt, whose Fokker D.VII collided with a staffel-mate's; Loewenhardt attempted to use his parachute, but it malfunctioned and he fell to his death.[74] And Ltn Paul Billik, a thirty-one-victory ace who commanded Jasta 52, was shot down and taken prisoner that day.[75]

But Berthold clung to the hope of flying again. To emphasise the point, on the evening of 12 August he showed up at Leffincourt Airfield. With his usual air of entitlement, Berthold had persuaded a driver at the field hospital that he needed to return to JG 2 to resume his responsibilities. Once inside Jasta 15's pilots' mess, he announced: "Here, I am the boss." The newly-appointed Geschwader commander, Rittmeister Heinz Freiherr von Brederlow, who had seniority and administrative experience, but only one victory to his credit, reportedly 'acquiesced and left' the room. Berthold said he would return to bed and give orders from there.[76]

He was so convincing that the Geschwader war diary entry for the day noted:

'The Berthold luck has proven itself once again. He is under the care of one of Professor Bier's assistants, who is at Kriegslazarett 19E in Montcornet, and will spend his recovery time here.'[77]

The next morning, however, Berthold's condition worsened. He ran a high fever and was wracked by excruciating pains. A doctor was summoned and he ordered the wounded ace sent back to Montcornet – over fifty kilometres away – immediately. Given Berthold's high visibility within the Luftstreitkräfte, news of his latest escapade travelled quickly and to the highest levels. Upon hearing it, *'der Oberste Kriegsherr'*[78] [supreme warlord – Kaiser Wilhelm II] ordered swift action to prevent a recurrence. On 14 August, the commanding general of the Luftstreitkräfte sent a telegram to JG 2 staff officers at Leffincourt to clarify how Berthold's future convalescence would progress:

> 'The commander of Jagdgeschwader 2, Hauptmann Berthold, is to submit to official orders to be conveyed immediately in hospital care and is to remain there until properly discharged. Confirmation of the name and location of the requested hospital is to be wired [to Kogenluft] via the commander of aviation, 9th Army. Geschwader leadership will be assumed by Leutnant Veltjens until further notice.'[79]

The officer in charge of 9th Army aviation, Hptm Genée, a pre-war flyer and early wartime unit commander,[80] was not susceptible to Berthold's charms. He would assure these orders were carried out to the letter.

Two days later, on Friday, 16 August, Berthold protégé 'Seppl' Veltjens assured that his mentor was made comfortable on a train that took him from the battlefield rear area in France to the quieter and more accommodating Viktoria-Lazarett Universitäts-Klinik in Berlin.

Germany's deteriorating war effort was rapidly losing heroes and needed to retain its older renowned veterans for propaganda purposes, if not for humanitarian reasons. For the foreseeable future, Rudolf Berthold's battles would be against his own impatience and self-dissatisfaction while he continued to nurture impossible dreams of further glory.

CHAPTER TEN
THE FINAL BATTLE

'Is it not a pity that such men, who risked their lives
countless times over the frontlines, must perish in this way?'[1]

ANONYMOUS WITNESS

It soon became clear to Rudolf Berthold that his precipitous move to regain authority over Jagdgeschwader 2 – so erratic, but so typical for him – had cost him the good-will he had in the higher echelons of the German Luftstreitkräfte. Now he was back in Berlin for medical treatment, but his days as a somewhat indulged, national hero were over. The war was going badly for Germany and his superiors no longer had the time, patience or desire to accommodate his ego.

His sister Franziska, once again composing his diary entries, wrote about this development:

'Berthold was in the hospital and followed, with growing concern, the affairs at the frontlines and at home. Soon after his last crash he was briefly informed that ... he would be assigned other service within Germany. Nothing further! He had to put part of his life's work behind him ... He became sad and bitter that they treated him that way and dismissed him so summarily.'[2]

Berthold was last mentioned in the national press on 13 August 1918, when the widely-read Wolff'schen Telegraph-Bureau news service included his last two aerial victories in that day's summary.[3] A final courtesy from the Luftstreitkräfte came when he was apprised that, on 31 August, command of JG 2 had passed to twenty-five-year-old Oblt Oskar Freiherr von Boenigk, a highly-decorated regular army officer, long-time flyer and twenty-one-victory ace.[4] After that, Berthold had to rely on newspaper accounts to learn about the war. Out of a sense of patriotism, news articles of the period tended to magnify Germany's success and downplay its defeats. Those accounts were generally accurate, but lacked the candour of the battlefront reports to which Berthold was accustomed.

Back to Ditterswind

Rudolf Berthold completed his treatments at Dr. Bier's clinic in early October. His arm pain was alleviated and he was sent home to his family in Ditterswind to continue his convalescence. Franziska, who remained in Berlin, noted that: 'in the forest of his homeland, in beautiful Franconia, he gradually regained his inner equilibrium, although he was no longer as physically robust.'[5] She made no further mention of his drug addiction.

Schloss Ditterswind in Bayern.

An old postcard view of Ditterswind shows the pastoral beauty in which Rudolf Berthold tried to find peace at war's end. (Heinz J. Nowarra)

In any event, Rudolf had not lost his capacity for big dreams – or delusions. On 14 October, he wrote to Franziska:

'I am eager to get going again! Externally, the consequences of my last crash have been overcome. Unfortunately, my right arm remains paralysed. But in the spring and summer I shot down aeroplanes with it. The will and the skill must still be there! I want to have my Jagdgeschwader 2 once again ...'[6]

Just over a week later, Berthold was encouraged by a newspaper account about the thirty-fifth aerial victory scored by his protégé Ltn.d.Res Josef Veltjens.[7] His joy ceased, however, on reading the 23 October article devoted to US President Woodrow Wilson's third reply to the German government about peace proposals.[8] That news was disastrous to Berthold, who returned to keeping his diary. He wrote:

'Wilson has responded. We are going on the downward path again. I want to go back out to the frontlines! I sit ... and wait. If only I had my healthy bones – but I can still do it. As long as the battle rages ... everyone with experience belongs out there ...

'These days I am in the confines of my hometown near Bamberg. It is a beautiful patch of German soil. In the splendid German forest, the solemn spruce trees seem to me to be more melancholy than before – indeed, sad. They mourn with me the weakness and humiliation of our people ...'[9]

The news of 6 November was more depressing. Reports of mutinies of Imperial Navy forces in Hamburg, Kiel and Lübeck[10] led Berthold to compare those uprisings with events in Russia of a year earlier. He wrote:

'Bolshevism continues to spread ... and, to add the final touch to this measure of shame, the troops are going over in clusters to the revolutionaries. The dress uniform jacket that I wore with pride for so long is now disgraced. How difficult it is, how hard it will be for me to continue to live.'[11]

A day later, Rudolf Berthold tried to describe the destruction of the old public order and the collapse of the military establishment and civilian support for the kaiser – all social systems to which he remained totally committed:

'It has happened! Revolution has broken out. Fate, now go your own way! How paralysed the thinking is. Hopefully, the reckoning will come soon for the villains who have used our misery [for their gain]. The kaiser and the princes have been deposed ... The mind cannot grasp how terrible it all is ...'[12]

The tumultuous events of November 1918 – the Armistice, armed clashes in the streets between German civilians and police – brought with them miserable times for Rudolf Berthold. He admitted to being so sad that, for a while, he could not even pour out his despair to his diary.[13] Meanwhile, he also learned that many other military veterans joined private paramilitary units known as Freikorps [free corps], encouraged and supported financially by the central government to counter Arbeiter-und Soldatenräter [Workers' and Soldiers' Councils] that were perceived as being in league with the Bolsheviks. There was turmoil in the cities, but in the Bavarian countryside, the hours dragged on for Berthold and, even in the Christmas season, he wrote that the 'bells ring so sadly, as if they were tolling only to awaken memories of peoples' woes ...'[14]

The new year brought reports of street fighting in Berlin involving rifles, machine guns and light artillery. The left-wing 'Spartakus' revolutionary movement tried to bring down the government of Social Democrat Chancellor Friedrich Ebert and was finally suppressed on 15 January 1919 by army and Freikorps troops.[15]

A New Beginning
Despite the turmoil that swept Germany, 1919 seemed to offer hope to Rudolf Berthold. Within the new government in Berlin were many people from the old régime, including people in the new Reichswehr [armed force] who remembered Berthold. Consequently, he was summoned to the German capital for a physical examination to release him from disability leave and qualify him for an aviation-related active duty posting.

A Reichswehr position seemed to be an honourable use of Hauptmann Rudolf Berthold's professional military training. On 24 February, he was assigned to command

Döberitz Airfield on the southeast edge of Berlin.[16] Being back in uniform raised his spirits and 'enabled him to endure any bitterness'.[17] Berthold soon had the once bedraggled airfield and its hangars looking like a military facility again. He knew how to motivate men and build such trust that even resentful Workers' and Soldiers' Council members worked willingly for him. It was noted that 'they trusted the one-armed flyer with the *Pour le Mérite*. His appearance, resolute and brooking no contradiction, impressed them.'[18]

But that brief idyll came to an end when Berthold was ordered to close the airfield and dismiss the workers. His diary notes that he 'saw great danger in pushing the destitute and unemployed men into the arms of the Spartakus movement,'[19] but he lacked the power to change such a potentially-disastrous social development.

All around him signs, placards and newspaper articles proclaimed '*Deutschland in Not*' [Germany in peril]. That message became the harshest reality in April 1919, when Munich, the capital of Rudolf Berthold's Bavarian homeland, was taken over first by socialists and anarchists,[20] and then by Communists, who proclaimed a Bavarian 'soviet republic'.[21] Order was restored on 3 May by a combined force of 9,000 Reichswehr troops and 30,000 members of various Freikorps – after fierce street fighting resulted in over 1,700 civilian casualties.[22]

Berthold Joins the Freikorps

The putsch [coup d'état] in Munich and its subsequent suppression by Freikorps units was a defining moment for Rudolf Berthold. He felt drawn to a form of service he now considered to be higher than that of the Reichswehr and, following his own sense of mission, he joined the Freikorps.[23] One of his comrades, Hans Wittmann, wrote:

> 'Berthold ... put out a call to patriotic Bavarian youth, especially in the Franconia area, to enlist in the Freikorps unit that was being established not far from Bad Kissingen in the former army training ground in Hammelburg. Enthusiastic young Bavarian men responded in large numbers. Especially numerous was the amount of big, brawny Franconian farmers who reported in ...
>
> 'Within a short time Berthold had at his disposal 1,200 men in a unit that he named the "Fränkisches Bauerndetachement Eiserne Schar Berthold" [Franconian Farmers' Detachment – the Iron Troop Berthold]. Absolute obedience to the leaders and iron discipline were the foundations of the group.'[2]

Berthold promised his men hard work in a worthy cause and they responded enthusiastically. They cleaned up the barracks and rehabilitated the old training ground. Unlike regular army soldiers, however, Berthold's troops 'did not swear an oath of allegiance and anyone could be let go at the leader's discretion'.[25] But, just as he had led his pre-war youth groups by the force of his strong personality, Berthold continued to inspire his men to want to remain with him in service to Germany.

Berthold's men completed their training at the end of May and headed south by train for Munich, which already had enough Freikorps units to dissuade any further unrest. The troops were kept busy with long marches and sports activities. Without a purpose in Germany, in early August they answered the call for Freikorps volunteers in the Baltic states to fight Bolsheviks.

Gaunt and weary beyond his twenty-eight years, Berthold posed in his new Freikorps uniform with the identification patch of the Iron Troop Berthold on his left sleeve. Note he tried to conceal his paralysed right hand. (Lance J. Bronnenkant)

Berthold's men left Munich for a northward journey that ended a month later when they crossed the border into Lithuania.[26] There, the Iron Troop Berthold joined the Iron Division, a large, mostly German, volunteer force keeping Red Army forces out of newly-independent Lithuania, Estonia and Latvia. The division, led by Major Josef Bischoff, eventually found itself fighting against local troops that wanted Russian and German forces out of their countries. The conflict was marked by brutality on all sides.

Berthold's unit, officially the 3rd Company of the 2nd Kurländisches [Courland] Regiment,[27] was in combat at Mitau and the Latvian capital, Riga. Berthold's disability kept him from active fighting, but he rallied and inspired his men as they endured harsh weather and fierce fighting. By the year's end, a combination of defeats and orders from Berlin – at the request of victorious wartime Allies – to leave the Baltic area and return to Germany led Berthold's men to a camp on the Lithuanian-German border. There were no honours for the men, only harsh criticism in the German press that reviled them as 'Baltic criminals'.[28] For the moment, though, the Iron Troop Berthold

Commemorative badge of the Iron Troop Berthold Freikorps unit. (Greg VanWyngarden)

enjoyed the 'luxury' of a three-week rest before their return to Germany. Rudolf Berthold knew his unit would be disarmed and disbanded – and possibly further dishonoured[29] – and he planned to resist that dissolution.

On New Year's Day 1920, Berthold and his men were in the Lithuanian port city of Memel [now Klaipėda] and feeling much refreshed. He had received orders to proceed by train to Stade, a city on the Elbe river, west of Hamburg, and to remain there pending further directions. Some of his men would have preferred to go south to Bavaria, but Berthold exercised his iron discipline and reinforced that they would go where they were ordered.[30] It was an enormous logistical undertaking to move all the men and equipment of the Iron Division, which had not yet been ordered to disband, and this only added to a general public nervousness.

Return to Germany

Finally, Berthold's unit moved to locations in the area near Stade. The presence of Freikorps units so close to the city created a delicate situation at a time when neighbouring communities had varying allegiances. People in conservative communities wanted to restore the old social order; those of a liberal persuasion wanted a fully-democratic society. There was great fear of a right-wing military-backed putsch in Berlin. Such anxiety was stoked when it became known that Berthold's unit had been ordered to proceed to a military campsite at Zossen, just south of Berlin, to be demobilised on 15 March. That location was already home to the 6,000-man 3rd Marine-Brigade,[31] commanded by

Korvettenkapitän [Lieutenant-Commander] Hermann Ehrhardt, a fervent nationalist and a Freikorps founder.

Initially, officials in Stade requested that Berthold's men be disarmed. As an expression of good faith, he agreed to turn over 'a portion' of the unit's weapons to the local armoury.[32] Then, on the morning of Saturday, 13 March 1920, it was the Iron Troop's time to head for Zossen. Berthold ordered his force – now down to some 800 men, equipped with 300 rifles and a few machine guns[33] – to form up for the eighteen-kilometre march from their camp in Drochtersen to Stade. They would travel the rest of the way to Zossen by train.

On their arrival in Stade, however, Berthold and his men learned that a military-backed putsch had been launched in Berlin against the government of Chancellor Friedrich Ebert. Now it became imperative for Berthold to reach Zossen. He claimed to want no role in the insurrection, even though he acknowledged being responsible to General Walther Freiherr von Lüttwitz, Reichswehr commander in Berlin and one of the putsch leaders.[34]

At this point, Germany teetered on the brink of civil war, as General von Lüttwitz and political right-wing activist Wolfgang Kapp called for order to be maintained by Reichswehr and Freikorps units. Chancellor Ebert countered by urging Germany's workers to launch a general strike to thwart the take-over. When Berthold's men tried to board the train, they felt the sting of the strike, as the train crew at Stade refused to get under way. Berthold then ordered his men to occupy the city's post office, telegraph office, city hall and train station; and they spent the night in the local girl's high school.[35]

The following day, Berthold was determined to use the train to move his men and equipment to Zossen. His comrade Hans Wittmann summarised the next course of action: 'Therefore, the watchword for us became "help yourself!"'[36] And the Iron Troop, which had already voted to support the putsch, took over the train and forced the crew to transport them and their equipment eastward. In response, other striking railroad workers turned off all signal lights on the rail line, requiring the train to proceed slowly and cautiously to avoid a collision on the rails. It was dark when the commandeered train rolled into the small community of Harburg, southeast of Hamburg, at about 9:00 on Sunday night. Berthold ordered the train to halt.

Town officials in Harburg, alerted that Berthold's unit was heading their way, arrested the commander of Pionier-Bataillon 9 [combat engineer battalion], to neutralise his 900 Reichswehr troops.[37] Harburg was governed by Independent Socialists, who were bent on obstructing Berthold's plans, and were prepared to use their own armed force to do so. When Berthold met with town officials, he was assured his troops could be housed safely in the Heimfelder Middle School, its residence facilities and adjacent buildings in the Woellmerstrasse – but that assurance was a ruse.

Clash in the Streets

By the following morning, Harburg was on high alert. Local trade union leaders tried to motivate the resident Reichswehr soldiers to convince Berthold to disarm his men and leave peacefully.[38] But the soldiers were wary of disobeying orders of their officers, who supported the putsch. Labour leaders then armed their own men to face the battle-hardened Freikorps members.

Berthold overplayed his hand and stubbornly refused Harburg Oberbürgermeister [Lord Mayor] Heinrich Denicke's offer of safe passage. By noon on Monday, 15 March, groups of armed workers approached the school area. There are several versions of what happened next, but all agree that Berthold's men demanded the crowd clear a path in front of the school – and sent a burst of machine-gun fire over the heads of the civilians. Instead of being frightened off, men in the crowd returned fire and Berthold's men withdrew into the school buildings. The citizens militia encircled the school area and many shots were exchanged, eventually resulting in fatalities on both sides: 'Thirteen civilians and eleven military personnel, of whom three fell in actual fighting, the remainder were murdered after being disarmed.'[39]

The stand-off lasted into the late afternoon. With little ammunition left, Berthold ordered a white flag be shown and called on the mayor for further negotiations. Denicke and other town leaders steadfastly offered only assurance of safe passage back to Stade for all Freikorps members who were disarmed. Realising he was defeated, Berthold gave in. Then, at about 6:00 p.m., as Berthold's men began to file out of the school buildings, the crowd – not part of the negotiations and now outraged at the sight of their own dead – attacked the Freikorps men. More shots rang out.[40]

Berthold and some of his men sought refuge back inside the main school building. By one account, Berthold escaped through a back door and moved safely down a side street when a civilian spotted the *Pour le Mérite* medal around his neck and called out to his comrades. An angry mob chased Berthold down and, as he disappeared from sight, more shots were heard. It was reported that, with his one good arm, Berthold pulled out a pistol to defend himself, but lost it in the struggle and was shot with his own sidearm.[41]

When Hans Wittmann arrived at the spot, as he later wrote, he saw only:

'In the dirt of the street lay, lifeless, Hauptmann Berthold, his shoes and his overcoat robbed from him, his face crushed into a formless mass by the mob's feet, his paralysed arm torn out of its socket, his bloody body punctured by gunshot wounds ...'[42]

The putsch in Berlin ended the following day and, when cooler heads prevailed in Harburg, the unarmed Iron Troop men were taken to an area military base. Berthold's body was removed to a hospital in Wandsbek, a suburb of Hamburg, where an autopsy confirmed that he died from gunshot wounds – two to the head and four to the chest.[43] Upon learning of Berthold's death, two old flying comrades in nearby Hamburg, former Leutnants Lohmann and Tiedje, rushed to the hospital.[44] They awaited the arrival of Franziska Berthold, who confirmed she was travelling from Berlin to claim her brother's remains and personal effects. Meanwhile, decorations stolen from Berthold's corpse – his *Pour le Mérite*, Iron Cross 1st Class and pilot's badge – were retrieved from a rubbish heap at an ironworks in Harburg.[45]

Another Funeral in Berlin

Friends and former comrades gathered first at a chapel in the Wandsbek hospital, while arrangements were made for Berthold's funeral to be held in Berlin. In addition to helping plan that ceremony, Lohmann and Tiedje negotiated for Berthold's men to be released from Harburg[46] to a more friendly Reichswehr facility in Altona, closer to Hamburg. Then they proceeded to Berlin, where, despite the collapse of the putsch, people remained wary of events involving armed uniformed men.

The Berthold family announced Rudolf's death and funeral arrangements in this Berlin newspaper obituary. (Heinz J. Nowarra)

Thus, at about 3:00 p.m. on Tuesday, 30 March – six days after what would have been Rudolf Berthold's twenty-ninth birthday[47] – he was buried in the Invalidenfriedhof, the national heroes' cemetery. Protocol called for his pall bearers to be of Berthold's rank, but his family requested that members of his cortège be sergeants from his Iron Troop.[48] His wish to be buried with his comrades[49] was honoured and his remains now lie in a triangular arrangement next to the grave of onetime JG 2 pilot Ltn Oliver Freiherr von Beaulieu-Maconnay, whose plot abuts that of Berthold's best friend, Hptm.d.Res Hans Joachim Buddecke.[50]

Many long speeches were made over Berthold's grave, but a simpler tribute came from an anonymous woman from Bremen who was in Harburg during the street battle. She wrote to a friend in Erlangen:

> 'Berthold was killed in the fighting. You will read about it in the newspaper. Is it not a pity that such men who risked their lives countless times over the frontlines must perish in this way?'[51]

Originally, Berthold's grave had an ornate cover decorated with his flying sword insignia and a *Pour le Mérite* likeness. Reportedly, it disappeared about a year before the infamous Berlin Wall was erected around the eastern part of the city. (Lance J. Bronnenkant)

Tributes and Retribution

Responding to complaints that Rudolf Berthold had been the victim of lynch mob justice, police in Stade investigated the events of 15 March 1920. The following February, two men were charged with murder: Johannes Bremer, a thirty-six-year-old coppersmith from Harburg, and forty-year-old fishmonger Otto Noack from Hamburg.[52] Both men were put on trial and were acquitted. Bremer later gained a minor post in the local Social Democratic Party. After Adolf Hitler's National Socialist German Workers Party (NSDAP) came to power in 1932, Bremer was arrested and spent time in several jails. He ended up in Buchenwald concentration camp, where, on 1 December 1937, he was killed while reportedly attempting to escape.[53]

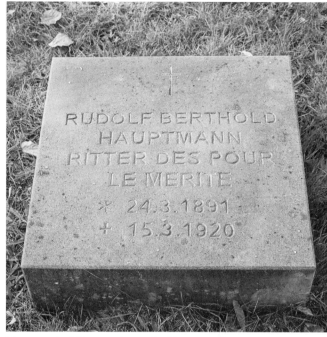

Now, Berthold's grave is marked by a small stone monument. (Kilduff Collection)

Even though Rudolf Berthold held conservative views and favoured a restoration of the monarchy – which was anathema to the NSDAP – his life and achievements were lionised during the Third Reich period. He was touted as a nationalist hero, whose sacrifices were held up as worthy of emulation. Various cities named streets in his honour. Two noteworthy examples are Rudolf-Berthold-Strasse in Bamberg, where he attended school, and Hauptmann-Berthold-Strasse in Wittenberg, where he joined the army. After World War II, however, the streets were renamed.

Berthold's historical legacy suffered a further blow in 1960. Officials in, then, Communist-dominated East Berlin altered the Invalidenfriedhof, which straddled its border with West Berlin. The eastern government 'cleared' many of the historic gravesites on its side to reinforce its defences by gaining an unobstructed view of the border. Thus, Rudolf Berthold's plot lost its once ornate gravestone, which has not been recovered. Four years after Germany was reunified, in 2003, independent donors paid for Berthold's grave to be restored and for a modest stone grave marker to be erected there.

Perhaps Rudolf Berthold – the tempestuous Iron Man of early German fighter aviation – has finally found the peace that eluded him in life.

APPENDIX I:
AERIAL VICTORY LIST OF RUDOLF BERTHOLD

[Author's note: The following victory list was compiled from Rudolf Berthold's own accounts, Hanns Möller's JG 2 history, and official German daily, weekly and monthly reports, as well as comparable RFC/RNAS/RAF, French and US Air Service reports. The final assumptions are the author's. In researching which units and airmen were involved in these aerial combats, several factors were considered: dates, times, places of the victory/loss, as well as proximity of the opposing air units' airfields. Other more recent research provided additional corresponding casualty information to determine the most likely identities of Berthold's victims. Dates are stated in the German style (day and month) and times are expressed in military time, with sub-headings to clarify whether a victory claim was an hour ahead of British/French time, or matched it. In two-seater claims, pilots are listed first, observers second. Condition of the aircrew is indicated by the abbreviations: WiA = Wounded in Action; DoW = Died of Wounds; KiA = Killed in Action; PoW = Prisoner of War. When no abbreviation is given, it is assumed the man was uninjured and returned to his own lines. Claims that were not confirmed are indicated by n/c.]

1916

Date	Time	Location	Aircraft Type	Victor & Aircraft	Vic. No.	Crew/Disposition
2.2		Chaulnes	Voisin LA	Oblt Berthold, KEK Vaux Fokker E.III 411/15	1	Cpl A. Jacquin (PoW), S/Lt P. Ségaud (KiA), Escadrille VB 108
5.2		near Irles	B.E.2c 4091	Oblt Berthold, KEK Vaux Fokker E.III 411/15	2	2/Lt L.J. Pearson (PoW), 2/Lt E.H.E.J. Alexander (WiA / PoW), 13 Sqn, RFC
13.3		near Bourlon	B.E.2c 4151	Oblt Berthold, KEK Vaux Fokker E.III 411/15	3	2/Lt M.A.J. Orde (WiA/PoW), 1AM P. Shaw (PoW) 8 Sqn, RFC
1.4		near Lihons	Farman F.40	Oblt Berthold, KEK Vaux Fokker E.III 411/15	4	Sgt L. Paoli (KiA), Lt A. Braut (KiA), Esc MF 54
16.4		south of Maurepas	B.E.2c 2097	Oblt Berthold, KEK Vaux Fokker E.III 411/15	5	2/Lt W.S. Earle (KiA), 2/Lt C.W.P. Selby (WiA / PoW), 9 Sqn, RFC
1.5		German time one hour ahead of Allied time				
24.8		Péronne	Nieuport 17 1552	Oblt Berthold, KEK Vaux Fokker E.III 411/15	6	Cpl H. Dangueuger (KiA) Esc N 37
17.9		Cambrai	Martinsyde G.100 7286	Oblt Berthold, Ja 4	7	Lt W.H.S. Chance (PoW), 27 Sqn, RFC

Date	Time	Location	Aircraft Type	Victor & Aircraft	Vic. No.	Crew/Disposition
22.9		Bertincourt	B.E.12	Oblt Berthold, Ja 4	n/c	19 Sqn, RFC
24.9	1100	Rancourt	Nieuport 17	Oblt Berthold, Ja 4	n/c	Esc N 103
26.9		Bertincourt	B.E. 2c 7079	Oblt Berthold, Ja 4	8	Lt B.T. Coller (KiA) 2/Lt T.E.G. Scaife (KiA) 9 Sqn, RFC

1917

Date	Time	Location	Aircraft Type	Victor & Aircraft	Vic. No.	Crew/Disposition
24.3		La Ferme Folemprix (Aisne)	Farman 61 No. 4100	Oblt Berthold, Ja 14 Albatros D.II D.1717/16	9	Cpl J. Peinaud (KiA), Lt M. Vernes (KiA), Esc MF 7
25.3		German time synchronised with Allied time				
6.4	1315	La Ferme de Malval, Braye-en-Laonnois	Caudron R.4 No. 1559	Oblt Berthold, Ja 14 Albatros D.III D.2182/16	10	S/Lt P. Desbordes (MiA), Lt J. Borgoltz (MiA) & Sold A. Lebleu (MiA), Esc F 35
11.4	1145	south of Corbeny	SPAD VII 370	Oblt Berthold, Ja 14 Albatros D.III D.2182/16	11	Adj A. Barioz (MiA), Esc N 73
14.4	1200	Beau Marais wood	Sopwith 1A2	Oblt Berthold, Ja 14 Albatros D.III D.2182/16	12	S/Lt A. Arnoux de Maison-Rouge (WiA/DoW), S/Lt R. Levi (WiA) Esc N 15
17.4		German time one hour ahead of Allied time				
21.8	0817	Dixmuide	Airco D.H.4 A.7577	Oblt Berthold, Ja 18 Albatros D.III	13	Lt C. Barry (KiA), 2/Lt F.B. Falkiner (KiA), 57 Sqn, RFC
4.9	0825	northern edge of Ypres	R.E.8 B.3411	Oblt Berthold, Ja 18 Albatros D.III	14	2/Lt T.E. Wray (KiA), 2/Lt W.S.L. Payne (KiA), 7 Sqn, RFC
	1700	St. Jean, north of Ypres	R.E.8 A.4372	Oblt Berthold, Ja 18 Albatros D.III	15	2/Lt G.M. Moore (WiA) Lt F.F. Munro, 9 Sqn, RFC
5.9	1528	near Thielt	Airco D.H.4 A.7530	Oblt Berthold, Ja 18 Albatros D.III	16	Lt J.W.F. Neill (WiA/PoW), 2/Lt T.M. Webster (WiA/PoW), 55 Sqn, RFC
15.9	1410	near Zillebeke lake	Airco D.H.4 A.2130	Oblt Berthold, Ja 18 Albatros D.III	17	Lt E.E.F. Loyd (PoW), Lt T.G. Deason (PoW), 55 Sqn, RFC
16.9	1800	west of Becelaere	R.E.8 A.4693	Oblt Berthold, Ja 18 Albatros D.III	18	2/Lt H. Haslam (KiA), L/Cpl A.J. Linay (KiA), 6 Sqn, RFC
	1825	Zonnebeke	R.E.8 A.4728	Oblt Berthold, Ja 18 Albatros D.III	19	2/Lt L.G. Humphries (KiA), 2/Lt F.L. Steben (WiA), 4 Sqn, RFC
19.9	1000	Becelaere	R.E.8 B.3427	Oblt Berthold, Ja 18 Albatros D.III	20	2/Lt J.S. Walthew (KiA), Lt M.C. Hartnett (KiA), 4 Sqn, RFC
20.9	0950	west of Menin, north of Wervicq	Airco D.H.5 A.9179	Oblt Berthold, Ja 18 Albatros D.III	21	2/Lt W.O. Cornish (KiA) 32 Sqn, RFC
21.9	1130	west of Menin	SPAD 7 B.3533	Oblt Berthold, Ja 18 Albatros D.III	22	2/Lt F.W. Kirby (KiA), 19 Sqn, RFC
22.9	0900	east of Zillebeke lake	Bristol F.2B A.7205	Oblt Berthold, Ja 18 Albatros D.III	23	2/Lt E.A. Bell (KiA), 2/Lt R.E. Nowell (KiA), 22 Sqn, RFC
25.9	1630	Gheluvelt	SPAD 7 B.3520	Oblt Berthold, Ja 18 Albatros D.III	24	Lt B.A. Powers (KiA), 19 Sqn, RFC

Date	Time	Location	Aircraft Type	Victor & Aircraft	Vic. No.	Crew/Disposition
26.9	1200	Becelaere	Sopwith Camel B.2358	Oblt Berthold, Ja 18 Albatros D.III	25	Lt W.H.R. Gould (KiA), 70 Sqn, RFC
28.9	1230	south of Zillebeke lake	Bristol F.2B A.7210 or A.7241	Oblt Berthold, Ja 18 Albatros D.III	26	20 Sqn, RFC
30.9	1150	Deûlémont	Sopwith Pup B.2185 or B.1768	Oblt Berthold, Ja 18 Albatros D.III	27	66 Sqn, RFC
2.10	1330	Roulers	Airco D.H.4 A.7581	Oblt Berthold, Ja 18 Albatros D.III	28	2/Lt C.G.O. MacAndrew (KiA), 2/Lt L.P. Sidney (KiA), 57 Sqn, RFC

1918

Date	Time	Location	Aircraft Type	Victor & Aircraft	Vic. No.	Crew/Disposition
10.3		German time synchronised with Allied time				
16.4		German time one hour ahead of Allied time				
28.5	1130	Crouy, northeast of Soissons	SPAD XVI 2-seater	Hptm Berthold, Ja 15 Fokker D.VII	29	Esc Sop 278
29.5	1830	south of Soissons	SPAD XIII	Hptm Berthold, Ja 15 Fokker D.VII	30	Sgt A. Géhin (MiA), Esc Spa 77
	1840	Salmson 2A2		Hptm Berthold, Ja 15 Fokker D.VII	31	M.d.L. Tussing (MiA), Lt C. Lemmery (WiA/PoW), Esc Sal 27
5.6		north of St. Just-en-Chaussée	Airco D.H.9 C.6203	Hptm Berthold, Ja 15 Fokker D.VII	32	Capt H. Turner (KiA), 2/Lt G. Webb (KiA), 103 Sqn, RAF
11.6			French 2-seater	Hptm Berthold, Ja 15 Fokker D.VII	33	
12.6			SPAD XIII	Hptm Berthold, Ja 15 Fokker D.VII	34	Cpl J. Monod (WiA/DoW), Esc Spa 96
18.6	1150	Villers-Bretonneux	S.E.5a C.1923	Hptm Berthold, Ja 15 Fokker D.VII	35	Lt P. Nielsen (KiA), 84 Sqn, RAF
	1155	Villers-Bretonneux	S.E.5a D.259	Hptm Berthold, Ja 15 Fokker D.VII	36	2/Lt R.J. Fyfe (KiA), 84 Sqn, RAF
27.6	1906	Villers-Bretonneux	Bristol F.2B in flames C.935	Hptm Berthold, Ja 15 Fokker D.VII	37	Lt E.A. Foord (KiA), Sgt L. James (KiA) 48 Sqn, RAF
19.7		near Soissons	Salmson 2A2	Hptm Berthold, Ja 15 Fokker D.VII	38	Capt H. Denis (KiA) Lt Chappius, Esc Sal 40
20.7	1905	southeast of Dormans (Marne)	French 2-seater	Hptm Berthold, Ja 15 Fokker D.VII	39	
1.8	0945	northeast of Château Thierry, near Fère-en-Tardenois	Salmson 2A2	Hptm Berthold, Ja 15 Fokker D.VII	40	1/Lt W.P. Erwin, 1/Lt E.B. Spencer (WiA) 1st Aero Sqn, USAS
9.8	1800	Tricot	SPAD XVI 2-seater	Hptm Berthold, Ja 15 Fokker D.VII	41	Esc Spa 289
	1830	Beaucourt-en-Santerre	SPAD XVI 2-seater	Hptm Berthold, Ja 15 Fokker D.VII	42	Esc Spa 289
10.8	1220	Licourt	S.E.5a in flames	Hptm Berthold, Ja 15 Fokker D.VII	43	Lt P. Macfarlane (KiA), 32 Sqn, RAF
	1230	Ablaincourt	Airco D.H.9 B.9344	Hptm Berthold, Ja 15 Fokker D.VII	44	2/Lt H. Hartley (PoW), Sgt O.D. Beetham (PoW), 49 Sqn, RAF

Daily Victory and Casualty Lists of JG 2 Units

Jagdstaffel 12

1916

Date	Time	Location	Aircraft Type	Victor & Aircraft	Vic. No.	Crew/Disposition
1.5		German time one hour ahead of Allied time				
18.9		Attached: 7. Armee Location: Vaux Airfield				
15.10		Attached: 1. Armee Location: Epinoy Airfield				
1.11		Attached: 6. Armee Location: Riencourt Airfield				
16.11	IiC	Riencourt Airfield		Off.Stv Malz Fokker D.I 1905/16		landing accident
17.11	WiA	Riencourt		Off.Stv Angst Fokker D.I 216/16		sent to Reserve- Feldlazarett 6
22.11	KiC	Gueudecourt		Gefr. R. Michaelis Fokker D.I 218/16		crashed during test flight
28.11		Riencourt		Fokker D.I 179/16		landing accident, pilot uninjured
4.12		near Bailleul / 8 km east of Arras	F.E.2b 7022	Ltn.d.R Splitgerber Fokker D.I	1	25 Sqn, RFC
	KiA	Meschede near Bailleul		Vfw Hennebeil Fokker D.I 169/16		combat with F.E.s
11.12	1245	near Annequin / 6 km west of La Bassée	B.E.2g 7153	Ltn.d.R Schulte Fokker D.I	1	10 Sqn, RFC
23.12		Attached: Armee-Abt A Location: Niederum Airfield				

1917

Date	Time	Location	Aircraft Type	Victor & Aircraft	Vic. No.	Crew/Disposition
6.2		near La Grande Rang-Ferme	Nieuport 1-seater	Ltn.d.R Schulte	2	
19.2		Attached: 1. Armee Location: Epinoy Airfield Attached: Grufl N				

Date	Time	Location	Aircraft Type	Victor & Aircraft	Vic. No.	Crew/Disposition
6.3	0945	near Albert	Sopwith	Ltn.d.R Schöck	n/c	
	1330	near Vraucourt, south of Boiry	F.E.2d in flames 1953	Ltn.d.R Schulte	3	57 Sqn, RFC
7.3		near Brancourt	F.E. 4803	Vzfw Schorisch	1	
11.3		near Grévillers forest	Airco D.H.2	Vfw Grigo	1	32 Sqn, RFC
	1105	near Gueudecourt-Ligny	F.E.2d	Ltn.d.R Schulte	4	18 Sqn, RFC
	WiA			Ltn Erkenbrecht		
17.3	1145	between Vaulx & Quéant	E.A.	Vfw Schorisch	n/c	
	1145	near Grévillers	E.A.	Uffz Jörke	n/c	
	1240	between Ligny & Grévillers	E.A.	Ltn Frowein	n/c	
18.3		Attached: Grufl 2				
19.3	0915	near Roisel-Templeux	SPAD 7 in flames A.6633	Hptm von Osterroht	1	19 Sqn, RFC
	0915	near Roisel	Sopwith	Ltn Frowein	n/c	
23.3	0845	near Havrincourt	F.E. biplane	Ltn Roth	n/c	
24.3	1045	near Croisilles, southwest of Hendecourt	F.E.2b A.5442	Ltn.d.R Schulte	5	11 Sqn, RFC
	1045	near Croisilles	F.E.2b A.5472	Uffz Jörke	1	11 Sqn, RFC
	1045	near Croisilles	Vickers FtL	Fwb Grigo	n/c	
25.3		German time synchronized with Allied time				
28.3		Attached: Grufl A				
	0905	Vaulx-Lagnicourt road	Vickers 1-seater	Ltn.d.R Schulte	n/c	
3.4	1700	direction of Bapaume	F.E.2b	Hptm von Osterroht	n/c	
	1710	northeast of St. Leger	F.E.2b FtL 4897	Ltn.d.R Schulte	6	23 Sqn, RFC
	1730	near Bullecourt	B.E.2c 7236	Hptm von Osterroht	2	15 Sqn, RFC
5.4	0940	direction of Inchy	F.E.2b			pilot unidentified, victory reported by Grufl A
	1105	near La Paré / Gouzeaucourt	F.E.2b	Ltn.d.R Friedrich Roth	1	
	1110	Honnecourt	F.E.2b	Ltn.d.R Splitgerber	2	
	1140		Lattice tail			pilot unidentified, victory reported by Grufl A
	1150	near Vraucourt	F.E.2b	Vfw Schorisch	n/c	victory reported by Grufl A
6.4	0745	north of Cambrai	F.E.2b A.21	Ltn.d.R Splitgerber	3	57 Sqn, RFC
	0830	near Anneux	F.E.2b	Ltn.d.R Schulte	n/c	
	0830	near Lagnicourt	F.E.2b	Hptm von Osterroht	3	

Date	Time	Location	Aircraft Type	Victor & Aircraft	Vic. No.	Crew/Disposition
6.4	0830	near Pronville	F.E.2b	Ltn.d.R F. Roth	n/c	
	0940	direction of Pronville	Bristol	Ltn.d.R F. Roth	2	
	1215	between Bourlon & Marcoing, near Malakow RR station	Sopwith Triplane N.5448	Hptm von Osterroht	4	1 Sqn, RNAS
9.4	1900	near Lagnicourt-Boursies	Bristol F.2A A.3315	Hptm von Osterroht & Ltn.d.R Schulte	n/c	48 Sqn, RFC (reported by Kofl 1. Armee)
11.4	0855	near Tilloy	B.E.2d 5849	Ltn.d.R Schulte	7	4 Sqn, RFC
		west of Neuvireuille	Sopwith Pup 5185	Ltn.d.R Schulte	8	3 Sqn, RNAS
		northeast of Abancourt, near Hem-Lenglet	B.E.2c 2769	Ltn.d.R F. Roth	3	4 Sqn, RFC
12.4		Attached: 6.Armee				
		Location: Roucourt Airfield between Rumaucourt & F.E. Baralle				pilot unidentified, victory confirmed in *Nachrichtenblatt Nr 11*
		between Marquion & Bourlon	Sopwith Pup N.6172	Hptm von Osterroht	5	3 Sqn, RNAS
	1035	near Bourlon	Sopwith 2-seater	Hptm von Osterroht	n/c	
	1035	between Dury & Eterpigny	F.E. 2b 4984	Vzfw Schorisch	2	18 Sqn, RFC
	1040	near Bourlon	F.E. 2b 4995	Ltn.d.R Schulte Albatros D.III 1996/16	9	18 Sqn, RFC
	KiA	over Croisilles		Ltn.d.R Schulte Albatros D.III 1996/16		collided with F.E.2b 4995
13.4		Attached: Grufl 4				
17.4		German time one hour ahead of Allied time				
20.4	0940	near Écoust-St. Mein	B.E.2f 2553	Vzfw Schorisch	3	16 Sqn, RFC
22.4	1830	north of Croisilles	B.E.2	Uffz Gille	n/c	
	2005	2 km south of Marcoing	SPAD 7 A.6695	Hptm von Osterroht	6	23 Sqn, RFC
	2005	south of Marcoing	SPAD 7	Ltn Roth	4	23 Sqn, RFC
	2010	south of Marcoing, west of Havrincourt	SPAD 7	Uffz Jörke	2	23 Sqn, RFC
		Havrincourt	"Vikkers"			pilot unidentified, victory confirmed in *Nachrichtenblatt Nr 12*
23.4	0835	near Haplincourt	Sopwith 1-seater	Uffz Gille	n/c	
	1200	west of Fontaine	Sopwith 1-seater	Hptm von Osterroht Albatros D.III 1958/16	7	
	1200	between Wancourt & Neuville	Sopwith	Vfw Schorisch	4	
	1205	near Damville	Sopwith 2-seater	Ltn.d.R Schöck	1	
	1205	near Neuville	Sopwith 2-seater	Vfw Grigo	2	

Date	Time	Location	Aircraft Type	Victor & Aircraft	Vic. No.	Crew/Disposition
23.4	MiA	near Écoust-St. Mein		Hptm von Osterroht Albatros D.III 1958/16		about 1800 hours; KiA
	2000	near St. Martin-Neuville	British 1-seater	Uffz Jörke	5	
	2000	near St. Martin-Neuville	British 1-seater	Vfw Grigo	4	
	2035	near Haplincourt	Sopwith	Uffz Gille	n/c	
29.4		Location: Epinoy Airfield				
	1055	near Baralle	F.E.2d A.6355	Uffz Gille	1	57 Sqn, RFC
30.4	0847	near Izel	F.E.2d A.6402	Oblt Ritter von Tutschek Albatros D.III	4	57 Sqn, RFC
	1725	near Baralle / Rumaucourt	Sopwith Pup N.6175	Ltn Billik	1	3 Sqn, RNAS
	1820	near Recourt	E.A.	Uffz Gille	n/c	
1.5	1140	between Cantaing & Cambrai	Sopwith Pup	Oblt Ritter von Tutschek Albatros D.III	5	3 Sqn, RNAS
	KiA	over Epinoy		Ltn Strehl Albatros D.III		combat with Sopwith Pups and F.E.2bs
4.5		Fresnes-Vitry, Baralle	Sopwith Pup	Oblt Ritter von Tutschek Albatros D.III	6	3 Sqn, RNAS
5.5	1205	east of Chérisy	SPAD 7 B.1525	Ltn.d.R Schöck Albatros D.III	2	23 Sqn, RFC
10.5	1320	west of Monchy	Sopwith Pup FtL	Oblt Ritter von Tutschek Albatros D.III	n/c	
11.5	1330	near Tilloy	F.E.2b	Uffz Rosenfeld Albatros D.III	1	
	1535	southeast of Haynecourt	Sopwith Pup	Vfw Riessinger Albatros D.III	1	54 Sqn, RFC
	1540	near Croisilles	Sopwith Pup N.6464	Oblt Ritter von Tutschek Albatros D.III	7	3 Sqn, RNAS
12.5	0800	near Inchy	Nieuport 17 B.1544	Uffz Gille Albatros D.III	2	29 Sqn, RFC
	0825	near Lagnicourt	E.A.	Uffz Jörke Albatros D.III	n/c	
	1050	between Baralle & Marquion	Sopwith Pup A.664	Oblt Ritter von Tutschek Albatros D.III	8	66 Sqn, RFC
	2020	near Fresnoy /Izel	SPAD 7 B.1560	Ltn Billik	2	19 Sqn, RFC
18.5	2020	near Vraucourt	Parasol monoplane	Uffz Jörke	n/c	
19.5	0905	near Dury	Sopwith Triplane N.5461	Oblt Ritter von Tutschek Albatros D.III 2274/16	9	1 Sqn, RNAS
	KiA	over Dury		Ltn.d.R Schöck Albatros D.III		hit by anti-aircraft fire
20.5	0807	near Riencourt	F.E.2b	Uffz Rosenfeld Albatros D.III	2	
	1110	near Riencourt	SPAD 7 B.1587	Oblt Ritter von Tutschek Albatros D. III 2274/16	10	23 Sqn, RFC
25.5		Monchy	SPAD 7	Uffz Gille	3	

Date	Time	Location	Aircraft Type	Victor & Aircraft	Vic. No.	Crew/Disposition
26.5	0810	near Cagnicourt	Sopwith Pup A.6186	Ltn Hochstetter	1	66 Sqn, RFC
	2015	near Etaing	Sopwith Pup	Uffz Jörke	3	66 Sqn, RFC
	2050	near Etaing	Sopwith	Uffz Rosenfeld	3	66 Sqn, RFC
3.6	1750	near Epéhy	F.E.2b	Vfw Jörke	4	
6.6.	1310	southeast of Inchy, near Moeuvres	Sopwith Pup	Vfw Riessinger	2	
	1310	near Moeuvres	Sopwith Pup A.7306	Uffz Rosenfeld	4	54 Sqn, RFC
	1320	near Sains-lès-Marquion	Sopwith Pup B.1730	Ltn.d.R Becker	1	54 Sqn, RFC
12.6	WiA			Uffz Rosenfeld		
13.6	2105	near Arras	Sopwith Triplane	Uffz Gille	4	
15.6	1415	near Quéant	R.E. 8	Vfw Riessinger	3	
	1545	near Bullecourt	British monoplane FtL	Ltn Billik	n/c	
16.6	2130	near Buissy	Nieuport 17 B.1610	Vfw Riessinger	4	60 Sqn, RFC
	KiA	near Buissy		Vfw Riessinger		collided with Nieuport
17.6		Goldbach	SPAD 7	Vfw Albert Hurrle	1	
27.6	2000	near Vis-en-Artois / south of Haucourt	Nieuport 17 B.1572	Ltn von Nostitz	2	29 Sqn, RFC
		near Croisilles	Nieuport 1-seater	Ltn.d.R Knake	1	
29.6	0910	near Plouvain / Bullecourt	Nieuport 17 B.1677	Ltn Billik	3	29 Sqn, RFC
3.7	1035	north of Vaulx	Sopwith 1½ Strutter	Oblt Ritter von Tutschek Albatros D.V 2005/17	11	
	1920	near Lagnicourt	Nieuport 17 B.1585	Ltn Billik	4	60 Sqn, RFC
11.7	1815	near Thélus	R.E.8	Oblt Ritter von Tutschek Albatros D.V	12	5 Sqn, RFC
	1845	near Monchy	F.E.2d	Oblt Ritter von Tutschek Albatros D.V	13	25 Sqn, RFC
12.7	1800	northwest of Lens	British Balloon	Oblt Ritter von Tutschek Albatros D.V	14	36th Balloon Wing 16th Company 1st Section, RFC
13.7	0800	Noeux-les-Mines, near Lens	Nieuport 1-seater	Oblt Ritter von Tutschek Albatros D.V	15	
14.7	1650	near Boursies	F.E.	Vfw Oefele Albatros D.V	1	
15.7	2025	south of Douai	Nieuport 23 B.1575	Oblt Ritter von Tutschek Albatros D.V	16	60 Sqn, RFC
21.7	2130	near Moeuvres / Cambrai-Bapaume road	Nieuport 23 B.1695	Oblt Ritter von Tutschek Albatros D.V	17	40 Sqn, RFC
22.7	2040	west of Hulluch	Sopwith 1-seater	Ltn.d.R Knake	2	
	KiA	over Oppy		Vfw Oefele		
23.7	1755	near Neuville	Balloon in flames	Oblt Ritter von Tutschek Albatros D.V	18	

Date	Time	Location	Aircraft Type	Victor & Aircraft	Vic. No.	Crew/Disposition
23.7	1800	north of Arras	Balloon in flames	Ltn.d.R Knake	3	
24.7	KiA	near Epinay		Ltn.d.R Knake		
27.7		Location: Roucourt Airfield				
28.7	0730	near Méricourt	Sopwith Triplane	Oblt Ritter von Tutschek Albatros D.V	19	
	1040	northeast of Lens	Nieuport 1-seater	Oblt Ritter von Tutschek Albatros D.V	20	
29.7	0750	near Hénin-Liétard	S.E.5a in flames	Oblt Ritter von Tutschek Albatros D.V	21	
9.8	2100	near Feuchy	Bristol F.2B A.7114	Ltn Schobinger	1	11 Sqn, RFC
11.8	0910	east of Biache	Bristol F.2B	Oblt Ritter von Tutschek Albatros D.V	22	22 Sqn, RFC
	1830	near Noyelle-Godault near Hénin-Liétard	Bristol F.2B A.7179	Oblt Ritter von Tutschek Albatros D.V	23	22 Sqn, RFC
	WiA	Acheville		Oblt Ritter von Tutschek		shot down by Sopwith Triplane N.5482; hospitalized
	2040	near Farbus	Sopwith Triplane N.5482	Ltn Schobinger	2	8 Sqn, RNAS
18.8	0755	south of Lallaing, near Brebières	Bristol F.2B	Ltn Schobinger	3	11 Sqn, RFC
20.8	0920	near Vitry	Sopwith 1½ Strutter A.8336	Vfw Jörke	5	43 Sqn, RFC
22.8	1950	near Bauvin	Nieuport 1-seater	Uffz Gille	n/c	
4.9	1120	near Tilloy / Monchy	R.E.8	Ltn Schobinger	4	
5.9	1945	near Lens	Sopwith Camel	Vfw Jörke	6	
15.9	1810	near Guémappe / Wancourt	R.E.8 A.3773	Uffz Gille	5	12 Sqn, RFC
16.9	1400	near Monchy	Sopwith Pup A.673	Vfw Jörke	7	46 Sqn, RFC
	1410	near Lécluse	Sopwith Pup A.673	Ltn Schobinger	5	46 Sqn, RFC
17.9	0700	near Feuchy	Sopwith Pup	Vfw Jörke	8	
18.9	0800	near Mory	R.E.8 4319	Ltn Schobinger	6	52 Sqn, RFC
	1100	north of Wambaix	Airco D.H.5 A.9208	Ltn Ewers	1	41 Sqn, RFC
	1105	west of Moeuvres	Airco D.H.5	Vfw Jörke	9	41 Sqn, RFC
19.9	0900	south of Sailly	Bristol F.2B A.7130	Vfw Gille	6	11 Sqn, RFC
21.9	0915	near Monchy-le-Preux	Sopwith Pup A.7321	Gefr Neckel	1	46 Sqn, RFC
23.9	1655	near Gavrelle / between Oppy & Willerval	Nieuport 1-seater	Ltn.d.R Becker	2	
26.9		Pinon	SPAD	Vfw A. Hurrle	2	
28.9	1815	Biache	Airco D.H.5	Uffz Neckel	2	41 Sqn, RFC

Date	Time	Location	Aircraft Type	Victor & Aircraft	Vic. No.	Crew/Disposition
30.9	1205	near Fresnes-Plouvain	R.E.8	Vfw Hamster		
10.10	1705	near Hendecourt	Airco D.H.5	Ltn Ewers	2	41 Sqn, RFC
11.10	1745	east of Sains-lès-Marquion	Sopwith Pup	Ltn Ewers	3	46 Sqn, RFC
13.10	1100	near Quéant	Airco D.H.5	Ltn Staats	1	
18.10	1640	northeast of Boursies	Airco D.H.5	Uffz Neckel	3	41 Sqn, RFC
21.10	1540	southwest of Lécluse	R.E.8 A.3859	Ltn Schobinger	7	59 Sqn, RFC
31.10	1115	south of Boiry-Notre Dame	Sopwith Camel	Ltn.d.R Becker	3	
	1710	near Inchy / south of Marquion	Bristol F.2B	Ltn Schobinger	8	11 Sqn, RFC
5.11	Attached: 4. Armee					
	Location: Erkeghem Airfield					
16.11	Attached: 2. Armee					
	Location: Phalempin Airfield					
26.11	Attached: 6.Armee					
	Location: Roucourt Airfield					
30.11	KiA	near Moeuvres - Bourlon wood		Ltn von Senger und Etterlin		combat at 1700 hours with 46 Sqn, RFC

1918

Date	Time	Location	Aircraft Type	Victor & Aircraft	Vic. No.	Crew/Disposition
3.1	MiA			Ltn Wigan		PoW
18.1	1145	near Loos	A.W. FK8	Vfw Neckel	4	2 Sqn RFC
19.1	1145	east of Mauville-Ferme, near Biache	Sopwith Camel	Ltn Koch	1	
24.1		Izel	Sopwith Camel FtL	Uffz Jakob	n/c	
	KiA	Izel		Uffz Jakob		
29.1		near Méricourt	Sopwith Camel	Ltn Hoffmann		
		Rémigny	Caudron G 4	Vfw A. Hurrle	3	
30.1	KiA	Laveregny Ferme		Vfw A. Hurrle		
2.2	Attached: 7. Armee					
	Location: Marle Airfield					
6.2	1600	Remy	Sopwith Camel C.6706	Ltn.d.R Becker	4	3 Sqn, RFC
		Lécluse	Sopwith 1-seater	Off.Stv Dobberahn	1	
13.2	Location: Toulis Airfield					
14.2	Jagdeschwader II's first combat flight led by			Oblt Ritter von Tutschek Albatros D.V 2194/17		
26. 2		east of Vauxaillon, near Pinon	S.E.5a	Vfw Neckel B.548	5	24 Sqn, RFC
	1120	near Athies, 2 km northeast of Laon	SPAD 7 B.6732	Hptm Ritter von Tutschek Fokker Dr.I	24	23 Sqn, RFC

Date	Time	Location	Aircraft Type	Victor & Aircraft	Vic. No.	Crew/Disposition
27.2		near Essigny-le-Grand	SPAD XI	Oblt Blumenbach Fokker Dr.I	1	
28.2		St. Gobain	S.E.5a	Ltn Koch Albatros D.V	2	
		St. Gobain wood	S.E.5a	Vfw Neckel Albatros D.V	6	
		St. Gobain wood	S.E.5 C.5379	Ltn.d.R Becker Albatros D.V	5	84 Sqn, RFC
	collision			Hptm Ritter von Tutschek Fokker Dr.I 404/17		struck Oblt Blumenbach's Fokker Dr.I, landed uninjured
	collsion			Oblt Blumenbach Fokker Dr.I		struck Ritter von Tutschek's Fokker Dr.I, landed uninjured
1.3	0845	near Terny	Balloon	Hptm Ritter von Tutschek Fokker Dr.I 404/17	25	
6.3	1440	Gropy Wood	S.E.5a C.1057	Hptm Ritter von Tutschek Fokker Dr.I 404/17	26	24 Sqn, RFC
	1445	Bertaucourt	S.E.5a FtL C.9535	Ltn.d.R Becker Albatros D.V	6	24 Sqn, RFC
	KiA	Rony		Ltn Staats Albatros D.III 1788/16 (G.145)		collision with S.E.5a C.9535, 24 Sqn, RFC
10.3		German time synchronized with Allied time				
10.3	1745	west of Fort Malmaison, near Chavignon	SPAD 1-seater	Hptm Ritter von Tutschek Fokker Dr.I 404/17	27	Esc Spa 86
15.3	1113	KiA near Brancourt		Hptm Ritter von Tutschek Fokker Dr.I 404/17		shot down by S.E.5a B.79, 24 Sqn, RFC
19.3		Attached: 18. Armee				
		Location: Guise Airfield				
22.3	WiA			Off.Stv Dobberahn		hospitalized
23.3		Location: Roupy Airfield				
		near Ham	Sopwith Camel C.8244	Vfw Neckel	7	70 Sqn, RFC
24.3		Location: Gouzeaucourt Airfield				
25.3		near St. Christ	Sopwith Camel C.8216	Ltn.d.R Becker Albatros	7	43 Sqn, RFC
28.3		Location: Balâtre Airfield				
31.3		west of Montdidier	SPAD XIII	Ltn.d.R Becker	8	Esc Spa 57
			SPAD XIII	Vfw Neckel	8	
1.4	WiA			Ltn Hoffmann		DoW on 2.4 in Nesle
		Location: Bonneuil-Ferme Airfield				
12.4		southeast of Thilloy	SPAD XIII	Ltn.d.R Becker	9	
	1530	east of Arvillers	SPAD XIII	Ltn.d.R Neckel	9	Esc Spa 94
16.4		German time one hour ahead of Allied time				
21.4		Location: Le Mesnil (Nesle) Airfield				
	1145	Bussy	Bréguet 14 B2	Ltn.d.R Neckel	10	Esc Br 127

Date	Time	Location	Aircraft Type	Victor & Aircraft	Vic. No.	Crew/Disposition
3.5		near Morisel-Hailles	SPAD XI	Ltn.d.R Becker	n/c	
6.5		north of Montdidier	SPAD XIII	Ltn.d.R Becker	10	Esc Spa 57
9.5		southwest of Faverolles	SPAD XIII	Ltn.d.R Becker	11	
27.5	KiC	near Mesnil		Gefr Dombrowe		accident
30.5		Montbré	French Balloon	Off.Stv Grigo	3	50ème Cie Aérostieres
11.6		Montdidier	Sopwith Camel B.235	Ltn Hildebrandt	5	73 Sqn, RAF
12.6		Attached: 2. Armee				
		Location: Mesnil-Bruntel Airfield				
	KiA	Laigne Wood (Plessis-Biron)		Ltn.d.R Hugo Schulz		
14.6	2010	Dreslincourt	Sopwith Camel D.6420	Ltn.d.R Neckel	11	80 Sqn, RAF
	2015	Dreslincourt	Sopwith Camel D.6597	Ltn.d.R Neckel	12	80 Sqn, RAF
16.6	1855		Sopwith Camel B.2524	Ltn.d.R Neckel	13	80 Sqn, RAF
17.6			SPAD XIII	Ltn.d.R Neckel	14	
25.6	1240	east of Albert	Bristol F.2B C.4719	Ltn.d.R Neckel	15	48 Sqn, RAF
	2000	east of Villers-Brettoneux	Sopwith Camel B.7278	Ltn.d.R Neckel	6	201 Sqn, RAF
27.6	1905	Villers-Brettoneux	Bristol F.2B C.877	Ltn.d.R Neckel	17	48 Sqn, RAF
		Villers-Brettoneux	S.E.5a B.8408	Ltn.d.R Neckel	18	84 Sqn, RAF
3.7		northeast of Warfusée	Sopwith Camel	Ltn.d.R Neckel	19	
	KiA	near Corbie		Vfw Vietzen		
7.7		northeast of Warfusée	Sopwith Camel C.8279	Ltn.d.R Neckel	20	209 Sqn, RAF
12.7		Attached: 3. Armee				
		Location: Leffincourt Airfield				
24.7		Attached: 9. Armee				
		Location: Chéry-lès-Pouilly Airfield				
10.8	MiA	Cuvilly		Ltn Muhs Fokker D.VII		aerial combat, PoW
11.8	1730	Guyencourt, north of Roye	SPAD XIII	Ltn.d.R Neckel	21	Esc Spa 37
	1830	north of Roye	SPAD XIII	Ltn.d.R Becker	12	Esc Spa 37
13.8	1300	near Le Quesnel	Sopwith Camel D.9642	Ltn.d.R Neckel	22	201 Sqn, RAF
	KiA	over Roye		Ltn Schickler Fokker D.VII		
14.8	1200	Villers-Carbonnel	S.E.5a C.1888	Ltn.d.R Becker Fokker D.VII	13	92 Sqn, RAF

Date	Time	Location	Aircraft Type	Victor & Aircraft	Vic. No.	Crew/Disposition
14.8	1205	Chaulnes / Villers-Carbonnel	S.E.5a in flames D.6173	Ltn.d.R Neckel Fokker D.VII	23	92 Sqn, RAF
	FtL	Foreste	(engine hit in aerial combat)	Ltn.d.R Greven		pilot uninjured
16.8	crash			Ltn Koch SSW D.III		pilot uninjured
21.8		Attached: 18. Armee				
		Location: Fontaine-Notre-Dame Airfield				
	1400	south of Quierzy	SPAD XIII FtL	Ltn.d.R Neckel	24	
28.8		Attached: 1. Armee				
		Location: Neuflize Airfield				
3.9		Attached: Armee-Abt C				
		Location: Doncourt Airfield				
4.9		Location: Giraumont Airfield				
13.9	KiA	west of Longeville, near Mars-la-Tour		Ltn.d.R Kelber		in fight with two SPADs, shot down in flames
14.9		Lüttingen, northeast of Metz	Bréguet 14 B2 FtL	Ltn.d.R Becker	14	Esc Br 243
15.9	1235		Bristol F.2B E.2512	Ltn.d.R Neckel Fokker D.VII	25	20 Sqn, RAF
18.9	1730	west of Conflans	Bréguet 14 B2	Ltn.d.R Besser Fokker D.VII	1	11th Aero Sqn, USAS
	1730	southwest of Conflans	Bréguet 14 B2	Ltn.d.R Greven Fokker D.VII	1	11th Aero Sqn, USAS
	1730	southwest of Conflans	Bréguet 14 B2 Fokker D.VII	Flgr Wilke	1	11th Aero Sqn, USAS
	1730	near Conflans	D.H.4	Ltn.d.R Neckel Fokker D.VII	26	11th Aero Sqn, USAS
	1730	near Lüttingen, northeast of Metz	Bréguet 14 B2 FtL	Ltn.d.R Becker Fokker D.VII	15	11th Aero Sqn, USAS
	1730	between Conflans – St. Jean	Bréguet 14 B2	unidentified	n/c	11th Aero Sqn, USAS
	1732	west of Conflans	Bréguet 14 B2	Ltn.d.R Becker Fokker D.VII	16	11th Aero Sqn, USAS
26.9		southeast of Longuyon	D.H.4	Ltn.d.R Becker Fokker D.VII	17	20th Aero Sqn, USAS
		Anoux	D.H.4 in flames	Ltn.d.R Becker Fokker D.VII	18	20th Aero Sqn, USAS
		Landres	D.H.4 32792	Ltn.d.R Besser Fokker D.VII	n/c	20th Aero Sqn, USAS observer seen to jump, aircraft's bombs exploded in the air
		Giraumont Airfield	D.H.4 FtL 32286	Ltn.d.R Greven Fokker D.VII	2	20th Aero Sqn, USAS
	FtL			Ltn.d.R Greven Fokker D.VII		hit in fuel tank, pilot uninjured, landed at Giraumont Airfield

Date	Time	Location	Aircraft Type	Victor & Aircraft	Vic. No.	Crew/Disposition
26.9	1000	southwest of Longuyon	D.H.4	Vfw Klaiber Fokker D.VII	2	11th Aero Sqn, USAS
		Giraumont, east of Conflans	D.H.4 32286	Ltn.d.R Greven Fokker D.VII	2	20th Aero Sqn, USAS
28.9		Attached: 5. Armee				
		Location: Charmolis (Stenay) Airfield				
3.10	1630	Doulcon, northeast of Aincreville	SPAD S.13 FtL	Ltn.d.R Becker Fokker D.VII	19	94th Aero Sqn, USAS SPAD just shot down BZ 64 balloon
4.10	0915	west of Villers-devant-Dun	SPAD S.13	Ltn.d.R Becker Fokker D.VII	20	28th Aero Sqn, USAS
10.10	1730	Beauvessaire	SPAD S.13	Ltn.d.R Becker Fokker D.VII	21	139th Aero Sqn, USAS
	1730	La Croix	D.H.4 in flames 32904	Vfw Klaiber Fokker D.VII	3	20th Aero Sqn, USAS
	1731	La Croix	D.H.4	Vfw Klaiber Fokker D.VII	4	
18.10		Location : Carignan Airfield				
23.10	1615		A.R.2	Ltn.d.R Neckel Fokker D.VII	27	
30.10	1220	northeast of Landres	SPAD XI	Ltn.d.R Becker Fokker D.VII	22	
	1225	Champigneulle	SPAD XI	Vfw Klaiber Fokker D.VII	5	
	1230	Verpel	SPAD XI	Vfw Wittchen Fokker D.VII	1	
	1630		SPAD S.13	Vfw Klaiber Fokker D.VII	6	22nd Aero Sqn, USAS
	1645		SPAD XIII	Ltn.d.R Neckel Fokker D.VII	28	
			SPAD S.13	Ltn Bertling Fokker D.VII	1	22nd Aero Sqn, USAS
31.10	1245		Salmson 2A2	Ltn.d.R Neckel Fokker D.VII	29	
	1630	Villers-devant-Dun	SPAD XIII in flames	Ltn Bertling Fokker D.VII	2	
		Villers-devant-Dun	SPAD XIII in flames	Ltn.d.R Greven Fokker D.VII	3	
3.11		Location: Florenville Airfield				
	1620	east of Joncq	SPAD XIII	Ltn.d.R Becker Fokker D.VII	23	2nd Aero Sqn, USAS
	1620	Beaumont	SPAD XIII	Ltn Telge Fokker D.VII	1	
	1625	Summauthe	SPAD XIII	Vfw Wittchen Fokker D.VII	2	
	1625	Summauthe	SPAD XIII	Uffz Rossbach Fokker D.VII	1	

151

Date	Time	Location	Aircraft Type	Victor & Aircraft	Vic. No.	Crew/Disposition
3.11	1625	Beaumont	SPAD XIII	Ltn Bertling Fokker D.VII	3	
		Pouilly	SPAD XIII	Ltn.d.R Greven Fokker D.VII	4	
6.11		Bethelainville	SPAD XIII	Ltn.d.R Neckel Fokker D.VII	30	28th Aero Sqn, USAS
10.11		Attached: 5. Armee				
		Location: Trier Airfield				

Jagdstaffel 13

1916

Date	Time	Location	Aircraft Type	Victor & Aircraft	Vic. No.	Crew/Disposition
28.9		Attached : Armee-Abt C				
		Location: Mars-la-Tour Airfield				

1917

Date	Time	Location	Aircraft Type	Victor & Aircraft	Vic. No.	Crew/Disposition
22.1		near Nixeville, west of Verdun	Caudron	Oblt Dostler	2	
20.2		Attached: 5. Armee				
5.3		Attached: 7. Armee				
		Location: La Selve Airfield				
11.3		near Moulin, south of Vendresse	Caudron	Vfw Ruckdeschel	1	
18.3		northwest of Beaurieux	Caudron	Ltn de Payebrune	1	
25.3		German time synchronized with Allied time				
6.4		south of Vailly	Farman	Ltn Kreuzner	1	
17.4		German time one hour ahead of Allied time				
20.4		Landricourt	Farman	Ltn Schürz	1	
1.5		Location : Le Clos-Ferme (Boncourt) Airfield				
3.5		Septmons, south of Soissons	Caudron	Ltn.d.R Dannenberg	1	
9.5	IiC	(made forced landing)		Vfw Kairis		
11.5		southeast of Vendresse	Caudron	Vfw Ruckdeschel	1	
26.5	WiA			Fwb Grigo		
24.6		Versigny	Nieuport 1-seater	Ltn.d.R Dannenberg	2	
17.8		east of Varennes	Nieuport	Ltn Büchner	1	
20.8		southeast of Malancourt	SPAD	Ltn Schröder	1	
		near Esnes	SPAD	Uffz. Hiob	1	
29.9		Douaumont	A.R.2	Uffz Goretski	1	
15.10		Margival, south of Vauxaillon	SPAD	Ltn Büchner	2	
30.10		Pargnan	SPAD	Ltn Güttler	5	

Date	Time	Location	Aircraft Type	Victor & Aircraft	Vic. No.	Crew/Disposition
1.11		Attached: 2. Armee				
		Location: Marle Airfield				
22.11		Location: Cambrai area Airfield				
2.12		Villeret	A.W. FK.8	Ltn Güttler	6	8 Sqn, RFC
29.12		Cerny	Caudron	Ltn Golz	1	

1918

Date	Time	Location	Aircraft Type	Victor & Aircraft	Vic. No.	Crew/Disposition
3.1		south of Pargnan	SPAD	Ltn.d.R Kämpfe	1	
		northwest of Pargnan	Balloon	Ltn.d.R Kämpfe	2	
5.1		Staubecken	Paul Schmitt	Vfw Hiob	2	
28.1		Vendenil	Caudron	Vfw Kramer	4	
29.1		Sansy	Balloon	Vfw Brunnengräber	1	
2.2		Attached: 7 Armee				
		Location: Reneuil-Ferme Airfield				
12.2		Attached: 7. Armee				
		Location: Autremencourt Airfield				
17.2	1450	northeast of La Fère	British Balloon	Oblt Thomas	2	3rd Balloon Wing 13th Company 5th Section, RFC
19.2		Guise	Bréguet 14 B2	Ltn Güttler	8	3 Sqn, RFC
20.2	KiC	southeast of Reneuil-Ferme Airfield		Ltn Güttler & Vfw Hiob Halberstadt		
21.2			S.E.5a B.619	Vfw Jörke	10	2 Sqn, AFC
	1635	northwest of La Fère	British Balloon	Ltn.d.L Pippart	7	3rd Balloon Wing 13th Company 6th Section, RFC
5.3		Verneuil-Geny	Caudron FtL	Ltn.d.R Hermann Schmidt	n/c	
6.3	1040	Fort Mayot	S.E.5a A.8946	Ltn.d.L Pippart	8	84 Sqn, RFC
9.3		southwest of Laon	SPAD S.13	Ltn Hildebrandt	1	95th Aero Sqn, USAS
10.3		German time synchronized with Allied time				
19.3		Attached: 18. Armee				
		Location: Guise Airfield				
23.3		Location: Roupy Airfield				
24.3		Location: Gouzeaucourt Airfield				
28.3		Location: Balâtre Airfield				
		Montdidier, Poudry	SPAD XIII	Ltn Hildebrandt	2	Esc Spa 57
		near Proyart	Bristol F.2B	Ltn.d.R H. Schmidt	1	
30.3	FtL		(engine disabled by enemy fire)	Ltn.d.L Pippart		uninjured

Date	Time	Location	Aircraft Type	Victor & Aircraft	Vic. No.	Crew/Disposition
1.4	1820	west of Montdidier	Balloon	Ltn.d.L Pippart	9	89ème Cie Aérostieres
2.4	1850	Ourscamp	British 2-seater	Ltn.d.R Wilhelm Schwartz	2	
13.4		Location: Boneuil-Ferme Airfield				
16.4		German time one hour ahead of Allied time				
20.4	1500	west of Chauny	Bréguet 14 B2	Ltn.d.L Pippart	10	Esc Br 127
21.4		Location: Le Mesnil (Nesle) Airfield				
23.4	KiA	near Moreuil		Uffz Dassenies		
4.5	1800	between Ham & Aubigny	Bréguet 14 B2	Ltn Hildebrandt	3	Esc Br 29
6.5	1710	near Frières	Bréguet 14 B2 in flames	Ltn.d.R W. Schwartz	3	
	1730	near La Fère	Bréguet 14 B2 in flames	Ltn Hildebrandt	4	
15.5		near Quesnoy	Bréguet 14 B2 in flames	Ltn.d.R W. Schwartz	4	
30.5		north of Vic	Balloon	Ltn.d.R W. Schwartz	5	
9.6		Thiescourt	S.E.5a B.8391	Ltn.d.R Hencke	1	32 Sqn, RAF
		Thiescourt	SPAD XIII	Uffz Piel	1	
		Dreslincourt	SPAD XIII	Vfw Haussmann	7	
		Ribecourt	Bréguet 14 B2	Ltn.d.R Niethammer	1	
10.6		south of Vauxaillon	SPAD XIII	Ltn.d.R Büchner	3	
		Château Sorel	S.E.5a C.9626	Gefr Laabs	1	32 Sqn, RAF
11.6	1200	Montener-Méry Lataule	SPAD XIII	Ltn Hetze	1	Esc Spa 94
		Méry	SPAD VII	Ltn.d.R Büchner	4	Esc Spa 159
			SPAD XIII	Uffz Piel	2	
			S.E.5a	Uffz Hertzsch	1	
12.6		Attached : 2. Armee				
		Location: Mesnil-Bruntel Airfield				
14.6	2000	Dreslincourt	Sopwith Camel D.6581	Ltn.d.R W. Schwartz	6	
15.6	WiA		Balloon attack	Ltn.d.R W. Schwartz		
25.6	1250	south of Albert	Bristol F.2B C.4719	Ltn Hetze	2	48 Sqn, RAF
	KiA	Chaulnes	(shot down in flames)	Ltn.d.R Hilberer		
	IiC	Ennemain Airfield		Uffz Hertzsche Fokker D.VII		DoI at Marchélepot on 26.6.18
27.6	1900	Villers Brettoneux / Amiens	R.E.8 A.3661	Vzfw Haussmann	8	3 Sqn, AFC
		Villers Brettoneux	Bristol F.2B	Uffz Fritzsche	n/c	

Date	Time	Location	Aircraft Type	Victor & Aircraft	Vic. No.	Crew/Disposition
28.6	2100	over Amiens	S.E.5a D.6086	Ltn.d.R Büchner	5	56 Sqn, RAF
29.6			Bréguet 14 B2 in flames	Uffz Fritzsche		
	KiA	Amiens	(aerial combat with Spads)	Uffz Piel Fokker D.VII 373/18		
1.7			Sopwith	Ltn.d.R Büchner	6	
		south of Albert	Sopwith Camel B.6369	Ltn.d.R Niethammer	2	209 Sqn, RAF
2.7	1045	Contay	Sopwith Dolphin D.3671	Ltn.d.R Büchner	7	87 Sqn, RAF
7.7	1115	near Hamel	Sopwith Camel D.3329	Ltn.d.R Büchner	8	209 Sqn, RAF
13.7		Attached: 3. Armee				
		Location: Leffincourt Airfield				
16.7			Bréguet 14 B2	Ltn.d.R Büchner	9	
			Bréguet 14 B2	Ltn.d.R Büchner	10	
	KiA	Semide	(jumped from burning aircraft)	Uffz Laabs		
19.7			SPAD XIII	Ltn.d.R Büchner	11	
24.7		Attached: 9. Armee				
		Location: Chéry-lès-Pouilly Airfield				
28.7	1850	Chaudun	SPAD XIII	Ltn.d.R Grimm	1	
29.7	1840	near Vénizel	Sopwith Camel in flames D.9498	Ltn.d.R Büchner	12	73 Sqn, RAF
9.8	1820	Lignières	SPAD XI	Ltn.d.R Büchner	13	
10.8	1125	near Laon	Bristol F.2B	Ltn.d.R Büchner	14	
	FtL	near Laon	(fuel tank hit in aerial combat)	Ltn.d.R Büchner		uninjured
	FtL	Roman Road from St. Quentin to Amiens	(hit by ground fire)	Ltn.d.R Niethammer		uninjured
11.8	1908	Roye, near Estrées	Sopwith	Ltn.d.R Büchner	15	
	1910	near Estrées	SPAD XIII	Ltn.d.R Büchner	16	
13.8	MiA	Lake Lachaussée	(shot down at 1510)	Ltn.d.R P. Wolff Fokker D.VII	PoW	
14.8	1840	Chaulnes	Sopwith Camel F.2112	Ltn.d.R Büchner	17	46 Sqn, RAF
	1840	Chaulnes	Sopwith Camel D.6631	Vfw Haussmann	9	46 Sqn, RAF
	1840	Chaulnes	Sopwith Camel F.2086	Off.Stlv Ledermann	1	46 Sqn, RAF
15.8	0920	Crapeaumesnil	SPAD XIII	Ltn Hetze	3	
	1925	Liaucourt	SPAD XIII	Ltn Hetze	4	
18.8		Attached: 18. Armee				
		Location: Foreste Airfield				

Date	Time	Location	Aircraft Type	Victor & Aircraft	Vic. No.	Crew/Disposition
19.8	1006	Pertain	Bréguet 14 B2 / D.H.9	Ltn.d.R Büchner	18	
20.8			SPAD XIII	Ltn.d.R Büchner	19	Esc Spa 155
			Bréguet 14 B2	Ltn.d.R Büchner	20	
	1600	Blérancourt	EA 2-seater	Vfw Haussmann	10	
	MiA		(with two SPADs)	Off.Stlv Ledermann		PoW
21.8	1800		Bréguet 14 B2	Vfw Haussmann	11	
22.8	1410	Carlepont	Balloon	Vfw Haussmann	12	93ème Cie Aérostieres
26.8		Location: Fontaine-Notre-Dame Airfield				
28.8		Attached: 1. Armee				
		Location: Neuflize Airfield				
3.9		Attached: Armee-Abt C				
		Location: Tichémont Airfield				
	2010	Rony-le-Petit	Sopwith Camel	Ltn.d.R Hencke	2	
7.9	1230	Jeandélize	Salmson 2A2 FtL	Vfw Haussmann	13	
12.9		north of Hattonville	D.H.4 in flames	Ltn.d.R Büchner	21	8th Aero Sqn, USAS
		Vieville-en-Haye	D.H.4 in flames	Ltn.d.R Büchner	22	50th Aero Sqn, USAS
		east of Thiaucourt	Bréguet 14 B2 in flames	Ltn.d.R Büchner	23	Esc Br 132
		Thiaucourt	Bréguet 14 B2 in flames	Ltn.d.R Grimm	2	
	1000	Thiaucourt	Bréguet 14 B2 in flames	Ltn Hetze	5	96th Aero Sqn, USAS
	1002	Thiaucourt	Salmson 2A2	Ltn Hetze	n/c	12th Aero Sqn, USAS
	1850	Thiaucourt	Bréguet 14 B2	Ltn.d.R Grimm	2	Esc Br 128
13.9		Allamont	SPAD XIII	Ltn.d.R Franz Büchner	24	
		Allamont	SPAD XIII	Vfw Haussmann	14	
		Allamont	SPAD XIII	Ltn.d.R Felix Büchner	1	
	WiA		strafed by SPAD while riding in car	Ltn.d.R Hetze		taken to Kriegslazarett B 37 at Vallroy
14.9		Mars-la-Tour	Bréguet 14 B2	Ltn.d.R Franz Büchner	25	Esc Br 132
		Latour	Bréguet 14 B2	Ltn.d.R Franz Büchner	26	Esc Br 132
		Conflans	Bréguet 14 B2	Ltn.d.R Grimm	3	Esc Br 132
		Puxe	Bréguet 14 B2	Ltn.d.R Niethammer	3	Esc Br 132
		Conflans	Caudron R.11	Ltn.d.R Felix Büchner	2	
	MiA	over Lake Lachaussée	(combat at 1500 hours)	Ltn.d.R Paul Wolff Fokker D.VII		PoW
15.9		Thiaucourt	SPAD XIII	Ltn.d.R Franz Büchner	27	Esc Spa 92
		Lachaussée	SPAD XIII	Ltn.d.R Franz Büchner	28	
17.9		Dampvitoux	Salmson 2A2	Ltn.d.R Franz Büchner	29	
18.9		Dampvitoux	SPAD XIII	Ltn.d.R Franz Büchner	30	

Date	Time	Location	Aircraft Type	Victor & Aircraft	Vic. No.	Crew/Disposition
18.9	1725	Chambley	SPAD S.13 S.15252	Ltn.d.R Franz Büchner	31	213th Aero Sqn, USAS
	1730	west of Chambley	SPAD S.13	Ltn.d.R Franz Büchner	32	
20.9	WiA	Chambley	(jumped with parachute, hit by ground MG fire)	Ltn.d.R Kämpfe		to Festungslazarett II in Metz – DoW 20.9
26.9		Consenvoye	SPAD S.13 S.7519	Ltn.d.R Franz Büchner	33	27th Aero Sqn, USAS
		Charpenterie	SPAD S.13 S.4505	Ltn.d.R Franz Büchner	34	94th Aero Sqn, USAS
		Gercourt	SPAD S.13	Ltn.d.R Franz Büchner	35	22nd Aero Sqn, USAS
		Etreillers	SPAD S.13	Ltn.d.R Franz Büchner	36	49th Aero Sqn, USAS
		Bertincourt	SPAD S.13	Vfw Haussmann	15	139th Aero Sqn, USAS
28.9		Attached: 5. Armee: Location Stenay Airfield				
		Nantillois	Salmson 2A2	Ltn.d.R Franz Büchner	37	88th Aero Sqn, USAS
		Pagny	Salmson 2A2	Ltn.d.R Niethammer	4	
1.10			Salmson 2A2 in flames	Ltn.d.R Franz Büchner	38	
9.10			Salmson 2A2 in flames	Ltn.d.R Niethammer	5	
10.10			SPAD XIII	Vfw Haussmann	n/c	Esc Spa 89
		crash	(collided with aircraft of Gefr Michaelis; escaped harm with parachute)	Ltn.d.R Franz Büchner		uninjured
	KiC		(collided with aircraft of Ltn.d. R Büchner; escaped harm with parachute)	Gefr Michaelis		
16.10	KiC	Romagne	(aircraft caught fire for no apparent reason, pilot jumped, parachute failed to open)	Vfw Haussmann Fokker D.VII		
21.10		Argonne	E.A.	Ltn.d.R Franz Büchner	39	
22.10			E.A. 2-seater	Ltn.d.R Franz Büchner	40	
			E.A. 2-seater in flames	Ltn.d.R Niethammer	6	
1.11		Location: Carignan Airfield				
3.11		Location: Florenville Airfield				
10.11		Attached: 5. Armee				
		Location: Trier Airfield				

157

Jagdstaffel 15

1916

Date	Time	Location	Aircraft Type	Victor & Aircraft	Vic. No.	Crew/Disposition
1.5		German time one hour ahead of Allied time				
29.9		Attached: Armee-Abt B				
		Location: Habsheim Airfield				
12.10		Offenburg	Sopwith 1½ Strutter	Ltn Haber	5	3 Wing, RNAS
		Bremgarten	Bréguet BM 4	Ltn.d.R Pfältzer	2	
	1530	Rustenhart	Bréguet BM 4	Ltn.d.R Udet	2	Esc BM 120
18.12		Niederaspach	Nieuport	Ltn.d.R Weitz	1	
24.12	1100	Oberaspach	Caudron G 4	Ltn.d.R Udet	3	Esc C 34

1917

Date	Time	Location	Aircraft Type	Victor & Aircraft	Vic. No.	Crew/Disposition
20.2	1200	Aspach	Nieuport Scout	Ltn.d.R Udet	4	Esc N 81
5.3		Attached: 7. Armee				
		Location: La Selve Airfield				
25.3		German time synchronized with Allied time				
16.4		near Prouvais	Nieuport	Ltn Hellmuth Wendell	1	
	1040	Juvincourt	Farman FtL	Off.Stv Glinkermann	n/c	
17.4		German time one hour ahead of Allied time				
24.4	1930	Chavignon	Nieuport	Ltn.d.R Udet	5	
26.4	KiA	Lierval	(combat with SPADs at 1930 hours)	Oblt M. Reinhold		
29.4	WiA			Ltn.d.R Peckmann		
1.5		Location : Le Clos-Ferme (Boncourt) Airfield				
4.5		between La Ville au Bois & Craonne wood	SPAD VII	Ltn.d.R Gontermann	18	
5.5	1930	near Villers wood	SPAD VII	Ltn.d.R Udet	6	
10.5	1230	Berry-au-Bac	SPAD VII	Ltn.d.R Gontermann	19	
	1820	Berry-au-Bac	Caudron R.4	Ltn.d.R Gontermann	20	Esc C 46
11.5	1030	Berry-au-Bac	SPAD VII	Ltn.d.R Gontermann	21	
22.5		Berrieux	SPAD VII	Vfw Glinkermann	2	
25.5	KiC	Mortiers Airfield	(crashed after take-off)	Vfw Heinrich Müller		
26.5	KiA	Laon, Chermizy		Ltn.d.R Haenisch		
29.5	KiA	Orgeval		Vfw Glinkermann		
4.6	KiA	Filian	(attacked by SPADs after balloon attack)	Vfw Eichenauer		
16.6		Laon	Nieuport	Ltn.d.R Esser	1	
	KiA	Winterberg, near Laon		Ltn.d.R Esser		
24.6	15.5	Pontavert	French Balloon	Ltn.d.R Gontermann	22	65ème Cie Aérostieres

Date	Time	Location	Aircraft Type	Victor & Aircraft	Vic. No.	Crew/Disposition
27.6	1200	southeast of Reims	French Balloon	Ltn.d.R Gontermann	23	51ère Cie Aérostieres
16.7	1400	south of Reims	Balloon	Ltn.d.R Gontermann	24	
24.7	0945	Stadecken	SPAD VII	Ltn.d.R Gontermann	25	
5.8	1940	Braye/Grund	Nieuport 1-seater	Ltn.d.R Gontermann	26	
9.8		Forêt de Hesse	French Balloon	Ltn.d.R Gontermann	27	46ème Cie Aérostieres
		Forêt de Hesse	French Balloon	Ltn. d.R Gontermann	28	51ère Cie Aérostieres
13.8	0945	Monampteuil	Caudron	Ltn Arntzen	5	
	1115	Hurtébise-Ferme south of Laon	Caudron	Ltn von Budde	1	
	1155	near Braine	Balloon	Vfw Haussmann	5	43ème Cie Aérostieres
		Braine	Nieuport 1-seater	Vfw Haussmann	6	
		near Pontavert	French Balloon	Ltn.d.R Mendel	1	43ème or 71ère Cie Aérostieres
14.8	2030	Pont-à-Vendin	Airco D.H.4	Ltn.d.R Udet	7	25 Sqn, RFC
15.8	1025	Pont-à-Vendin	Sopwith 1½ Strutter	Ltn.d.R Udet	8	43 Sqn, RFC
17.8	1205	south of Aisne	French Balloon	Ltn.d.R Gontermann	29	28ème Cie Aérostieres
		south of Aisne	French Balloon	Ltn.d.R Gontermann	30	39ème Cie Aérostieres
19.8	1040	between Spancy & Jouy	SPAD VII	Ltn.d.R Gontermann	31	
	1923	south of Aisne valley	Balloon	Ltn.d.R Gontermann	32	
	1924	south of Aisne valley	Balloon	Ltn.d.R Gontermann	33	
	1925	south of Aisne valley	Balloon	Ltn.d.R Gontermann	34	
	1926	south of Aisne valley	Balloon	Ltn.d.R Gontermann	35	
	KiA	Boncourt		Uffz Paul		
20.8		near Mourmelon-le-Grand	Balloon	Ltn Brandt	2	
21.8	0845	Ascq	Airco D.H.4	Ltn.d.R Udet	9	27 Sqn, RFC
15.9	0720	over Cerny	Caudron	Ltn.d.R Gontermann	36	
17.9	0730	south of Izel	Airco D.H.5	Ltn.d.R Udet	10	41 Sqn, RFC
22.9	1825	west of La Fère	Balloon	Ltn Förster	1	
24.9	1220	east of Loos	Sopwith Camel	Ltn.d.R Udet	11	43 Sqn, RFC
28.9	1800	west of Wingles	Sopwith Camel B.6209	Ltn.d.R Udet	12	43 Sqn, RFC
	1805	Vermelles	Sopwith Camel	Ltn.d.R Udet	13	43 Sqn, RFC
30.9	1145	east of Stadecken	SPAD VII	Ltn.d.R Gontermann	37	
	1200	west of Stadecken	SPAD VII	Ltn Förster	2	
	1250	northeast of La Fère	Caudron R.11	Ltn.d.R Gontermann	38	
2.10	1335	Laon	SPAD VII	Ltn.d.R Gontermann	39	
14.10	1645	south of Stadecken	French Balloon	Ltn Hebler	1	27ème Cie Aérostieres
15.10	1300	Crony-Bucy	French Balloon	Ltn Arntzen	6	8ème Cie Aérostieres

Date	Time	Location	Aircraft Type	Victor & Aircraft	Vic. No.	Crew/Disposition
18.10	1035	Deulemont	S.E.5a	Ltn.d.R Udet	14	84 Sqn, RFC
21.10		south of the Aisne	Balloon	Ltn Förster	3	
23.10		southwest of Stadecken	SPAD VII (or 2-seater)	Ltn.d.R Mendel	2	
1.11	Attached: 2. Armee					
		Location: Marle Airfield				
22.11	Location: Cambrai area Airfield					
28.11	1340	Passchendaele-Poelcapelle	Airco D.H.5	Ltn.d.R Udet	15	32 Sqn, RFC
5.12	1430	Westrozebeke - Poelcapelle	S.E.5a	Ltn.d.R Udet	16	

1918

Date	Time	Location	Aircraft Type	Victor & Aircraft	Vic. No.	Crew/Disposition
6.1	1615	Bixschoote	Nieuport	Ltn.d.R Udet	17	
9.1	1200	Stadecken	A.R.2	Ltn Hans Müller	1	
28.1	1635	southeast of Bixschoote	Sopwith	Ltn.d.R Udet	18	
29.1	1200	Zillebeke	Bristol F.2B	Ltn.d.R Udet	19	
		south of Staubecken	A.R.2	Ltn H. Müller	2	
		south of Staubecken	A.R.2 FtL	Ltn H. Müller	n/c	
12.2	Attached: 7. Armee					
		Location: Autremencourt Airfield				
18.2	1050	Zandvoorde	Sopwith Camel	Ltn.d.R Udet	20	
26.2	MiA	La Fère	(FtL after combat with S.E.5a B664, 24 Sqn, RFC)	Vfw Hegeler Pfalz D.III 4184/17		(G.141)
9.3	1040	west of Houthem	Sopwith Camel	Ltn.d.R Udet	n/c	
10.3	German time synchronized with Allied time					
19.3	Attached: 18. Armee					
		Location: Guise Airfield				
23.3		Location: Roupy Airfield				
24.3		Location: Gouzeaucourt Airfield				
28.3		Location: Balâtre Airfield				
	1235	Foucaucourt	R.E.8 B.6571	Ltn Hugo Schäfer	1	52 Sqn, RFC
	1730	southeast of Amiens	Bréguet 14 B2	Ltn.d.R Rahn	4	
30.3	0850	Montdidier	Bréguet14 B2 in flames	Off.Stv Johannes Klein	3	
31.3	1130	west of Montdidier	SPAD 1-seater	Ltn H. Schäfer	2	
	1130	west of Montdidier	SPAD 1-seater	Off.Stv J. Klein	4	
1.4	1045	west of Moreuil, near Ailly	S.E.5a B.174	Ltn H. Schäfer	3	84 Sqn, RAF
	1810	southeast of Montdidier	SPAD VII S.1419	Off.Stv J.Klein	5	Esc Spa 94

Date	Time	Location	Aircraft Type	Victor & Aircraft	Vic. No.	Crew/Disposition
10.4	0930	near Rouvrel	R.E.8	Ltn.d.R Veltjens	11	35 Sqn, RAF
12.4	1525	near Orvillers	SPAD XI	Off.Stv J.Klein	6	
13.4		Location: Boneuil-Ferme Airfield				
16.4		German time one hour ahead of Allied time				
21.4		Location: Le Mesnil (Nesle) Airfield				
10.5	1545	near Braches	SPAD XIII	Ltn.d.R Veltjens	12	Esc Spa 94
18.5	1255	near Cauny	Bréguet 14 B2	Ltn.d.R Veltjens	13	
28.5	1115	north of Crouy, northeast of Soissons	SPAD XVI	Hptm Berthold Fokker D.VII	29	Esc Sop 278
	1115	near Soissons	SPAD XVI in flames	Ltn von Beaulieu-Marconnay Fokker D.VII	1	Esc Sop 278
		La Gorgue	Bristol F.2B	Ltn Baier	1	
29.5	1830	southwest of Soissons	SPAD XIII	Hptm Berthold Fokker D.VII	30	Esc Spa 77
	1830	south of Soissons	SPAD XIII	Ltn.d.R Veltjens Fokker D.VII	14	
	1830	south of Soissons	SPAD XIII FtL	Ltn von Hantelmann Fokker D.VII 2469/18	n/c	
	1840	southeast of Soissons	Salmson 2A2	Hptm Berthold Fokker D.VII	31	Esc Sal 27
	FtL	south of Soissons	(propeller and machine-gun problems)	Hptm Berthold Fokker D.VII		
2.6	1330	southwest of Soissons	Bréguet 14 B2	Ltn.d.R Veltjens Fokker D.VII	15	
5.6		north of St. Just-en-Chaussée	Airco D.H.9 C.6203	Hptm Berthold Fokker D.VII	32	103 Sqn, RAF
6.6	1105	Assainvillers	Airco D.H.4	Ltn von Beaulieu-Marconnay Fokker D.VII	2	27 Sqn, RAF
	1140	Ferrières	Airco D.H.4	Ltn von Hantelmann Fokker D.VII	1	27 Sqn, RAF
	1140	Maignelay	Airco D.H.4 B.2080	Ltn von Ziegesar Fokker D.VII	1	27 Sqn, RAF
	1950	southwest of Montdidier	S.E.5a	Ltn von Beaulieu-Marconnay Fokker D.VII	3	32 Sqn, RAF
	1950	southwest of Montdidier	S.E.5a	Ltn.d.R Veltjens Fokker D.VII	16	
	1950	southwest of Montdidier	S.E.5a	Vzfw J.Klein Fokker D.VII	7	32 Sqn, RAF
7.6	1150	south of Noyon	Airco D.H.9	Ltn.d.R Veltjens Fokker D.VII	17	49 Sqn, RAF
	1150	south of Noyon	Sopwith Camel	Ltn von Beaulieu-Marconnay Fokker D.VII	4	80 Sqn, RAF
9.6	1215	south of Méry	A.R.2	Ltn.d.R Veltjens Fokker D.VII	18	
		Thiescourt	S.E.5a	Ltn.d.R Hencke	1	
10.6	2010	Le Plessis-Brion	SPAD XIII	Ltn von Hantelmann Fokker D.VII 2469/18	2	

Date	Time	Location	Aircraft Type	Victor & Aircraft	Vic. No.	Crew/Disposition
11.6			French 2-seater infantry aircraft	Hptm Berthold Fokker D.VII	33	
	1510	Méry	Sopwith Camel D.1962	Ltn von Beaulieu-Marconnay Fokker D.VII	5	73 Sqn, RAF
	1525	west of Courcelles	Bristol F.2B	Ltn.d.R Veltjens Fokker D.VII	19	
	1550	west of Tricot	Airco D.H.4	Ltn.d.R Veltjens Fokker D.VII	0	
12.6		Attached: 2. Armee				
		Location: Mesnil-Bruntel Airfield				
	1300	near Compiègne	Sopwith Camel	Ltn von Ziegesar Fokker D.VII	n/c	
	1315	northeast of Compiègne	Sopwith Camel D.1917	Ltn von Beaulieu-Marconnay Fokker D.VII	6	43 Sqn, RAF
	1315	near Compiègne	Sopwith Camel	Ltn von Hantelmann Fokker D.VII 2469/18	3	43 Sqn, RAF
	1315	northeast of Compiègne	Sopwith Camel	Ltn.d.R Veltjens Fokker D.VII	21	43 Sqn, RAF
			SPAD XIII	Hptm Berthold Fokker D.VII	34	Esc Spa 96
	1900	Méry	Bréguet 14 B2	Ltn H. Schäfer Fokker D.VII	4	
	1900	Méry	Bréguet 14 B2	Ltn von Hantelmann Fokker D.VII 2469/18	u/c	
16.6	1150	Braches	Airco D.H.4 C.6109	Ltn H. Schäfer Fokker D.VII	5	27 Sqn, RAF
	1150	near Grivesnes	Airco D.H.9	Uffz Weischer Fokker D.VII	1	27 Sqn, RAF
	1200	Roye	Airco D.H.9 in flames C.6346	Ltn von Beaulieu-Marconnay Fokker D.VII	7	27 Sqn, RAF
	1200	Orvillers near Grivesnes	Airco D.H.9 D.469	Vfw J. Klein Fokker D.VII	8	27 Sqn, RAF
	1315	Erches	Airco D.H.4 in flames A.7597	Ltn.d.R Veltjens Fokker D.VII	22	27 Sqn, RAF
	FtL	within German lines	(fight with S.E.5a)	Ltn H. Schäfer Fokker D.VII		uninjured
17.6	1200	MiA over Cachy	(shot down in combat with S.E.5s)	Ltn.d.R Wüsthoff Fokker D.VII 2469/18		PoW 23 & 24 Sqns, RAF
18.6	1135	Ressons	SPAD XIII	Ltn von Hantelmann Fokker D.VII	4	
	1150	Villers-Bretonneux	S.E.5a C.1923	Hptm Berthold Fokker D.VII	35	84 Sqn, RAF
	1155	Villers-Bretonneux	S.E.5a D.259	Hptm Berthold Fokker D.VII	36	84 Sqn, RAF
	1155	southeast of Abancourt	S.E.5a	Ltn von Beaulieu-Marconnay Fokker D.VII	8	
25.6	1850	Roye	Bréguet 14 B2	Ltn.d.R Veltjens Fokker D.VII	23	
	1900	south of Rony-le-Grand	Bréguet 14 B2	Ltn.d.R Borck	1	

Date	Time	Location	Aircraft Type	Victor & Aircraft	Vic. No.	Crew/Disposition
25.6			Bréguet 14 B2	Ltn von Hantelmann	5	
27.6	1906	Villers-Bretonneux	Bristol F.2B in flames C.935	Hptm Berthold Fokker D.VII	37	48 Sqn, RAF
12.7		Attached: 3. Armee				
		Location: Leffincourt Airfield				
19.7		near Soissons	Salmson 2A2	Hptm Berthold Fokker D.VII	38	Esc Sal 40
20.7	1905	south of Dormans (Marne)	French 2-seater	Hptm Berthold Fokker D.VII	39	
24.7		Attached: 9. Armee				
		Location: Chéry-lès-Pouilly Airfield				
31.7	2020	Château Thierry	SPAD S.13	Ltn.d.R J. Klein Fokker D.VII	9	47th Aero Sqn, USAS
1.8	0945	north of Château Thierry, near Fère-en-Tardenois	Salmson 2A2	Hptm Berthold Fokker D.VII	40	1st Aero Sqn, USAS
9.8	1800	near Tricot	SPAD XVI 2-seater	Hptm Berthold Fokker D.VII	41	Esc Spa 289
	1800	northwest of Tricot	SPAD 2-seater	Ltn von Beaulieu-Marconnay Fokker D.VII	9	
	1815	north of Beaucourt-en-Santerre	Sopwith Camel D.9589	Ltn von Beaulieu-Marconnay Fokker D.VII	10	201 Sqn, RAF
	1830	near Beaucourt-en-Santerre	SPAD XVI 2-seater	Hptm Berthold Fokker D.VII	42	Esc Spa 289
	1830	near Beaucourt-en-Santerre	Sopwith Camel	Ltn.d.R J. Klein Fokker D.VII	10	
	1830	west of Le Quesnel	Sopwith Camel	Ltn von Ziegesar Fokker D.VII	n/c	
10.8	1200	north of Roye	S.E.5a	Ltn.d.R Borck Fokker D.VII	2	32 Sqn, RAF
	1220	Licourt	S.E.5a in flames	Hptm Berthold Fokker D.VII	43	32 Sqn, RAF
	1230	Ablaincourt	Airco D.H.9 B.9344	Hptm Berthold Fokker D.VII	44	49 Sqn, RAF
	WiA	Ablaincourt, southwest of Peronne	(broken arm)	Hptm Berthold Fokker D.VII		to Feldlazarett 10
	1245	Arvillers	S.E.5a D.6094	Ltn.d.R Veltjens Fokker D.VII	24	56 Sqn, RAF
	1830	Beuvraignes	SPAD XI	Ltn.d.R Veltjens Fokker D.VII	25	
		northeast of Chaulnes	S.E.5a	Ltn von Beaulieu-Marconnay Fokker D.VII	n/c	56 Sqn, RAF
11.8	1220	Fescamps, west of Roye	Caudron R.9	Ltn.d.R Veltjens Fokker D.VII	26	Esc R 239
	1225	Remaugies, west of Roye	Caudron R.9	Ltn.d.R Veltjens Fokker D.VII	27	Esc R 239
	1235	west of Nesle	S.E.5a	Ltn.d.R J. Klein Fokker D.VII	11	

Date	Time	Location	Aircraft Type	Victor & Aircraft	Vic. No.	Crew/Disposition
11.8	1240	north of Roye, near Nesle	S.E.5a D.375	Ltn.d.R Veltjens Fokker D.VII	28	92 Sqn, RAF
	KiA	near Nesle / Rethonvillers	(shot down in flames)	Ltn.d.R Borck Fokker D.VII		
	1240	near Gruny / Rethonvillers	S.E.5a	Ltn von Beaulieu-Marconnay Fokker D.VII	11	56 Sqn, RAF
	1945	southwest of Noyon	Bréguet 14 B2 in flames	Ltn H. Schäfer Fokker D.VII	6	
14.8	1215	Chaulnes	Bréguet 14 B2	Ltn.d.R J. Klein Fokker D.VII	12	
15.8	1220	Cannectancourt	Caudron R.11	Ltn Klaudat Fokker D.VII	1	Esc C 46
16.8	1220	south of Noyon	SPAD XI	Ltn.d.R Veltjens Fokker D.VII	29	
	1220	southeast of Tracy-le-Val	SPAD XIII	Ltn von Beaulieu-Marconnay Fokker D.VII	12	
	1220	Carlepont	SPAD XIII	Ltn von Hantelmann Fokker D.VII	n/c	
	1930	west of Lassigny	SPAD XIII	Ltn.d.R Veltjens Fokker D.VII	30	
17.8	1710	Beuvraignes, south of Roye	SPAD S.13	Ltn Klaudat Fokker D.VII	2	94th Aero Sqn, USAS
	1720	west of Roye	SPAD S.13	Ltn von Hantelmann Fokker D.VII	6	
	1720	Roye	SPAD S.13	Ltn.d.R Veltjens Fokker D.VII	31	94th Aero Sqn, USAS
18.8		Attached: 18. Armee				
		Location: Foreste Airfield				
21.8	1650	Chauny	Bréguet 14 B2	Ltn von Beaulieu-Marconnay Fokker D.VII	13	
	1650	Chauny	SPAD XIII	Ltn.d.R J. Klein Fokker D.VII	n/c	
	1650	south of Chauny	Bréguet 14 B2	Ltn Klaudat Fokker D.VII	3	
	1650	south of Chauny	Bréguet 14 B2	Ltn Siebert Fokker D.VII	n/c	
	1652	south of Chauny	Bréguet 14 B2	Ltn.d.R J. Klein Fokker D.VII	13	
26.8		Location: Fontaine-Notre-Dame Airfield				
28.8		Attached: 1. Armee				
		Location: Neuflize Airfield				
3.9		Attached: Armee-Abt C				
		Location: Doncourt Airfield				
4.9		Location: Giraumont Airfield				
12.9		south of Thiaucourt	Salmson 2A2 3203	Oblt von Boenigk Fokker D.VII	22	1st Aero Sqn, USAS
	1135	west of Conflans	Bréguet 14 B2 in flames	Ltn von Hantelmann Fokker D.VII	7	96th Aero Sqn, USAS

Date	Time	Location	Aircraft Type	Victor & Aircraft	Vic. No.	Crew/Disposition
12.9	1935	Limey	SPAD S.13	Ltn von Hantelmann Fokker D.VII	8	139th Aero Sqn, USAS
13.9		Location: Tichémont Airfield (north of Giraumont)				
	1355	Vionville	SPAD S.13	Ltn Klaudat Fokker D.VII	4	103rd Aero Sqn, USAS
	1805	southwest of Thiaucourt	SPAD S.13 in flames	Ltn von Hantelmann Fokker D.VII	9	103rd Aero Sqn, USAS
	1815	south of Thiaucourt	SPAD XIII	Oblt von Boenigk Fokker D.VII	23	Esc Spa 155
	1820	Metz	SPAD S.13	Ltn Klaudat Fokker D.VII	5	28th Aero Sqn, USAS
	1840	southeast of Pont-à-Mousson	Airco D.H.9	Ltn.d.R H. Schäfer Fokker D.VII	6	99 Sqn, IF, RAF
	IiC	Tichémont Airfield	crash landing	Ltn Siebert Fokker D.VII		
14.9	0900	north of Gorze	D.H.4	Ltn von Hantelmann Fokker D.VII	10	11th Aero Sqn, USAS
	0900	Bayonville-sur-Mad	D.H.4	Vfw Weischer Fokker D.VII	2	11th Aero Sqn, USAS
	1140	north of Lachaussée	SPAD S.13 FtL Fokker D.VII	Ltn.d.R J. Klein	14	22nd Aero Sqn, USAS
	1140	northwest of Lachaussée	SPAD S.13	Oblt von Boenigk Fokker D.VII	24	22nd Aero Sqn, USAS
	1145	St. Benoit en Woëvre	SPAD XIII	Ltn von Hantelmann Fokker D.VII	11	
	1615	Lachaussée	D.H.4	Ltn von Hantelmann Fokker D.VII	12	11th Aero Sqn, USAS
	1620	St. Benoît-en-Woëvre	SPAD S.13	Vfw Schmückle Fokker D.VII	5	13th Aero Sqn, USAS
		north of Lachaussée	SPAD S.13 Fokker D.VII	Oblt von Boenigk	25	28th Aero Sqn, USAS
15.9	1210	southwest of Metz	Airco D.H.9	Ltn H. Schäfer Fokker D.VII	8	104 Sqn, IF, RAF
	WiA	(flesh wound on leg)		Ltn J. Klein Fokker D.VII		not hospitalized
	1215	south of Metz	Airco D.H.9 D.3245	Ltn von Hantelmann D.VII	13	104 Sqn, IF, RAF
	1215	south of Metz	Airco D.H.9	Vfw Weischer Fokker D.VII	3	104 Sqn, IF, RAF
		Lachaussée	SPAD XIII	Oblt von Boenigk Fokker D.VII	25	
16.9	1120	southwest of Conflans	SPAD XIII	Ltn von Hantelmann Fokker D.VII	14	Esc Spa 77
	1125	St. Hilaire-en-Woëvre	SPAD XIII FtL S.493	Ltn Klaudat Fokker D.VII	6	Esc Spa 77
17.9	1510	north of Gorze	SPAD S.13 S.15199	Ltn von Hantelmann Fokker D.VII	15	95th Aero Sqn, USAS
18.9	1645	Vionville	SPAD S.13 S.7555	Ltn von Hantelmann Fokker D.VII	16	27th Aero Sqn, USAS

Date	Time	Location	Aircraft Type	Victor & Aircraft	Vic. No.	Crew/Disposition
22.9		Urcourt	Salmson 2A2	Oblt von Boenigk Fokker D.VII	26	
23.9	1120	south of Metz	D.H.4	Ltn von Hantelmann Fokker D.VII	17	
24.9	1615	Lachaussée	SPAD XIII	Ltn.d.R J. Klein Fokker D.VII	15	
26.9	1215	Etain	SPAD S.13	Ltn von Hantelmann Fokker D.VII	18	139th Aero Sqn, USAS
	1215	southwest of Etain	SPAD S.13	Ltn H. Schäfer	9	139th Aero Sqn, USAS
		Verny, south of Metz	SPAD S.13	Ltn.d.R J. Klein Fokker D.VII	16	13th Aero Sqn, USAS
	1740	Pont-à-Mousson	SPAD S.13	Ltn von Ziegesar Fokker D.VII	2	13th Aero Sqn, USAS
28.9		Attached: 5. Armee				
		Location: Charmois (Stenay) Airfield				
1.10	1640	southeast of Buzancy	SPAD XIII	Ltn.d.R Veltjens Fokker D.VII	32	
	1640	Buzancy	SPAD XIII	Ltn von Hantelmann Fokker D.VII	19	
2.10	IiC		(collided with aircraft of Ltn.d.R Klieforth, Jasta 19)	Ltn Siebert Fokker D.VII		remained with Staffel despite injuries
3.10	1745	Brieulles	Bréguet 14 B2	Ltn.d.R Veltjens Fokker D.VII	33	
4.10	0915	Meuse valley	SPAD S.13	Vfw Schmückle Fokker D.VII	6	28th Aero Sqn, USAS
	0955	Brieulles	SPAD S.13	Ltn.d.R Veltjens Fokker D.VII	34	49th Aero Sqn, USAS
5.10	1605	Montfaucon	SPAD S.13	Vfw Weischer Fokker D.VII	4	22nd Aero Sqn, USAS
	1605	Nantillois	SPAD S.13	Ltn H. Schäfer Fokker D.VII	10	22nd Aero Sqn, USAS
9.10	1615	east of Montfaucon	SPAD XIII	Ltn von Hantelmann Fokker D.VII	20	
	1615	Montfaucon	SPAD XIII	Ltn H. Schäfer Fokker D.VII	11	
18.10		Location: Carignan Airfield				
	1625	south of Grandpré	Airco D.H.4	Ltn von Hantelmann Fokker D.VII	21	
	1630	south of Grandpré	Airco D.H.4	Ltn.d.R Veltjens Fokker D.VII	35	
21.10	1615	Rémonville	SPAD XIII	Ltn von Hantelmann Fokker D.VII	22	Esc Spa 159
22.10	1700	Brieulles	SPAD S.13 S.7708	Ltn von Hantelmann Fokker D.VII	23	94th Aero Sqn, USAS
23.10	WiA	Bois de Money	(combat with a SPAD)	Ltn Klaudat Fokker D.VII		received broken arm

Date	Time	Location	Aircraft Type	Victor & Aircraft	Vic. No.	Crew/Disposition
29.10	1740	Champigneulles	Salmson 2A2	Ltn von Ziegesar Fokker D.VII	3	12th Aero Sqn, USAS
30.10		Buzancy	Salmson 2A2	Ltn von Hantelmann Fokker D.VII	24	12th Aero Sqn, USAS
3.11		Location: Florenville Airfield				
4.11			SPAD XIII	Ltn von Hantelmann Fokker D.VII	25	
10.11		Attached: 5. Armee				
		Location: Trier Airfield				

Jagdstaffel 19

1916

Date	Time	Location	Aircraft Type	Victor & Aircraft	Vic. No.	Crew/Disposition
25.10		Attached: Armee-Abt A				
		Location: Ronssoy (Épéhy) Airfield				
4.12		Attached 1. Armee				
		Location: Lagnicourt				
28.12		Attached: Armee-Abt A				
		Location: Bühl (Saarburg) Airfield				

1917

Date	Time	Location	Aircraft Type	Victor & Aircraft	Vic. No.	Crew/Disposition
25.3		German time synchronized with Allied time				
6.4		south of Berry-au-Bac	French lattice-tail	Ltn Böning	1	
8.4		Loivre	Caudron G 4	Oblt Hahn	2	Esc C46
12.4		near Orainville	Caudron G 4	Oblt Hahn	3	
15.4		over Reims	Nieuport 1-seater	Ltn Dotzel	1	
16.4		La Neuville	Lattice-tail FtL	Ltn Oertel	n/c	
17.4		German time one hour ahead of Allied time				
22.4		Aumenancourt / St. Etienne	Caudron	Ltn Gerlt	1	
26.4		Brimont	SPAD VII	Oblt Hahn	4	Esc Spa 76
29.4		near Courcy	Caudron R.9	Ltn Böning	3	
30.4		Guyencourt	French Balloon	Oblt Hahn	5	
		Guyencourt	French Balloon	Oblt Hahn	6	
		Reims	French Balloon	Vfw Rahn	1	
		Reims	French Balloon	Vfw Rahn	2	
4.5		north of Reims	SPAD VII	Ltn.d.R Brandt	1	Esc Spa 12
5.5		near Cormicy	Caudron	Vfw Rahn		
10.5	1910	south of Dury, near Berry-au-Bac	SPAD VII	Uffz Ruppert	1	
12.5		near Berry-au-Bac	SPAD VII	Ltn Leusch	1	
30.6		Attached: 1. Armee				
		Location: St. Loup Airfield				

Date	Time	Location	Aircraft Type	Victor & Aircraft	Vic. No.	Crew/Disposition
17.8		near Cornillet	Caudron	Ltn Böning	4	
21.8		Mourmelon-le-Grand	French Balloon	Ltn.d.R Brandt	2	87ème Cie Aérostieres
23.8		near Loivre	Caudron	Ltn Scheller	1	
3.9		Pontavert	Balloon	Uffz Mallmann	1	
		Pontavert	Balloon	Uffz Tybelsky	1	
4.9	KiA	northeast of Beine		Oblt Hahn		(16th victim of Capt G. Madon, Esc Spa 38)
19.9		Grand Brimont	Caudron	Uffz Mallmann	2	
22.9		west of La Fère	Balloon	Ltn Förster	1	
23.9		near the Merlet Mill	Nieuport 1-seater	Ltn Böning	5	
		near Hiller Wood	Nieuport 1-seater	Ltn Böning	6	
13.10	1730	Bourgogne	A.R.2 1123	Ltn.d.R Ernst Hess	15	Esc AR 230
16.10	1200	Asfeld-la-Ville	A.R.2	Ltn.d.R E. Hess	16	Esc AR 52
	1200	Hochberg	Caudron FtL	Ltn.d.R E. Hess	n/c	
30.10	1230	south of Moronvilliers	Letord	Ltn.d.R E. Hess	17	
23.12	KiA	east of Fresnes		Ltn.d.R E. Hess Albatros D.Va 5547/17		(1st victim of Adj De Kergolay, Esc N 96)

1918

Date	Time	Location	Aircraft Type	Victor & Aircraft	Vic. No.	Crew/Disposition
20.1	KiC	near Ecly	(collision in training flight)	Gefr C. Schiller		
2.2		Attached: 7. Armee				
		Location: Cuirieux Airfield				
26.2		Location: Toulis Airfield				
3.2		Berru	Bréguet 14 B2	Ltn Konrad von Bülow-Bothkamp	2	
1.3	KiC	St. Loup Airfield		Vfw Korioth		
6.3		near St. Quentin	Sopwith 1-seater	Ltn.d.R Rienau	1	
7.3		west of La Fère	Balloon in flames	Ltn.d.R Göttsch	n/c	
10.3		German time synchronized with Allied time				
17.3	crash		(following air combat)	Ltn.d.R Rienau		uninjured
23.3		Location: Roupy Airfield				
24.3		Location: Gouzeaucourt Airfield				
28.3		Location: Balâtre Airfield				
30.3	FtL		(engine disabled by enemy fire)	Vfw Richard Schneider		uninjured
31.3		east of Montdidier	SPAD XIII	Ltn Körner	4	Esc Spa 100
		near Montdidier	A.R.2	Ltn.d.R Göttsch	18	
		near Montdidier	Bréguet 14 B2	Vfw Gerdes	1	
		Guerbigny	Bréguet 14 B2	Ltn Jumpelt	2	Esc Br 117

Date	Time	Location	Aircraft Type	Victor & Aircraft	Vic. No.	Crew/Disposition
1.4		near Montdidier	Bréguet 14 B2	Ltn.d.R Göttsch	19	
		near Montdidier	Bréguet 14 B2	Ltn.d.R Rahn	5	
10.4		near Amiens	R.E.8 B.6641	Ltn.d.R Göttsch	20	52 Sqn, RAF
	KiA	near Gentelles		Ltn.d.R Göttsch Fokker Dr.I 419/17		
13.4		Location: Boneuil-Ferme Airfield				
16.4		German time one hour ahead of Allied time				
21.4		Location: Le Mesnil (Nesle) Airfield				
2.5	1315	east of Noyon – Roye road	Bréguet 14 B2	Ltn.d.L Pippart	1	Esc Br 126
4.5	2000	southeast of Montdidier	SPAD XIII S.3411	Ltn.d.L Pippart	12	Esc Spa 77
	2000	south of Montdidier	SPAD XIII	Ltn.d.R Rahn	6	Esc Spa 77
6.5	2030	northwest of Montdidier	SPAD XIII	Ltn.d.L Pippart	13	Esc Spa 96
7.5	MiA		(shot down in combat)	Flgr Görzel		PoW
30.5		between Cuts & Charlepont	Bréguet 14 B2	Ltn.d.L Pippart	14	Esc Br 29
1.6	crash	between Longpont & Parcy	(shot down in combat)	Ltn.d.R Rienau		uninjured
7.6		Rosières	S.E.5a B.611	Ltn.d.R Rahn	n/c	24 Sqn, RAF
	MiA		(shot down in combat)	Vfw Maschinsky		PoW
12.6		Attached: 2. Armee				
		Location: Mesnil-Bruntel Airfield				
		Lagny	S.E.5a in flames D.3960	Ltn.d.L Pippart	5	2 Sqn, AFC
17.6		west of Roye	SPAD XIII	Ltn.d.R Rienau	2	Esc Spa 3
		Rollot, west of Roye	SPAD XIII	Ltn Leusch	2	Esc Spa 3
8.7		Fismes	SPAD XIII	Vfw Richard Schneider	1	Esc Spa 86
12.7		Attached: 3. Armee				
		Location: Leffincourt Airfield				
15.7		northwest of St. Ménehould	SPAD XIII	Ltn.d.L Pippart	16	
16.7		Suippes	SPAD XIII	Ltn.d.L Pippart	17	Esc Spa 153
		Suippes	SPAD XIII	Vfw R. Schneider	2	Esc Spa 153
17.7	1215		Bréguet 14 B2	Ltn.d.L Pippart	18	
	WiA		(shot in hand)	Ltn.d.R Rahn		to hospital
19.7	1930	between Chassins & Dormans	SPAD XIII	Ltn.d.L Pippart	19	Esc Spa 85
22.7	1030	between Dormans & Mourmelon	Caudron R.11	Ltn.d.L Pippart	20	Esc R 240

Date	Time	Location	Aircraft Type	Victor & Aircraft	Vic. No.	Crew/Disposition
22.7	1035	near Mourmelon	SPAD XIII	Ltn.d.L Pippart	21	Esc Spa 93
24.7		Attached : 9. Armee				
		Location: Chéry-lès-Pouilly Airfield				
29.7	IiC	Chéry-lès-Pouilly Airfield	(engine stalled)	Ltn Hermann Müller		
11.8	1700	south of Vrély	British Balloon	Ltn.d.L Pippart Fokker D.VII	22	2th Balloon Wing 16th Company 5th Section, RFC
	1955	north of Noyon	Bréguet 14 B2	Gefr Felder	1	Esc Br 117
	KiA	Noyon	(shot down by anti-aircraft; parachute failed to deploy)	Ltn.d.L Pippart Fokker D.VII		
13.8	KiA	Roye		Ltn Schickler Fokker D.VII		
16.8	KiC	Chéry-lès-Pouilly Airfield	(test flying new aircraft; wing broke in flight)	Ltn Riedel Fokker E.V 107/18		
21.8		Location: Fontaine-Notre-Dame Airfield				
28.8		Attached: 1. Armee				
		Location: Neuflize Airfield				
3.9		Attached: Armee-Abt C				
		Location: Tichémont Airfield				
7.9	1325	northeast of Montsec	Salmson 2A2	Ltn von Beaulieu-Marconnay Fokker D.VII	14	Esc Sal 5
12.9		Thiaucourt	SPAD S.13	Ltn.d.R Kliefoth Fokker D.VII	1	22nd Aero Sqn, USAS
13.9	1720	Charey in flames	Bréguet 14 B2	Ltn von Beaulieu-Marconnay Fokker D.VII	15	Esc Br 225
	1720	Rembercourt	Bréguet 14 B2	Ltn Scheller Fokker D.VII	3	96th Aero Sqn, USAS
	1720	Charey	Bréguet 14 B2	Ltn.d.R Gewert Fokker D.VII	1	96th Aero Sqn, USAS
	1930	Jaulny	SPAD XIII	Ltn von Beaulieu-Marconnay Fokker D.VII	16	
	1930	Jaulny	SPAD XIII	Ltn.d.R Kliefoth Fokker D.VII	2	
	1930	north of Charey	(shot down but saved by successful parachute ascent)	Ltn.d.R Rienau Fokker D.VII		uninjured
14.9		Conflans	D.H.4	Ltn.d.R Kliefoth Fokker D.VII	3	91st Aero Sqn, USAS
		Conflans	Bréguet 14 B2	Ltn.d.R Rienau Fokker D.VII	3	
	1920	Beney	Salmson 2A2	Ltn Gewert Fokker D.VII	2	99th Aero Sqn, USAS
		Jonville	Bréguet 14 B2	Ltn von Beaulieu-Marconnay Fokker D.VII	17	24th Aero Sqn, USAS

Date	Time	Location	Aircraft Type	Victor & Aircraft	Vic. No.	Crew/Disposition
14.9	MiA	Lake La Chaussée		Ltn.d. R Paul Wolff Fokker D.VII		PoW
15.9		Pagny-sur-Moselle	SPAD XIII	Ltn Scheller Fokker D.VII	4	Esc Spa 95
		south of Pagny	SPAD XIII in flames	Ltn.d.R Rienau Fokker D.VII	4	Esc Spa 150
		Prény	SPAD XIII 4929	Ltn von Beaulieu-Marconnay Fokker D.VII.	n/c	Esc Spa 154
16.9	1755	southwest of Briey	Bréguet 14 B2	Ltn von Beaulieu-Marconnay Fokker D.VII	18	96th Aero Sqn, USAS
	1755	southwest of Briey	Bréguet 14 B2 in flames	Ltn.d.R Rienau Fokker D.VII	5	96th Aero Sqn, USAS
	1755	Conflans	Bréguet 14 B2	Gefr Felder Fokker D.VII	2	96th Aero Sqn, USAS
		Fléville, north of Conflans	Bréguet 14 B2	Ltn von Beaulieu-Marconnay Fokker D.VII	19	96th Aero Sqn, USAS
23.9	1010	Pont-à-Mousson	Salmson 2A2	Ltn von Beaulieu-Marconnay Fokker D.VII	20	Esc Sal 28
25.9		Pont-à-Mousson	Bréguet 14 B2	Ltn von Beaulieu-Marconnay Fokker D.VII	n/c	
27.9	1655	Pagny	SPAD XIII	Ltn Körner Fokker D.VII	5	
	IiC	Tichémont Airfield	(collided with another aircraft)	Ltn.d.R Steilung Fokker D.VII		severe head and arm injuries
28.9		Attached : 5. Armee				
		Location: Stenay Airfield				
	1030	Dannevoux	SPAD S.13	Ltn von Beaulieu-Marconnay Fokker D.VII	21	27th Aero Sqn, USAS
29.9	1855	Brieulles	SPAD S.13	Ltn.d.R Rienau Fokker D.VII	6	95th Aero Sqn, USAS
2.10	1130	Brabant	Bréguet 14 B2	Ltn von Beaulieu-Marconnay Fokker D.VII	22	96th Aero Sqn, USAS
	IiC		(collided with aircraft of Ltn Siebert, Jasta 15)	Ltn.d.R Klieforth Fokker D.VII		remained with Staffel despite injuries
3.10	1630	Liny	SPAD S.13	Ltn von Beaulieu-Marconnay Fokker D.VII	23	95th Aero Sqn, USAS
4.10	1745	Vilosnes	Salmson 2A2	Ltn Körner Fokker D.VII	6	91st Aero Sqn, USAS
	WiA		(lightly wounded in one eye)	Ltn von Beaulieu-Marconnay Fokker D.VII		remained with Staffel
6.10	1830	east of Cuisy	American Balloon in flames	Ltn Leusch	3	11 Co Bal Sec
9.10	1730	near Crépion	SPAD XIII	Ltn von Beaulieu-Marconnay Fokker D.VII	24	
10.10	1700	Landres	SPAD S.13	Ltn von Beaulieu-Marconnay Fokker D.VII	25	147th Aero Sqn, USAS

Date	Time	Location	Aircraft Type	Victor & Aircraft	Vic. No.	Crew/Disposition
18.10	WiA	Gouzeaucourt	(shot during combat, possibly by a fellow German)	Ltn von Beaulieu-Marconnay Fokker D.VII		DoW 26.10
25.10	crash	Stenay Airfield	(occurred while landing)	Ltn.d.R Klieforth Fokker D.VII		pilot uninjured
26.10	1705	near Dannevoux	SPAD S.XIII	Ltn Leusch	4	147th Aero Sqn, USAS
27.10	1640	shot down over Bois de Money by 94th Aero Sqn, USAS		Ltn.d.R Klieforth Fokker D.VII		PoW
29.10	1250	Barricourt	Bréguet 14 B2	Vzfw R. Schneider Fokker D.VII	3	96th Aero Sqn, USAS
1.11		Location: Carignan Airfield				
3.11		Location: Florenville Airfield				
	1610	Stenay	SPAD XIII in flames	Ltn Körner Fokker D.VII	7	
	1615	Beaumont	Bréguet 14 B2	Ltn Leusch Fokker D.VII	5	
6.11	1625	Stenay	SPAD XIII	Vzfw R. Schneider Fokker D.VII	4	
10.11		Attached: 5. Armee				
		Location: Trier Airfield				

ENDNOTES

CHAPTER ONE

1 Berthold, *Persönliches Kriegstagebuch*, pp. 42-43.

2 Short for *Grosskampfflugzeug* [large combat aeroplane].

3 Berthold, op.cit., p. 38.

4 The initials AEG stand for the name of the constructor, the *Allgemeine Elektricitäts-Gesellschaft* [General Electric Company, which has no connection to the U.S.-based corporation of that name].

5 Grosz, *AEG G.IV Windsock Datafile 51*, p. 1.

6 Bruce, *British Aeroplanes 1914-1918*, p. 664.

7 Ibid., p. 662.

8 Vickers F.B.5 serial numbered 5460 [Ref: Henshaw, *The Sky Their Battlefield*, p. 54].

9 Royal Flying Corps, *War Diary*, 2 October 1915, p. 1.

10 Woodman, *Early Aircraft Armament – The Aeroplane and the Gun up to 1918*, pp. 34, 37.

11 Berthold, op.cit., pp. 39-40.

12 Ibid., p. 39.

13 Weather report in RFC, op.cit.

14 Franks, Bailey & Duiven, *Casualties of the German Air Service 1914-1920*, p. 180.

15 O'Connor, *Aviation Awards of Imperial Germany and the Men Who Earned Them, Vol. IV – The Aviation Awards of the Kingdom of Württemberg*, pp. 57-60.

16 Royal Flying Corps, *War Diary*, 6 November 1915, p. 1.

17 Josef Georg Grüner was born on 11 December 1892 in Mariahilf, Bavaria [Ref: Zickerick, *Verlustliste der deutschen Luftstreitkräfte im Weltkriege in Unsere Luftstreitkräfte 1914-1918*, p. 28]; Haehnelt, *Ehrentafel der im Flugdienst während des Weltkrieges gefallenen Offiziere der Deutschen Fliegerverbände*, p. 26 lists Grüner as a member of FFA 32, an erroneous transposition of FFA 23.

18 Franks, Bailey & Duiven, op.cit., p. 181; once again, Grüner is erroneously noted as a member of FFA 32.

19 Walter Gnamm was born on 28 May 1895 in Alpirsbach, Württemberg. Commissioned into the 10. Württembergisches Infanterie-Regiment Nr. 180, he transferred to the Fliegertruppe and on 17 August 1915 was assigned to Feldflieger-Abteilung 23. He remained with that unit until 6 October 1916 [Ref: Deutscher Offizier-Bund, *Ehren-Rangliste des ehemaligen Deutschen Heeres*, p. 980; Hildebrand, K. *Die Generale der deutschen Luftwaffe 1935-1945*, Vol. I, p. 367].

20 Armee-Oberkommando der 2. Armee, *Täglicher Bericht*, 7 October 1915.

21 Royal Flying Corps, *Communiqué No. 19*, 9 November 1915, p. 1.

22 Ibid.

23 Gengler, *Rudolf Berthold – Sieger in 44 Luftschlachten Erschlagen im Bruderkampfe für Deutschlands Freiheit*, op.cit., p. 33.

24 Berthold began his army service in Prussian Infanterie-Regiment Reg. Graf Tauentzien von Wittenberg (3. Brandenburgischen) Nr. 20 and Grüner in Saxony's 13. Infanterie-Regiment Nr. 178 [Ref: Deutscher Offizier-Bund, op.cit., pp. 159, 909].

25 Anonymous, 'Leutnant Grüners Heldentod fürs Vaterland', p. 1.

26 O'Connor, *Aviation Awards of Imperial Germany and the Men Who Earned Them, Vol. III – The Aviation Awards of the Kingdom of Saxony*, p. 258.

27 Berthold, op.cit., p. 40.

28 Woodman, op.cit., p. 126.

29 Ernst Freiherr von Althaus was born on 19 March 1890 in Coburg in the Duchy of Saxe-Coburg-Gotha. In 1911, he was commissioned into Saxony's 1. Husaren-Regiment König Albert Nr. 18, with which he served early in World War I and was awarded the *Ritterkreuz des Militär-St.-Heinrichs-Orden* [Knight's Cross of the Military St. Henry Order] on 27 January 1915. After transferring to the Fliegertruppe and being trained as a pilot, Althaus was assigned to FFA 23 in September 1915 [Ref: Zuerl, *Pour-le-Mérite-Flieger*, p. 30].

30 The aircraft was from Escadrille N 3, which, at this time, was equipped with Nieuport Type 14 and 15 two-seaters and used both interchangeably [Ref: Jean, Rohrbacher, Palmieri, & Service historique de l'armée de l'air France. *Les escadrilles de l'aéronautique militaire française: Symbolique et histoire, 1912-1920*, p. 26].

31 Franks, *Sharks Among Minnows*, pp. 54-55.

32 Berthold, op.cit., pp. 42-44.

CHAPTER TWO

1 *Taufbuch*, p. 101.

2 Albert Oskar Arno was born and died on 23 April 1887; Although attended by three physicians, Frau Berthold suffered fatal secondary bleeding during the delivery. The other children were Friedrich Oskar Bertram, born on 30 December 1881, Anna Ida Gertrud on 17 December 1882, Amalia Franziska Ernestine on 14 June 1884 and Anna Ida Elsa on 11 August 1885 [Ref: *Bestattungsbuch*, Vol. 5, p. 141; Vol. 6, pp. 12, 91, 137].

3 The other siblings from the second marriage were Julius Wolfram, born on 26 July 1892, Armin Friedrich Johann on 19 July 1894 (who died on 29 December the same year) and Hermann Armin Julius, born on 24 February 1896 [Ref: *Taufbuch*, pp. 107, 117 and 126].

4 Heidelberger Akademie der Wissenschaften. *Deutsches Rechtswörterbuch – Wörterbuch der älteren deutschen Rechtssprache*, Vol. 10, p. 109.

5 Ibid., pp. 11-12.

6 Ibid.

7 Moncure, *Forging the King's Sword*, pp. 79-80.

8 Deutscher Offizier-Bund, *Ehren-Rangliste des ehemaligen Deutschen Heeres*, p. 789.

9 Ibid., p. 820.

10 Gengler, *Rudolf Berthold – Sieger in 44 Luftschlachten Erschlagen im Bruderkampfe für Deutschlands Freiheit*, p. 13.

11 Ibid.

12 Ibid. The original phrase '*Dulce et decorum est pro patria mori*' is from Horace's Odes (III.2.13) meaning, roughly, 'It is sweet and fitting to die for one's country'. The line is from a poem that urges Romans to develop their military strength to the extent that their enemies would become too frightened to challenge them.

13 Königl. Humanistische Gymnasium Schweinfurt. *Jahresbericht 1906/1907*, pp. 28-29.

14 Königl. Humanistische Gymnasium Schweinfurt. *Jahresbericht 1907/1908*, pp. 30-31.

15 Jordan, *Blätter der Erinnerung an die im Kriege 1914-1919* Gefallenen der Universität Erlangen, p. 84.

16 Gengler, op.cit., p. 14.

17 Abbreviated from Ibid., pp. 15-19, an over-abundant description of the event.

18 Ibid, p. 14.

19 Moncure, op.cit., p. 15.

20 Today in the State of Sachsen-Anhalt.

21 Gengler, op.cit.

22 Bogislav Friedrich Emanuel Graf [Count] Tauentzien (1760-1824) was granted the right to add the honorary title 'von Wittenberg' in honour of his leadership during the liberation of Wittenberg [Ref: Doerstling, *Kriegsgeschichte des Königlich Preussischen Infanterie-Regiment Graf Tauentzien v. Wittenberg (3. Brandenb.) Nr. 20*, pp. 1-2].

23 Gengler, op.cit., pp. 20-21.

24 Ibid., p. 22.

25 Supf, *Das Buch der deutschen Fluggeschichte*, Vol. II, p. 369.

26 Anonymous. 'Führende Männer im Weltkriege Nr. 8 – Generalfeldmarschall von der Goltz' in *Kriegs-Echo Nr. 66*, p. 14.

27 Ibid.

28 German newspaper on 15 December 1911, quoted from Bethge, *Bund Jungdeutschland in Fricke, Die bürgerlichen Parteien in Deutschland, Handbuch der Geschichte der bürgerlichen Parteien und anderer bürgerlicher Interessenorganisationen vom Vormärz bis zum Jahre 1945*, p. 164.

29 Ibid., p. 167.

30 Gengler, op.cit., pp. 22-23.

31 Anonymous. 'Führende Männer'. op.cit.

32 Neumann, *Die deutschen Luftstreitkräfte im Weltkriege*, p. 61, which also traces the Fliegertruppe's development from a provisional military flying school established at Döberitz in May 1910.

33 *Feldflieger-Abteilung 23 Kriegstagebuch* [war diary] quoted in Gengler, op.cit., p. 29.

34 Grosz, *Halberstadt CL.II Windsock Datafile 27*, p. 2.

35 Werner, *Boelcke der Mensch, der Flieger, der Führer der deutschen Jagdfliegerei*, p. 53.

36 MacDonogh, *The Last Kaiser: The Life of Wilhelm II*, p. 353.

37 Berthold, *Persönliches Kriegstagebuch*, p. 1.

38 Ibid., pp. 1-2.

39 Ibid., pp. 2-4.

40 Ibid., pp. 4-5.

41 Ibid., p. 5.

42 Subsequently designated as Royal Saxon *Flieger-Ersatz-Abteilung 6* on 1 December 1914 [Ref: Kriegsministerium, *Teil 10 Abschnitt B, Flieger-Formationen*, p. 348].

43 Berthold, op.cit.

CHAPTER THREE

1 Berthold, *Persönliches Kriegstagebuch*, p. 13.

2 Ibid., p. 7.

3 Täger, Heerde & Ruscher, *Flugplatz Grossenhain – Historischer Abriss*, p. 15.

4 Loewenstern & Bertkau, *Mobilmachung, Aufmarsch und erster Einsatz der deutschen Luftstreitkräfte im August 1914*, p. 104.

5 Four Prussian units included the other two Kompagnie at Flieger-Bataillon 1 at Döberitz; Flieger-Bataillon 2 at Posen, Graudenz und Königsberg; Flieger-Bataillon 3 at Cologne, Hannover and Darmstadt; and Flieger-Bataillon 4 at Strassburg, Metz and Freiburg im Breisgau; a Royal Bavarian Flieger-Bataillon was established at Oberschleissheim [Ref: Loewenstern & Bertkau, ibid.].

6 FFA 24 was commanded by Hptm Horst von Minckwitz, FFA 29 by Hptm Ferdinand von Jena, and EFP 3 by Major der Reserve Georg Mardersteig [Ref: Ibid., pp. 119-120].

7 Neumann, *Die deutschen Luftstreitkräfte im Weltkriege*, p. 62.

8   Otto Karl Ferdinand Freiherr Vogel von Falckenstein was born on 21 February 1883 in Berlin [Ref: Perthes, *Ehrentafel der Kriegsopfer des reichsdeutschen Adels 1914-1918*, p. 258] Zickerick, 'Verlustliste der deutschen Luftstreitkräfte im Weltkriege' in *Unsere Luftstreitkräfte 1914-1918*, p. 84].

9   3 July to 30 November 1911; Vogel von Falckenstein was a classmate of Job-Heinrich von Dewall, whose service record provided the dates of the course [Ref: Hildebrand, *K. Die Generale der deutschen Luftwaffe 1935-1945*, Vol. I, p. 191].

10   Supf, *Das Buch der deutschen Fluggeschichte*, Vol. I, pp. 468-469, 472, 555.

11   Supf, *Das Buch der deutschen Fluggeschichte*, Vol. II, p. 102; the other two Kompaniechefs were Hptm Wilhelm Grade and Hptm Jasper von Oertzen.

12   Neumann, op.cit.

13   Loewenstern & Bertkau, op.cit., pp. 119-120.

14   *Feldflieger-Abteilung 23 Kriegstagebuch* [war diary] quoted in Gengler, *Rudolf Berthold – Sieger in 44 Luftschlachten Erschlagen im Bruderkampfe für Deutschlands Freiheit*, p. 33.

15   Liddell Hart, B. *The Real War 1914-1918*, p. 54.

16   *FFA 23 Kriegstagebuch*, op.cit.

17   According to Imperial War Museum. *Handbook of the German Army in War. April 1918*, p. 20, generaloberst 'commands an army' and is one rank below generalfeldmarschall [field-marshal], the highest-ranked officer, who 'commands a group of armies'.

18   According to Esposito, *A Concise History of World War I*, p. 44:'The genesis of the final plan for the war on the Western Front was the Schlieffen Plan of 1905, compiled by Count Alfred von Schlieffen, then chief of the general staff ... [and] a disciple of Carl von Clausewitz ... Feeling certain the French would devote their energies to recapturing Alsace and Lorraine (which they did), [Schlieffen] envisioned a wide sweep to get behind them and pin them against the difficult terrain of the Vosges mountains' ...

19   Berthold, op.cit., pp. 8-9.

20   The pilots were: Oblt Otto Freiherr Vogel von Falckenstein, Oblt Gottfried Glaeser, Oblt Otto Freiherr Marschalck von Bachtenbrock, Oblt Willy Meyer, Ltn Franz Keller, Ltn Hans-Joachim von Seydlitz-Gerstenberg and Ltn Johannes Viehweger.

21   The observers included: Oblt Eberhard Bohnstedt, Oblt Karl von Gross, Ltn Rudolf Berthold and Ltn Aribert Müller-Arles.

22   Berthold, op.cit., p. 9.

23   Johannes Viehweger was an army officer when he received Deutsche Luftfahrer-Verband [German Air Travellers Association] pilots license No. 417 on 27 May 1913 [Ref: Supf, *Das Buch der deutschen Fluggeschichte*, Vol. II, p. 663].

24   Berthold, op.cit., pp. 10-12.

25   Ibid., pp. 12-13.

26   Ibid., p. 13.

27   Ibid., p. 38.

28   Hildebrand, *Die Generale der deutschen Luftwaffe 1935-1945*, Vol. II, p. 419.

29   Wolff'schen Telegraph-Bureaus, *Amtliche Kriegs-Depeschen nach Berichten des*, Vol. 1, p. 54.

30   *FFA 23 Kriegstagebuch*, op.cit., p. 38.

31   Ibid.

32   According to Perthes, op.cit., p. 83, Karl von Gross was born on 16 November 1895 and first served with Kurmärkisches Feldartillerie-Regiment Nr. 39.

33   Deutscher Offizier-Bund, *Ehren-Rangliste des ehemaligen Deutschen Heeres*, p. 500.

34   Franks, Bailey & Duiven, *Casualties of the German Air Service 1914-1920*, p. 172.

35   According to Perthes, op.cit., p. 155, Otto Freiherr Marschalck von Bachtenbrock was born on 12 February 1887 in Hutloh, Niedersachsen and first served with Grossherzoglich Mecklenburgisches Füsilier-regiment Nr. 90 Kaiser Wilhelm; Deutscher Offizier-Bund, op.cit., p. 272 notes that he was killed in a crash on 5 May 1916 near St. Quentin while attached to Armee-Flugpark 2.

36   *FFA 23 Kriegstagebuch*, op.cit.

37   Ibid.

38   Letter of 6 September 1914 quoted in Gengler, p. 39.

39   Berthold, op.cit., pp. 14-15.

40   Esposito, op.cit., pp. 62-65.

41   Berthold, op.cit., p. 16.

42   Ibid.

43   Anonymous, 'Führende Männer im Weltkriege Nr. 69 – Generalfeldmarschall von Bülow' in *Kriegs-Echo Nr. 129*, p. 270.

44   Berthold, op.cit., p. 17.

45   Esposito, op.cit., pp. 65-66.

46   O'Connor, *Aviation Awards of Imperial Germany and the Men Who Earned Them, Vol. II – The Aviation Awards of the Kingdom of Prussia*, p. 7.

47   Neubecker, *Für Tapferkeit und Verdienst*, p. 21.

48   O'Connor, op.cit.

49   Letter of 13 September 1914 quoted in Gengler, op.cit., p. 41.

50   Raleigh, *The War in the Air*, Vol. I, p. 336.

51   Ibid.

52   Both the Deutsche Waffen- und Munitionsfabrik P.08 7.65-mm pistol (better known as the Luger) and the Mauser C96 7.63-mm pistol could accommodate a rifle stock for added stability when being fired.

53   Berthold, op.cit., pp. 19-21.

54   Neumann, *Die deutschen Luftstreitkräfte im Weltkriege*, p. 187.

55   *FFA 23 Kriegstagebuch*, op.cit., p. 41.

56   Esposito, op.cit., p. 80.

57   Berthold, op.cit., p. 22.

58   Franks, Bailey & Duiven, op.cit., pp. 112, 173 and other sources list Ostermann's death date as 9 October 1914.

59   Berthold, op.cit., p. 26.

60   *FFA 23 Kriegstagebuch*, op.cit., p. 44.

61   Täger, Heerde & Ruscher, op.cit., pp. 24-25.

62   According to *Militär-Wochenblatt*, Vogel von Falckenstein's promotion was effective 17 October 1914.

63 Berthold, op.cit., p. 27.

CHAPTER FOUR

1   Berthold, *Persönliches Kriegstagebuch*, p. 27.

2   Normand Knackfuss was born on 13 June 1881 in Kassel, Grand Duchy of Hesse. He attained a regular army commission in the 1. Ober-Elsässisches Infanterie-Regiment Nr. 167 and he subsequently transferred to the Fliegertruppe, where he qualified as an observer. Early in World War I Knackfuss was assigned as commanding officer of EFP2, which on 18 March 1915 was renamed as Armee Flugpark 2. After the formation of Württembergische Flieger-Abteilung (A) 252 on 10 December 1916, he was appointed the unit's first commanding officer. On the evening of 15 March 1918, Knackfuss was killed during a French bombing raid on FAA 252w's airfield at Alincourt in the Champagne sector [Ref: *FAA 252w Monatsbericht* quoted in Kilduff, 'The History of Royal Württemberg Flieger-Abteilung (A) 252', p. 306; Deutscher Offizier-Bund, *Ehren-Rangliste des ehemaligen Deutschen Heeres*, p. 356].

3   Ernst Schlegel, born on 21 June 1882 in Konstanz, Grand Duchy of Baden. He was awarded Deutsche Luftfahrer-Verband pilot's license No. 209 on 20 May 1912 [Ref: Supf, *Das Buch der deutschen Fluggeschichte*, Vol. I, p. 568] and remained a civilian instructor of military pilots throughout the war.

4   Berthold, op.cit.

5   Hans Joachim Buddecke was born on 22 August 1890 in Berlin, the capital of Prussia. He attended school in Potsdam, Strassburg and Charlottenburg before entering the Prussian Cadet System in the spring of 1904. Buddecke qualified for inclusion among the *Selekta*, a special honour indicating he was a top student in his class. In spring 1910 he was commissioned a Leutnant in Leibgarde-Infanterie-Regiment (1. Grossherzoglich Hessisches) Nr. 115, a unit in which his father also served at the time. Three years later Buddecke was granted reserve status so he could travel to the USA, where he worked in an automotive plant and then learned to fly. At the beginning of World War I, he returned to Germany aboard a neutral ship. Buddecke was accepted into aviation training, first at Flieger-Ersatz-Abteilung 3 at Darmstadt and then Etappen-Flugzeug-Park 2 before being assigned to Feldflieger-Abteilung 23 [Ref: Zuerl, *Pour-le-Mérite-Flieger*, pp. 113, 124].

6   Established on 11 March 1621 [Ref: von Diersburg, *Geschichte des 1. Grossherzoglich Hessischen Infanterie-(Leibgarde-) Regiments Nr. 115, 1621-1899*, p. 1].

7   Alfred Keller went on to become Germany's premier night-bombing commander in World War I [Ref: Zuerl, op.cit., pp. 253-258].

8   Buddecke, *El Schahin (Der Jagdfalke): Aus meinem Fliegerleben*, pp. 42-43.

9   Berthold, op.cit., p. 31.

10 Ibid., pp. 28-29.

11 Ibid., pp. 32-33.

12 The *Militär-Flugzeugführer-Abzeichen* was promulgated on 27 January 1913 by order of Kaiser Wilhelm II. It was 'presented to officers, non-commissioned officers and non-rated men who, after completion of prescribed examinations and after completion of their training at a military aviation facility, have earned

certification as a military pilot' [Ref: Neubecker, *Für Tapferkeit und Verdienst*, p. 28].

13 Berthold, op.cit.. p. 35

14 Wolff'schen Telegraph-Bureaus, *Amtliche Kriegs-Depeschen nach Berichten des*, Vol. 1, p. 335.

15 Franz Keller was born on 22 September 1896 in Tübingen, Kingdom of Württemberg, and was commissioned into the 9. Württembergisches Infanterie-Regiment Nr. 127. Although no aviation training is listed in his service record, on 22 September 1914 he reported to EFP 2, from whence he was assigned to Feldflieger-Abteilung 23 on 15 October 1914. Keller was promoted to Oberleutnant on 24 December 1914. After he was shot down and wounded in the neck on 10 January 1915, he was sent to a French PoW camp in Entrevaux. Next, Keller was interned in Switzerland from 15 May 1916 until 14 July 1917, after which, as part of a prisoner exchange, he was repatriated to Germany. Forbidden to serve in a frontline unit by the repatriation agreement, Keller, who was promoted to Hauptmann on 19 October 1917 (with the date of rank of 18 August 1916), served in training duties with Flieger-Ersatz-Abteilung 10 in Böblingen, FEA 9 in Darmstadt and the Geschwaderschule [Multi-Engine Aircraft School] in Paderborn. His wartime awards were: the Kingdom of Württemberg's Goldene Militär-Verdienst-Medaille [Golden Military Merit Medal] on 10 June 1917, the Iron Cross 2nd Class on 29 January 1918 and the Verwundeten-Abzeichen [Wound Badge] in black, signifying one wound received in combat [Ref: Keller, *Kriegsranglisten-Auszug*, p. 3].

16 Lamberton, *Reconnaissance and Bomber Aircraft of the 1914-1918 War*, p. 140.

17 *Légion d'Honneur* citation quoted in Bailey, Kilduff & Vanoverbeke, 'General Service Unit: The History of Escadrille 23', p. 228.

18 Adrien Eugène Aimable Gilbert was born on 19 July 1889 in Riom (Puy-de-Dôme), France. He received instruction at the Blériot School at Étampes and qualified for *Aéro Club de France* [Aero Club of France] Pilot Brevet No. 240 on 24 September 1910. Gilbert qualified for Military Pilot's Brevet No. 165 on 31 August 1912, at which time he was posted to Escadrille Nr. 1. Having completed his military obligation, Gilbert became active in pre-war civilian air races and other events. He was recalled to active duty in the summer of 1914 and assigned to Escadrille MS 23, with which he participated in successful aerial combats on 2 November and 17 December 1914 and received full merit for aerial victories. His actions on 10 January 1915 resulted in credit for his third victory. [Ref: Pearce, "Eugène Gilbert – A Great French Fighter Pilot," pp. 57-70].

19 Ibid.

20 *Grossenhainer Tageblatt*, 8 August 1914, p. 1 quoted in Täger, Heerde, Franke & Ruscher, *Flugplatz Grossenhain – Historischer Abriss*, p. 22.

21 Karl Seber, born in 1883, served in the Garde-Fussartillerie-Regiment, a unit of the Guard Corps responsible for the monarch's defence, until he transferred to the Fliegertruppe [Ref: Deutscher Offizier-Bund, op.cit., p. 533].

22 Bailey & Cony, *The French Air War Chronology*, p. 6.

23 O'Connor, *Aviation Awards of Imperial Germany and the*

Men Who Earned Them, Vol. III – The Aviation Awards of the Kingdom of Saxony, pp. 17-18,

24 Ibid., p. 67.

25 Berthold, op.cit., pp. 29-30

26 Ibid., pp. 35-36.

27 Ibid., p. 35.

28 Welkoborsky, *Vom Fliegen, Siegen und Sterben einer Feldflieger-Abteilung*, p. 47.

29 Friedrich Schueler van Krieken was born on 10 October 1885 in Berlin. He served in a dragoons regiment before transferring to the Fliegertruppe, where he was trained as an observer and subsequently assigned to Feldflieger-Abteilung 23. He left FFA 23 in 1916 to become Kommandeur der Flieger (Kofl) [officer in charge of aviation] for the Turkish 5th Army.

30 Eberhard Bohnstedt was born on 22 July 1886 in Kassel, Grand Duchy of Hesse. He was commissioned into the Grenadier-Regiment Prinz Carl von Preussen (2. Brandenburgisches) Nr. 12, where he attained the rank of Hauptmann before transferring to the Fliegertruppe. He became an observer and was one of the founding members of FFA 23. On 26 November 1915, he was transferred to FFA 32 to become commanding officer [Ref: Deutscher Offizier-Bund, op.cit., p. 146; Welkoborsky, op.cit., p. 77].

31 Hans-Joachim von Seydlitz-Gerstenberg was born on 2 July 1891 in Dresden, the capital of Saxony. He was commissioned into the 2. Grenadier-Regiment Nr. 101 Kaiser Wilhelm, König von Preussen, and transferred to the Fliegertruppe. A founding member of FFA 23, he was wounded in action on 17 August 1914 and crashed behind French lines, but escaped to German territory. On 17 June 1916, he was transferred to train on R-type large, multi-engine bombers; he was killed in action while flying with Riesenflugzeug-Abteilung 501 on 26 July 1918 [Ref: Perthes, *Ehrentafel der Kriegsopfer des reichsdeutschen Adels 1914-1918*, p. 229; Deutscher Offizier-Bund, op.cit., p. 892].

32 Berthold's reference to von Seydlitz-Gerstenberg as 'Seidenspitz' is a play on words for the "German Kleinspitz", an old and popular species of dog, renowned for being very patient with children, totally loyal to its master's family and, with its acute hearing, always ready to defend the family's property.

33 Berthold, op.cit., pp. 36-37.

34 Ibid., p. 36.

35 Supf, *Das Buch der deutschen Fluggeschichte*, Vol. II, pp. 20, 250.

36 Neumann, *Die deutschen Luftstreitkräfte im Weltkriege*, p. 232.

37 Welkoborsky, op.cit., pp. 50-51.

38 Letter of 10 August 1915 quoted in Gengler, *Rudolf Berthold – Sieger in 44 Luftschlachten Erschlagen im Bruderkampfe für Deutschlands Freiheit*, p. 52.

39 Grosz, *Fokker E.III Windsock Datafile 15*, p. 3.

40 Lamberton, op.cit., p. 220.

41 Berthold, op.cit., p. 37.

42 Ibid.

43 AOK 3, *Stabsoffizier der Ballon-Abwehrkanonen Bericht Nr. 101*, 27 August 1915.

44 Berthold, op.cit., pp. 37-38.

45 Buddecke, op.cit., p. 43.

46 *Feldflieger-Abteilung 23 Kriegstagebuch* [war diary] quoted in ibid., p. 53.

CHAPTER FIVE

1 Buddecke, *El Schahin (Der Jagdfalke): Aus meinem Fliegerleben*, pp. 51-52.

2 Franks, Bailey & Guest, *Above the Lines*, p. 76.

3 Ibid., p. 134.

4 Ibid., p. 88.

5 *Feldflieger-Abteilung 23 Kriegstagebuch* [war diary] quoted in Gengler, *Rudolf Berthold – Sieger in 44 Luftschlachten Erschlagen im Bruderkampfe für Deutschlands Freiheit*, p. 53; the unit war diary also noted that, although promoted on 21 September 1915, Berthold's date of rank was 18 September.

6 Ibid.

7 According to weather reports in Royal Flying Corps, *War Diary*, 28, 29 and 30 September 1915.

8 Lamberton, *Reconnaissance and Bomber Aircraft of the 1914-1918 War*, p. 220.

9 Most likely, Lieutenant Herbert T. Kemp and Capt Cecil W. Lane in Vickers FB.5 5460 of 11 Squadron, RFC [Ref: Henshaw, op.cit., p. 54].

10 *FFA 23 Kriegstagebuch* quoted in Gengler, op.cit., p. 54.

11 Armee-Oberkommando der 2. Armee, *Tägliche Berichte* for 15, 18 and 22 October 1915.

12 Buddecke, op.cit., pp. 51-54.

13 Ibid., p. 59.

14 Ibid., p. 60; the aircraft was B.E.2c 2017 of 13 Squadron, RFC [Ref: Henshaw, op.cit., p. 56].

15 Hobson, *Airmen Died in the Great War 1914-1918*, pp. 71, 64.

16 Buddecke, op.cit., p. 63.

17 Neubecker, *Für Tapferkeit und Verdienst*, p. 15.

18 O'Connor, *Aviation Awards of Imperial Germany and the Men Who Earned Them, Vol. VII – The Aviation Awards of Eight German States and the Three Free Cities*, p. 46.

19 Ibid., p. 47.

20 AOK 2, op.cit., *Taglicher Bericht* for 3 November 1915.

21 Royal Flying Corps, *Communiqué No. 19*, 9 November 1915, p. 1; this account, from a slightly different perspective, relates the same aerial combat described in Chapter 1.

22 Ibid.

23 Lamberton, *Fighter Aircraft*, op.cit.

24 Ernst Freiherr von Althaus was promoted to Oberleutnant on 6 August 1915, over six weeks before Rudolf Berthold was promoted to that rank [Ref: Franks, Bailey & Guest, op.cit., p. 61].

25 Berthold, *Persönliches Kriegstagebuch* Berthold, p. 40.

26 Feldflieger-Abteilung 23. *Tägliche Berichte*, 14 October 1915-12 January 1916.

27 Jones, H. *The War in the Air*, Vol. II, p. 150.

28 Franks, Bailey & Guest, op.cit., p. 88.

29 Buddecke, op.cit., p. 64.

30 AOK 2. *Armee Bericht* 2/I Tc IIa Nr. 120, 1 January 1916.

31 Taeger, *Die verlorene Ehre des Ernst Freiherr von Althaus*.

32 Supf, *Das Buch der deutschen Fluggeschichte*, Vol. II, p. 308.

33 *FFA 23 Kriegstagebuch* quoted in Gengler, op.cit., p. 56.

34 Berthold, op.cit., pp. 40-42.

35 Quoted in Jones, op.cit., pp. 156-157.

36 Zuerl, *Pour-le-Mérite-Flieger*, p. 84.

37 Berthold, op.cit., pp. 42-43.

38 Arthur Jacquin was born on 8 November 1886 in Ville-sous-la-Ferté (Aube). He had been a mechanic before the war and entered military service in October 1907. He was mobilized in August 1914 and assigned to the 61è Régiment d'Infanterie [61st Infantry Regiment]. He transferred to aviation as a student pilot in the second quarter of 1915, trained at Ambérieu and received Military Pilot Brevet No. 1735 on 10 October 1915 while holding the rank of Soldat [Private]. He was assigned to the Réserve Générale de l'Aviation [General Aviation Reserve] on 14 November 1915 and the Groupe des Divisions d'Entraînement [Divisional Training Group] on 22 January 1916. Days later he was posted to Escadrille VB 108, where he served until he was shot down near Chaulnes (Somme) on 2 February 1916 and taken prisoner [Ref: http://www.memoiredeshommes.sga.defense.gouv.fr/spip.php?rubrique16 (link), *Personnels de l'aéronautique militaire / Personnels de l'aéronautique militaire*].

39 Pierre Ségaud was born on 11 March 1878 in Lalinde. He entered military service on 18 April 1896. He was mobilized in August 1914 with the 95è Régiment d'Infanterie Territorial. Transferred to the aviation branch as an observer on 30 August 1915, he was assigned to the Réserve Générale de l'Aviation on 5 September 1915 and then to VB 108 on 23 September 1915. He was killed in action near Chaulnes (Somme) on 2 February 1916 [Ref: http://www.memoiredeshommes.sga.defense.gouv.fr/spip.php?rubrique16 (link), *Personnels de l'aéronautique militaire / Personnels l'aéronautique militaire*].

40 Berthold, op.cit., p. 40.

41 Franks, *Sharks Among Minnows*, p. 55.

42 Letter of 5 February 1916, quoted in Gengler, op.cit., p. 59.

43 AOK 2, *Bericht Ic 2920*, 5 February 1916; while Berthold remained on the roster of FFA 23 (indicated here), he was in charge of its sub-unit, KEK Vaux; Berthold's rank listed here is incorrect, as by this time he had been promoted to Oberleutnant.

44 Ibid.

45 Royal Flying Corps, *Communiqué No. 30*, 4 March 1916, p. 1.

46 RFC, *Pilot & Observer Casualties*, 10 February 1916.

47 RFC, *Communiqué*, op.cit.

48 Ibid.

49 Ibid.

50 *FFA 23 Kriegstagebuch*, op.cit.

51 Ibid.

52 Liddell Hart, *The Real War 1914-1918*, p. 218.

53 O'Connor, *Aviation Awards of Imperial Germany in World War I, Vol. I – The Aviation Awards of the Kingdom of Bavaria*, p. 103.

54 2/Lt Michael Amyss Julian Orde was born on 18 December 1888 in Norfolk. He was commissioned a second lieutenant in the Army Service Corps and qualified as a pilot on 27 October 1915. Orde was shot down and listed as missing on 14 March 1916. He was taken prisoner and held until the end of the war. Orde died on 6 August 1920 in a flying accident on Salisbury Plain.

55 RFC, *War Diary*, 13 March 1916.

56 *FFA 23 Kriegstagebuch*, op.cit.

57 Ibid.

58 Louis Paoli was born on 6 January 1892 in à Bastia (Corsica). He joined the army on 3 September 1910 and, subsequently, was assigned to the 4e Régiment de Chasseurs à cheval [4th Mounted Rifles Regiment]. Paoli entered the aviation school at Étampes on 19 July 1915. On 25 September, he was sent to Bourget to fly a new type of bomber, but after a nearly fatal incident, he returned to flying Maurice Farman aircraft. He was posted to Escadrille MF 54 on 23 January 1915 and made his first flight over the enemy on 2 February 1916. Paoli was awarded the *Croix de Guerre* and had applied for fighter training shortly before he was killed [Ref: Anonymous, 'Les Héros Disparu: Paoli,' p. 284; http://www.memoiredes hommes. sga.defense.gouv.fr/spip.php?rubrique16 (link), *Personnels de l'aéronautique militaire / Personnels de l'aéronautique militaire*].

59 Jean, Rohrbacher, Palmieri & Service historique de l'armée de l'air France. *Les escadrilles de l'aéronautique militaire française: Symbolique et histoire, 1912-1920*, pp. 144-145.

60 Anonymous, 'Les Héros Disparu,' op.cit.

61 *FFA 23 Kriegstagebuch*, op.cit.

62 O'Connor, *Aviation Awards of Imperial Germany and the Men Who Earned Them, Vol. III – The Aviation Awards of the Kingdom of Saxony*, p. 83.

63 Ibid., p. 22.

64 Wallace Sinclair Earle was born on 8 February 1889 in Belleville, Ontario, Canada. On 14 December 1914 he enlisted as a sapper in the second contingent and was commissioned in the 6th Field Company, Canadian Engineers, 2nd Division, Canadian Expeditionary Force. Earle was attached to the RFC at Brooklands on 20 October 1915. After completing flight training, on 17 December 1915 he was assigned to 'B' Flight, 9 Squadron, RFC [Ref: S.K. Taylor notes].

65 Cuthbert William Prideaux Selby was born in (ca.) 1898 in Teynham, Kent. He was commissioned second lieutenant in the Royal West Kent Regiment and was later transferred to the RFC. After being shot down and wounded on 16 April 1916, Selby became a prisoner of war and, due to his wounds, was paroled to Switzerland on 24 December 1916. He was repatriated to Britain in September 1917.

66 RFC, *Communiqué No. 34*, 30 April 1916, p. 1.

67 Quoted in Franks, op.cit., p. 81.

CHAPTER SIX

1 Buddecke, *El Schahin (Der Jagdfalke): Aus meinem Fliegerleben*, p. 97.

2 Royal Flying Corps, *War Diary*, weather report, 25 April 1916, p. 1.

3   Jones, *The War in the Air*, Vol. II, p. 196.

4   Ibid., p. 197.

5   Davilla & Soltan, *French Aircraft of the First World War*, p. 312.

6   Grosz, *Pfalz E.I – E.VI Windsock Datafile 59*, p. 4.

7   Berthold, *Persönliches Kriegstagebuch*, pp. 44-45.

8   Berthold, *Lazarettkrankenbuch* entry, 18 May 1916.

9   Berthold, *Kriegstagebuch*, op.cit., p. 45.

10 Franks, *Sharks Among Minnows*, p. 81.

11 Etzel, *Das K.B. 9. Infanterie-Regiment Wrede: nach den amtlichen Kriegstagebüchern*, p. 77.

12 Jordan, *Blätter der Erinnerung an die im Kriege 1914-1919 Gefallenen der Universität Erlangen*, p. 84.

13 Etzel, op.cit., pp. 77-78.

14 Berthold, *Kriegstagebuch*, op.cit.

15 Haehnelt, *Ehrentafel der im Flugdienst während des Weltkrieges gefallenen Offiziere der Deutschen Fliegerverbände*, pp. 26, 57.

16 Grosz, *LVG B.I Windsock Datafile 98*, p. 3.

17 Goote, *Kamerad Berthold der 'unvergleiche Franke,'* p. 92.

18 Pietsch, 'Bernward Gross 1887-1916,' pp. 2-4 includes the text of a letter that FFA 23 commanding officer Hauptmann Hermann Palmer wrote to Gross' father, relating the known facts of the fight. That account matches facts stated in Royal Flying Corps Communiqué No. 37, 27 May 1916, p. 1.

19 Allerhöchste Führung des XIV. Reserve-Korps, *Bericht Ic 795 Geh*, 22 May 1916, p. 1.

20 Allerhöchste Führung des XIV. Reserve-Korps, op.cit., pp. 2-3.

21 Werner, *Boelcke der Mensch, der Flieger, der Führer der deutschen Jagdfliegerei*, p. 165.

22 Falls in Esposito, (ed.), *A Concise History of World War I*, p. 90.

23 Berthold, op.cit., pp. 45-46.

24 Armeegruppe Stein was assigned FFA 22 and Kampfstaffel S.2 at Bertincourt and Rocquigny; VI. Reserve-korps had FFA 26 and two staffeln of Kagohl 1 at Trejean and Essigny-le-Petit; Armeegruppe Quast had FFA 23, the other two staffeln of Kagohl 1 and three staffeln of Kagohl 4 at Roupy, Vaux, Essigny-le-Petit and Flesquières; and XVII. Armeekorps deployed Kampfstaffel T at Tergnier [Ref: Armee-Oberkommando der 2. Armee, *Taglicher Bericht* Nr. 130908/11452, 4 July 1916, p. 3].

25 Berthold, op.cit., p. 46

26 Berthold, op.cit., p. 47.

27 Werner, op.cit., p. 182.

28 Lamberton, *Fighter Aircraft of the 1914-1918 War*, p. 134.

29 *Feldflieger-Abteilung 23 Kriegstagebuch* [war diary] quoted in Gengler, *Rudolf Berthold – Sieger in 44 Luftschlachten Erschlagen im Bruderkampfe für Deutschlands Freiheit*, p. 63.

30 Henri Dangueuger was born on 18 June 1896 in Paris. He enlisted in the army in 1914 and then transferred to aviation and became qualified as a pilot. He joined Escadrille N 37 on 28 July 1916 [Ref: http://www.memoiredeshommes.sga.defense.gouv.fr/spip.php?rubrique16 (link), *Personnels de l'aéronautique militaire / Personnels de l'aéronautique militaire*].

31 Bailey & Cony, *The French Air War Chronology*, p. 67; Franks, op.cit., p. 133.

32 Davilla & Soltan, op.cit., p. 379.

33 *FFA 23 Kriegstagebuch*, op.cit., p. 64.

34 O'Connor, *Aviation Awards of Imperial Germany and the Men Who Earned Them, Vol. II – The Aviation Awards of the Kingdom of Prussia*, p. 132.

35 Kriegsministerium, *Teil 10 Abschnitt B, Flieger-Formationen*, p. 234.

36 Berthold, op.cit., pp. 48-49.

37 Buddecke, op.cit., pp. 92-93.

38 William Hugh Stobart Chance was born on 31 December 1896. When the war began in 1914, he left school and applied for an army commission. Serving first with the Worcestershire Territorial Regiment, in April 1916 he transferred to the Royal Flying Corps and was eventually posted to 27 Squadron on the Somme. Following his landing within German territory, Chance was confined in prisoner of war camps in Germany until December 1918. He was invested as a knight in 1945 and as a Commander, Order of the British Empire (C.B.E.) in 1958.

39 Quoted from Bowyer, *The Flying Elephants – A History of No. 27 Squadron*, p. 39.

40 *Jagdstaffel 4 Kriegstagebuch*, op.cit.

41 Bruce, *British Aeroplanes 1914-1918*, pp. 379-380.

42 19 Squadron, RFC, *Combat Report* by Capt Henderson, 22 September 1916.

43 RFC, *Pilot and Observer Casualties*, 22 September 1916.

44 Hobson, *Airmen Died in the Great War 1914-1918*, p. 55.

45 Ibid., p. 43.

46 Buddecke, op.cit., pp. 93-94.

47 André Steuer was born on 7 December 1894 in Versailles. He was one of six brothers to enlist and was accepted for aviation service on 3 September 1914. Following training at Le Plessis-Belleville and Belfort, he served as a two-seater pilot in Escadrille HF 1 and the MF 32. His brother Pierre became an aerial gunner with Escadrille C 46. In July and August, André Steuer trained as a fighter pilot and was assigned to N 103. In a twist of fate, Pierre Steuer was fatally wounded on 24 August, the day Berthold scored his sixth victory. On 24 September, André Steuer was killed by Berthold [Ref: Daçay, 'Les Frères Steuer,' p. 628; Jean, Rohrbacher, Palmieri & Service historique de l'armée de l'air France. *Les escadrilles de l'aéronautique militaire française: Symbolique et histoire, 1912 - 1920*, pp. 46, 246; http://www.memoiredeshommes.sga.defense.gouv.fr/spip.php?rubrique16 (link). op.cit.].

48 François Louis Roman was born on 11 June 1893 in Dieulefit (Drôme Provençale). He joined an army engineering unit in 1913 and transferred to aviation on 4 March 1916. He completed pilot training at Pau on 30 June 1916 and, after brief service with Escadrille MF 32, on 8 August he was assigned to N 103 [Ref: Daçay, op.cit., p. 628; Jean, Rohrbacher, Palmieri & Service historique de l'armée de l'air France, Ibid., p. 246; http://www.memoiredeshommes.sga.defense.gouv.fr/spip.php?rubrique16 (link), Ibid.].

49 Daçay, op.cit.

50 Buddecke, op.cit., p. 97.

51 *Jagdstaffel 4 Kriegstagebuch*, op.cit.

52 Weather report in RFC, *War Diary*, 26 September 1916.

53 *Jagdstaffel 4 Kriegstagebuch*, op.cit.

54 RFC, *Pilot & Observer Casualties*, 26 September 1916.

55 Hobson, op.cit., p. 34.

56 Ibid., p. 90.

57 Buddecke, op.cit., p. 98.

58 O'Connor, op.cit., p. 56 includes a photograph of Berthold's bestowal document.

59 According to Cron, *Imperial German Army 1914-18 – Organisation, Structure, Orders-of-Battle*, p. 84: Armee-Abteilung A 'was not under the command of an AOK, but itself formed a small army on the northern part of the front in Alsace-Lorraine'.

60 Buddecke, op.cit., p. 98.

61 *Jagdstaffel 4 Kriegstagebuch*, op.cit., p. 65.

62 Berthold, op.cit., p. 50.

63 *Kriegsministerium*, op.cit., p. 220.

64 Ibid., p. 236.

65 Berthold, op.cit., p. 51.

66 Ibid.

67 Grosz, *The Agile and Aggressive Albatros*, p. 37.

68 Grosz, *Albatros D.I/D.II Windsock Datafile 100*, p. 5.

69 Quoted in Gengler, op.cit., pp. 65-66.

70 Franks, Bailey & Duiven, *The Jasta Pilots*, p. 262.

71 Ibid., p. 66.

CHAPTER SEVEN

1 Berthold, *Persönliches Kriegstagebuch*, p. 56.

2 Neumann, *Die Deutschen Luftstreitkräfte im Weltkriege*, p. 4.

3 Ibid., p. 5; von Hoeppner previously commanded the 75th Reserve Division.

4 Berthold, op.cit., pp. 52-53.

5 Cron, *Imperial German Army 1914-18 – Organisation, Structure, Orders-of-Battle*, p. 189.

6 Berthold, op.cit., p. 53.

7 Jean, Rohrbacher, Palmieri & Service historique de l'armée de l'air France. *Les escadrilles de l'aéronautique militaire française: Symbolique et histoire, 1912-1920*, p. 391.

8 Kogenluft, *Nachrichtenblatt der Luftstreitkräfte*, Vol. I, Nr. 3, 15 March 1917, p. 10.

9 *Jagdstaffel 14 Kriegstagebuch* [war diary] quoted in Gengler, *Rudolf Berthold – Sieger in 44 Luftschlachten Erschlagen im Bruderkampfe für Deutschlands Freiheit*, p. 69.

10 Kogenluft, op.cit., p. 11 noted that the captured aircraft was Nieuport XVIIbis No. 2405.

11 Bailey & Cony, *The French Air War Chronology*, p. 96.

12 *Jasta 14 Kriegstagebuch*, op.cit.

13 Boelcke, *Hauptmann Boelckes Feldberichte*, p. 53.

14 Radloff & Niemann, 'The Ehrenbechers – Where Are They Now?' p. 366.

15 Lamberton, *Fighter Aircraft of the 1914-1918 War*, p. 110.

16 Berthold, op.cit., p. 53.

17 Jones, *The War in the Air*, Vol. III, p. 325.

18 Falls, 'Western Front, 1915-1917 Stalemate', p. 93.

19 Berthold, op.cit., pp. 54-55.

20 Kogenluft, op.cit., Nr. 7, 12 April 1917, p. 14.

21 Maréchal des Logis [Sergeant-Major] Jean Peinaud was born on 28 April 1888 in Saligny (Allier). He received his aviation training at Étampes and received Military Pilot Brevet 2508 on 26 January 1916. Lieutenant Marcel Vernes was born on 9 August 1886 in St. Germain-en-Laye (Seine-et-Oise). Following artillery service, he transferred to aviation and trained as an observer with Escadrille MF 7 [Ref.: http://www.memoiredeshommes.sga.defense.gouv.fr/spip.php?rubrique16 (link), *Personnels de l'aéronautique militaire / Personnels de l'aéronautique militaire*].

22 *Jasta 14 Kriegstagebuch*, op.cit., p. 72.

23 Kogenluft, op.cit., p. 15.

24 The crewmen, all members of Escadrille F 35, were: S/Lt Desbordes, Lt Borgoltz and Soldat Lebleu. Pierre Étienne Frédéric Desbordes was born 3 July 1886 in Jussy-le-Chaudrier (Jura). He began his military service with a dragoons regiment in 1904 and transferred to aviation eleven years later. He trained at Pau and, at the rank of sous-lieutenant, received Military Pilot Brevet 1205 on 18 July 1915. Jacques-Victor-Alexandré Borgoltz was born on 31 January 1894 in Chartres (Eure-le-Loir). Initially he served with an engineers regiment and transferred to Escadrille F 5 to become an observer. Alexandré Joseph Lebleu was born on 4 February 1892 in St. Symphorien (Indre-et-Loire). He entered military service with an armoured cavalry unit and transferred to aviation to become an aerial gunner [Ref.: http://www.memoiredeshommes.sga.defense.gouv.fr/spip.php?rubrique16 (link). op.cit.].

25 Kogenluft, op.cit., Nr. 11, 10 May 1917, p. 13.

26 Ibid., Nr. 9, 26 April 1917, p. 7.

27 Adjudant Albert Barioz was born on 29 April 1889 in Paris' 19e Arrondissement (Seine). He joined the army twenty years later and was in an artillery regiment at the beginning of the war. He transferred to aviation as an observer in April 1915. He served with Escadrille VB 110 until May 1915, when he began pilot training at Avord. He received Military Pilot Brevet 2024 in November. Promoted to adjutant on 16 August 1916, he was posted to Escadrille N 73 on 28 December and remained until his death on 11 April 1917 [Ref.: http://www.memoiredeshommes.sga.defense.gouv.fr/spip.php?rubrique16 (link). op.cit.].

28 *Jasta 14 Kriegstagebuch*, op.cit.

29 Kogenluft, op.cit., p. 14.

30 Franks, Bailey & Guest, *Above the Lines*, p. 223.

31 The Sopwith crewmen were S/Lts Antoine Arnoux de Maison-Rouge and Robert Levi. Antoine Valentin Roger Arnoux de Maison-Rouge was born on 3 May 1895 in Saumur (Maine-et-Loir). He enlisted in 1913 and, after ground service, was promoted to sous-lieutenant and accepted for pilot training on 8 March 1916. He received Military Pilot Brevet 3572 in May 1916. A year later he was invested as a Chevalier [Knight] of the *Légion d'Honneur*. He was wounded in

action on 14 April and died of his wounds on 29 May 1917 at Hôpital Complémentaire #1 at Troyes (Aube) [Ref.: http://www.memoiredeshommes.sga.defense. gouv.fr/spip.php?rubrique16 (link). op.cit.].

32   Kogenluft, op.cit., Nr. 11, p. 15.

33   Jones, op.cit., pp. 324-325.

34   Anonymous, *L'horreur des dévastations allemandes*, p. 550.

35   Berthold, op.cit., p. 55.

36   Kogenluft, op.cit., Nr. 9, 26 April 1917, p. 3.

37   Gengler, op.cit., p. 73.

38   Berthold, op.cit.

39   Gengler, op.cit.

40   Falls, op.cit., p. 94.

41   Kogenluft, op.cit., Nr. 15, 7 June 1917, p. 12; Nr. 16, 14 June 1917, p. 28; Nr. 20, 12 July 1917, p. 80.

42   Berthold, op.cit., p. 56.

43   Ibid.

44   Berthold, *Lazarettkrankenbuch* entry, 18 August 1917.

45   *Jasta 14 Kriegstagebuch*, op.cit., p. 73.

46   Berthold, *Kriegstagebuch*, op.cit., p. 56.

47   Strähle diary entry for 12 August 1917 quoted from Van Dorssen, Tubbs & Evans, *Paul Strähle – The War Diary of a German Aviator, 11 August 1917-22 April 1918*, p. 150.

48   Otto Gerbig qualified for Deutsche-Luftfahrer-Verband (DLV) license No. 805 on 3 July 1914 [Ref: Supf, *Das Buch der deutschen Fluggeschichte*, Vol. II, p. 667].

49   They included Ltn.d.Res Michael Paulin and Ltn Fritz Schabbel, who departed for Jasta 14 on 15 August 1917 [Ref: Kommandeur der Flieger der 4. Armee, *Tagesbefehl Nr. 51*, 22 August 1917].

50   VanWyngarden, *Jasta 18 – The Red Noses*, p. 27.

51   Deutscher Offizier-Bund. *Ehren-Rangliste des ehemaligen Deutschen Heere*s, p. 417.

52   Kriegsministerium, op.cit., pp. 236-237.

53   Franks, Bailey & Duiven, *The Jasta Pilots*, p. 33.

54   Jones, *The War in the Air*, Vol. IV, p. 109.

55   Berthold, op.cit.

56   Van Dorssen, Tubbs & Evans, op.cit., p. 151.

57   Henshaw, *The Sky Their Battlefield*, p. 211.

58   Kogenluft, op.cit., Nr. 30, 20 September 1917, p. 247.

59   Berthold, op.cit., pp. 53-54.

60   Kriegsministerium, op.cit., pp. 208-209.

61   von Hoeppner, *Deutschlands Krieg in der Luft*, p. 122.

62   Kommandeur der Flieger der 4. Armee, *Wochenbericht Nr. 116 op*, 30 August 1917, p. 2; the other groupings and their commanders were: Jagdgruppe Nord (Jastas 2, 20 and 28, and Kest 8), Hptm Otto Hartmann; Jagdgruppe 11 (Jastas 7, 29, 33 and 35), Oblt Otto Schmidt; and Jagdgruppe 15 (Jastas 3, 8, 26 and 27), Hptm Constantin von Bentheim).

63   Van Dorssen, Tubbs & Evans, op.cit., p. 152.

64   Bodenschatz, *Jagd in Flanderns Himmel – Aus den sechzehn Kampfmonaten des Jagdgeschwaders Freiherr von Richthofen*, p. 154.

65   Berthold letter of 20 August 1917 quoted in Gengler, op.cit., p. 74.

66   Van Dorssen, Tubbs & Evans, op.cit., p. 154.

67   Kogenluft, op.cit., p. 248.

68   Hobson, *Airmen Died in the Great War 1914-1918*, p. 22.

69   Ibid., p. 44.

70   Royal Flying Corps, *Pilot and Observer Casualties*, 21 August 1917.

71   Lamberton, *Reconnaissance and Bomber Aircraft of the 1914-1918 War*, p. 56.

72   Kogenluft, op.cit., Nr. 33, 11 October 1917, p. 308.

73   Ibid., p. 306.

74   Hobson, op.cit., p. 109.

75   Ibid., p. 81.

76   RFC, *War Diary*, 4 September 1917, p. 648.

77   Henshaw, op.cit., p. 220.

78   Kogenluft, op.cit., p. 306.

79   RFC, *War Diary*, 5 September 1917, p. 653.

80   Henshaw, op.cit., p. 221.

81   Kogenluft, op.cit., p. 307.

82   Ibid., p. 308.

83   Henshaw, op.cit., p. 224.

84   Hobson, op.cit., p. 54.

85   Ibid., p. 66.

86   RFC, *War Diary*, 16 September 1917, p. 688.

87   Hobson, op.cit., p. 56 notes that 19-year-old Leslie Glendower Humphries was buried not far from where he fell.

88   RFC, *Pilot and Observer Casualties*, 16 September 1917.

89   Kogenluft, op.cit., Nr. 34, 18 October 1917, p. 327.

90   Möller, *Kampf und Sieg eines Jagdgeschwaders*, p. 37.

91   Berthold, op.cit., p. 56.

92   Kogenluft, op.cit.

93   RFC, *Pilot and Observer Casualties*, 19 September 1917.

94   Hobson, op.cit., pp. 104, 54.

95   Berthold, op.cit., p. 57.

96   VanWyngarden, op.cit., p. 37.

97   Weather report in RFC, *War Diary*, 20 September 1917, p. 698.

98   There were no German anti-aircraft claims remotely near the area where this aeroplane came down [Ref: Kogenluft, op.cit., p. 330].

99   Hobson, op.cit., p. 36.

100 RFC, *Pilot and Observer Casualties*, 20 September 1917.

101 Kogenluft, op.cit., p. 328 erroneously lists it as Berthold's 20th chronological victory.

102 Ibid.

103 Kogenluft, op.cit., Nr. 39, 22 November 1917, p. 417, due to the late acceptance, erroneously lists it as Berthold's 28th chronological victory; in fact, it was his 22nd victory.

104 19 Squadron, RFC, *Squadron Record Book*, 21 September 1917, p. 1.

105 Lamberton, op.cit., p. 32.

106 Hobson, op.cit., pp. 23, 78.

107 Ibid., p. 84; Bernard Alexander Powers was commissioned 2/Lt in the Middlesex Regiment on 2 December 1915 [Ref: *Supplement to the London Gazette*, 1 December 1915, p. 12031].

108 19 Squadron, RFC, *Squadron Record Book*, 26 September 1917, p. 2.

109 Quoted from a letter to Gould's family from 70 Squadron's recording officer, 30 September 1917, courtesy of S.K. Taylor.

110 Henshaw, op.cit., p. 232.

111 RFC, *War Diary*, 26 September 1917, p. 736.

112 Hobson, op.cit., p. 50.

113 20 Squadron, RFC, *Squadron Record Book*, 28 September 1917, p. 2.

114 Hobson, op.cit., pp. 30, 99.

115 Ibid., pp. 101, 77.

116 RFC, *War Diary*, 28 September 1917, p. 746.

117 Kogenluft, op.cit., Nr. 39, p. 417; Berthold's victory is erroneously listed as his 25th.

118 RFC, *War Diary*, 30 September 1917, pp. 751-752.

119 Franks, Bailey & Duiven, *Casualties of the German Air Service 1914-1920*, p. 231.

120 Hobson, op.cit., p. 104.

121 RFC, *Pilot and Observer Casualties*, 30 September 1917.

122 Kogenluft, op.cit.

123 Berthold, op.cit.

124 Kogenluft, *Nachrichtenblatt*, Nrn. 33, 34, 39 as cited above.

CHAPTER EIGHT

1 Quoted in Berthold, *Persönliches Kriegstagebuch*, p. 58.

2 Kogenluft, *Nachrichtenblatt der Luftstreitkräfte*, Vol. I, Nr. 32, 4 October 1917, p. 273.

3 Royal Flying Corps, *War Diary*, 2 October 1917, p. 6.

4 VanWyngarden, *Jasta 18 - The Red Noses*, p. 40.

5 D.H.4 A.7451, the crew of nineteen-year-old 2/Lt Clifford Richard Brice Halley and Airman 1st Class Thomas Joseph Barlow, age twenty-four, perished [Ref: Hobson, *Airmen Died in the Great War 1914-1918*, pp. 52, 21].

6 Kogenluft, op.cit., Nr. 38, 15 November 1917, p. 397 incorrectly lists this victory as Berthold's twenty-seventh.

7 Hobson, op.cit., pp. 67, 92.

8 Their deaths were confirmed in RFC, *Pilot and Observer Casualties*, 2 October 1917.

9 D.H.4 A.7583; the pilot, 2/Lt C.G. Crane, was taken prisoner and his backseat man, 2/Lt William Logan Inglis, was killed [Ref: Ibid., p. 59].

10 *Jagdstaffel 18 Kriegstagebuch* quoted in Gengler, *Rudolf Berthold – Sieger in 44 Luftschlachten Erschlagen im Bruderkampfe für Deutschlands Freiheit*, p. 75.

11 Kleffel, letter of 25 October 1974, pp. 1-2.

12 Strähle diary entry for 5 October 1917 quoted from Van Dorssen, Tubbs & Evans, *Paul Strähle – The War Diary of a German Aviator, 11 August 1917 - 22 April 1918*, p. 156.

13 Confirmed in RFC, *Pilot and Observer Casualties*, 5 October 1917.

14 Kogenluft, op.cit., Nr. 34, 18 October 1917, p. 309.

15 RFC, *Communiqué No. 109*, 17 October 1917, p. 2.

16 Flown by Oblts Harald Auffarth and Ernst Wilhelm Turck, Ltns Walter Dingel, Arthur Rahn, Richard Runge, Otto Schober, Paul Strähle and Josef Veltjens, and Off.Stv Johannes Klein [Ref: Van Dorssen, Tubbs & Evans, op.cit.].

17 Revell, *High in the Empty Blue – The History of 56 Squadron, RFC/RAF 1916 to 1920*, p. 182.

18 56 Squadron, RFC, *Combat Report* by Capt Maxwell, 10 October 1917.

19 Van Dorssen, Tubbs & Evans, op.cit.

20 Berthold, *Kriegstagebuch*, op.cit., p. 57.

21 Berthold, *Lazarettkrankenbuch* entry, 10 October 1917.

22 Kogenluft, op.cit., Nr. 35, 25 October 1917, p. 340.

23 Berthold, *Lazarett*, op.cit., 31 October 1917.

24 Gengler, op.cit., p. 77.

25 Historische Kommission bei der Bayerischen Akademie der Wissenschaften, *Neue Deutsche Biographie*, Vol. II, pp. 230-231, which notes that Bier was also known for his work with Dr. Frederich Schwerd in developing the M16 *Stahlhelm* (the so-called 'coal scuttle' steel helmet) to provide better head protection for German ground troops.

26 Berthold, op.cit., 2 November 1917.

27 Quoted in Gengler, op.cit., p. 78.

28 Quoted in Berthold, *Kriegstagebuch*, op.cit., p. 58.

29 Quoted in Ibid., p. 59.

30 Ibid., pp. 59-60.

31 Van Dorssen, Tubbs & Evans, op.cit., p. 157.

32 Berthold, op.cit., p. 60.

33 Historische Kommission bei der Bayerischen Akademie der Wissenschaften, op.cit.

34 Berthold, op.cit., p. 60.

35 Ibid.

36 Berthold, *Lazarett*, op.cit., 1 March 1918.

37 Ibid., 6 March 1918.

38 *Luftwaffe Illustrierte Wochenschrift für die Gesamtinteresse der Luftstreitkräfte und des Luftverkehrs*, Nr. 8, 24 February 1918, p. 9.

39 According to RFC, *War Diary*, 10 March 1918, p. 163.

40 3 Squadron, RNAS, *Combat Report* by Flt/Lt Whealy, 10 March 1918.

41 Shores, C., Franks, N. & Guest, R. *Above the Trenches*, p. 380.

42 Esposito, *A Concise History of World War I*, pp. 104-106.

43 Kogenluft, *Nachrichtenblatt der Luftstreitkräfte*, Vol. II, Nr. 4, 21 March 1918, pp. 42, 49.

44 Möller, *Kampf und Sieg eines Jagdgeschwaders*, p. 27.

45 Kriegsministerium (organisational manual). *Teil 10 Abschnitt B, Flieger-Formationen*, pp. 208-209.

46 Möller, op.cit.

47 Ibid., p. 28.

48 VanWyngarden, op.cit., p. 66.

49 Thoms, *Invalidenfriedhof Berlin*, p. 1.

50 Buddecke, H. *El Schahin (Der Jagdfalke): Aus meinem Fliegerleben*, p. 124.

51 Berthold, *Kriegstagebuch*, op.cit.

52 Kommandeur der Flieger der 18. Armee, *Tagesbericht*, 24 March 1918.

53 Esposito, op.cit., p. 110.

54 Möller, op.cit., p. 29.

55 Ibid., p. 32.

CHAPTER NINE

1 Quoted in Möller, *Kampf und Sieg eines Jagdgeschwaders*, p. 56.

2 Berthold, *Persönliches Kriegstagebuch 1914-1920*, p. 61.

3 von Langsdorff, (ed.). *Flieger am Feind*, p. 338; Goote, *Kamerad Berthold der 'unvergleiche Franke'*, p. 215.

4 Berthold, 'Aus hinterlassenen Papieren' in von Langsdorff, ibid., pp. 105-106.

5 Ibid., p. 105

6 Berthold, *Kriegstagebuch*, op.cit.

7 Möller, op.cit., p. 35.

8 Esposito, *A Concise History of World War I*, p. 112.

9 Berthold, 'Papieren', op.cit., p. 106.

10 Quoted in Möller, op.cit., p. 37.

11 Berthold, 'Papieren', op.cit.

12 Bailey & Cony, *The French Air War Chronology*, p. 229; Jean, Rohrbacher, Palmieri, Service historique de l'armée de l'air France. *Les escadrilles de l'aéronautique militaire française: Symbolique et histoire, 1912-1920*, p. 452.

13 Kofl 18. Armee, *Wochenbericht*, 30 May 1918.

14 Möller, op.cit., p. 38.

15 Kofl 18, op,cit.; the SPAD pilot, Sgt André Louis Maurice Géhin of Escadrille Spa 77 was killed. He was born on 18 February 1893 in Bussang (Vosges) and entered military service in December 1913. Following service with the 1e Régiment de Zouaves, he began pilot training in August 1916 and in October received Military Pilot Brevet 4794. Géhin took part in shooting down three Albatroses over Montdidier on 8 February 1918. Of the Salmson crew from Escadrille Sal 27, the pilot, MdLTussing was killed, and the observer, Lt Camille Lemmery, was wounded and taken prisoner [Ref: Bailey & Cony, op.cit., p. 229; Jean, Rohrbacher, Palmieri, Service historique de l'armée de l'air France, op.cit., pp. 193, 84; http://www.memoiredeshommes.sga.defense.gouv. fr/spip. php?rubrique16 (link), *Personnels de l'aéronautique militaire / Personnels de l'aéronautique militaire*].

16 Berthold, 'Papieren' op.cit., pp. 106-107.

17 Möller, op.cit., p. 39.

18 Ibid., p. 40.

19 RAF, *Pilot and Observer Casualties*, 5 June 1918.

20 Hobson, *Airmen Died in the Great War 1914-1918*, pp. 198, 201.

21 Kogenluft, *Nachrichtenblatt der Luftstreitkräfte*, Vol. II, Nr. 24, 8 August 1918, p. 363.

22 Bardt, *Georg von Hantelmann: Erinnerungen aus dem Leben meines Bruders*, p. 24.

23 Esposito, op.cit., p. 114.

24 Kogenluft, op.cit., p. 364.

25 Bailey & Cony, op.cit., p. 242.

26 Quoted in Möller, op.cit., p. 44.

27 Ibid., pp. 44-45.

28 Ibid., p. 46.

29 Berthold, 'Papieren', op.cit., p. 107.

30 Bailey & Cony, op.cit., p. 243; Jacques Monod was born on 29 August 1896 in Livron (Drôme). He enlisted in the army on 21 September 1914 and served in ground units until he transferred to aviation on 15 March 1917. Monod trained at Longvic, Avord and Pau, and received Military Pilot Brevet No. 6810 on 4 June 1917. He succumbed to his wounds on 13 June 1918 at Hôpital d'Ognon (Oise) [Ref: gunner [Ref.: http://www.memoiredeshommes.sga.defense.gouv. fr/spip.php?rubrique16 (link). op.cit.].

31 Confirmed in Kogenluft, op.cit., p. 365.

32 Berthold, 'Papieren', op.cit.

33 84 Squadron, RAF, *Combat Report* by Capt Ralston, 18 June 1918.

34 RAF, *Pilot and Observer Casualties*, 18 June 1918.

35 Hobson, op.cit., pp. 173, 142.

36 Berthold, *Kriegstagebuch*, op.cit.

37 Berthold, 'Papieren', op.cit., pp. 107-108.

38 48 Squadron, RAF, *Combat Report* by Lt R.H. Little and 2/Lt E. Vickers, 27 June 1918.

39 Hobson, op.cit., pp. 140, 155.

40 Cron, 'Organization of the German Luftstreitkräfte', p. 55.

41 Lamberton, *Fighter Aircraft of the 1914-1918 War*, p. 118.

42 Möller, op.cit., p. 52.

43 Esposito, op.cit., p. 115.

44 Möller, op.cit., p. 53.

45 Bailey & Cony, op.cit., p. 267.

46 Kogenluft, *Nachrichtenblatt*, Nr. 29, 12 September 1918, p. 452.

47 Ibid., p. 453; Möller, op.cit.

48 Bailey & Cony, op.cit., p. 268.

49 Möller, op.cit., p. 54.

50 Ibid.; Cron, *Imperial German Army 1914-18 – Organisation, Structure, Orders-of-Battle*, p. 396.

51 Möller, op.cit.

52 Mortane, 'Les As Ennemis', p. 595.

53 Kogenluft, *Nachrichtenblatt*, Nr. 24, 8 August 1918, p. 352.

54 Kommandeur der Flieger der 9. Armee. *Wochenbericht Nr. 30157/18*, 8 August 1918, p. 18.

55 Henshaw, *The Sky Their Battlefield*, p. 462; Sloane, *Wings of Honor – American Airmen in World War I*, pp. 153, 155.

56 Quoted in Möller, op.cit., p. 56.

57 Esposito, op.cit., p. 116.

58 Ibid., p. 119.

59 Kogenluft, *Nachrichtenblatt*, Nr. 25, 15 August 1918, p. 368.

60 Jean, Rohrbacher, Palmieri, Service historique de

l'armée de l'air France, op.cit., p. 463.

61 Bailey & Cony, op.cit., p. 279; the crews were: Sgt Leger and Lt Flamming, and Sgt Pollet and S/Lt Bouvier.

62 Kogenluft, *Nachrichtenblatt*, op.cit.

63 Jones, *The War in the Air*, Vol. VI, p. 452.

64 Ibid., pp. 452-453; 12 S.E.5a aircraft from 32 Squadron, RAF, were in this air combat [Ref: 32 Squadron, RAF, *Squadron Record Book*, 10 August 1918, p. 303].

65 32 Squadron, RAF, *Combat Report* by 2/Lt J.O. Donaldson, 10 August 1918.

66 Möller, op.cit., p. 62.

67 Hobson, op.cit., p. 165.

68 32 Squadron, RAF, *Record Book*, op.cit.

69 RAF, *Pilot and Observer Casualties*, 10 August 1918.

70 Confirmed in Kogenluft, *Nachrichtenblatt*, Nr. 33, 10 October 1918, p. 528.

71 Möller, op.cit., pp. 62-63.

72 RAF, *Pilot and Observer Casualties*, op.cit.

73 Kofl 9. Armee. *Wochenbericht Nr. 30350/18*, 14 August 1918, p. 27.

74 Bodenschatz, *Jagd in Flanderns Himmel – Aus den sechzehn Kampfmonaten des Jagdgeschwaders Freiherr von Richthofen*, pp. 129, 198.

75 Zuerl, op.cit., p. 500.

76 Möller, op.cit., p. 66.

77 Quoted in Ibid.

78 Ibid., p. 67.

79 Quoted in Ibid.

80 Deutscher Offizier-Bund. *Ehren-Rangliste des ehemaligen Deutschen Heeres*, p. 601; von Loewenstern & Bertkau, *Mobilmachung, Aufmarsch und erster Einsatz der deutschen Luftstreitkräfte im August 1914*, p. 119.

CHAPTER TEN

1 Anonymous, Letter of 24 March 1920 [about Berthold's death], p. 3.

2 Berthold, *Persönliches Kriegstagebuch 1914-1920*, pp. 62-63.

3 Wolff'schen Telegraph-Bureau, *Amtliche Kriegs-Depeschen nach Berichten des*, Vol. 8, p. 2833.

4 Franks, Bailey & Guest, *Above the Lines*, p. 77.

5 Berthold, *Kriegstagebuch*, op.cit., p. 63.

6 Berthold, 'Aus hinterlassenen Papieren in von Langsdorff', (ed.). *Flieger am Feind*, p. 108.

7 Wolff'schen Telegraph-Bureau, op.cit., p. 2936.

8 Ibid., p. 2938.

9 Berthold, *Kriegstagebuch*, op.cit., p. 65.

10 Wolff'schen Telegraph-Bureau, op.cit., p. 2966.

11 Berthold, op.cit., p. 66.

12 Ibid., pp. 66-67.

13 Ibid., p. 67.

14 Ibid., p. 68.

15 Ullstein & Co., *Welt-Echo - Politische Wochen-Chronik*, 31 January 1919, p. 53.

16 Berthold, *Kriegslazarettenbuch* entry, 8 March 1919.

17 Berthold, *Kriegstagebuch*, op.cit., p. 82.

18 Ibid.

19 Ibid.

20 Ullstein & Co., *Welt-Echo*, op.cit., 17 April; 1919, p. 15.

21 Ibid., 24 April 1919, p. 15.

22 Ibid., 15 May 1919, p. 12.

23 Berthold, *Kriegstagebuch*, op.cit., p. 83.

24 Wittmann, *Erinnerungen der Eisernen Schar Berthold*, p. 15.

25 Ibid., p. 19.

26 Ibid., p. 25.

27 Ibid., p. 48.

28 Ibid., p. 92.

29 Ibid., p. 95.

30 Ibid., p. 96.

31 Ibid., p. 99.

32 Ibid., pp. 96-97.

33 Berlin, '"Lynchjustiz an Hauptmann Berthold" oder Abwehr des Kapp-Putsches?' in Berlin, J. (ed.). *Das andere Hamburg*, p. 223.

34 Wittmann, op.cit., pp. 100-101.

35 Berlin, op.cit.

36 Wittmann, op.cit., p. 103.

37 Berlin, op.cit., p. 221.

38 Zeit Online. 'Harburg und der Kapp Putsch – I. Teil', p. 4.

39 Ibid., p. 5.

40 Berlin, op.cit., p. 227.

41 Ibid., p. 228.

42 Wittmann, op.cit., pp. 139-140.

43 Zeit Online, op.cit., p. 5.

44 Berthold, *Kriegstagebuch*, op.cit., p. 106.

45 Ibid., p. 107.

46 Ibid.

47 Many sources state that Berthold was buried on the anniversary of his birth, but the family-sponsored newspaper obituary notice clearly gives the day of interment as 30 March 1920.

48 Ibid., p. 108.

49 Ibid., p. 107.

50 Thoms, *Invalidenfriedhof Berlin*, p. 56.

51 Anonymous, op,cit.

52 Zeit Online, op.cit., p. 3.

53 Röll, *Sozialdemokraten im Konzentrationslager Buchenwald 1937-1945*, pp. 49-52; Noack reportedly died in 1941.

BIBLIOGRAPHY AND SOURCES

Books:

Bailey, F. & Cony, C. *The French Air War Chronology*, London, 2001

Bardt, A-L. *Georg von Hantelmann: Erinnerungen aus dem Leben meines Bruders*, Pozna , ca. 1935

Berlin, J. (ed.). *Das andere Hamburg – Freiheitliche Bestrebungen in der Hansestadt seit dem Spätmittelalter*, Köln, 1981

Bodenschatz, K. *Jagd in Flanderns Himmel – Aus den sechzehn Kampfmonaten des Jagdgeschwaders Freiherr von Richthofen*, München, 1935

Boelcke, O. *Hauptmann Boelckes Feldberichte*, Gotha, 1916

Bowyer, C. *The Flying Elephants – A History of No. 27 Squadron*, London, 1972

Bronnenkant, L. *The Imperial Eagles in World War I – Their Postcards and Pictures*, Altglen, Pennsylvania, 2006
- *The Imperial Eagles in World War I – Their Postcards and Pictures, Vol. II*, Altglen, Pennsylvania, 2008
- *The Imperial Eagles in World War I – Their Postcards and Pictures, Vol. III*, Altglen, Pennsylvania, 2011

Bruce, J. *British Aeroplanes 1914-1918*, London, 1957

Bruce, J., Page, G. & Sturtivant, R. *The Sopwith Pup*, Tonbridge, Kent, 2002

Buddecke, H. *El Schahin (Der Jagdfalke): Aus meinem Fliegerleben*, Berlin, 1918

Cron, H. (C. Colton, transl). *Imperial German Army 1914-18 – Organisation, Structure, Orders-of-Battle*, Solihull, West Midlands, 2006 ed.

Cross & Cockade International. *Nieuports in RNAS, RFC and RAF Service*, London, 2007

Davilla, J. & Soltan, A. *French Aircraft of the First World War*, Stratford, Connecticut, 1997

Deutscher Offizier-Bund. *Ehren-Rangliste des ehemaligen Deutschen Heeres*, Berlin, 1926

Diersburg, C. von (ed F. Beck). *Geschichte des 1. 1st Grossherzoglich Hessischen Infanterie- (Leibgarde) Regiments Nr. 115, 1621-1899*, Berlin 1899.

Doerstling, O. *Kriegsgeschichte des Königlich Preussischen Infanterie-Regiment Graf Tauentzien v. Wittenberg (3. Brandenb.) Nr. 20*, Zeulenroda, 1933

Eberhardt, W. von (ed.). *Unsere Luftstreitkräfte 1914-1918*, Berlin, 1930

Esposito, V. (ed.), *A Concise History of World War I*, New York, 1965

Etzel, H. (ed.) *Das K.B. 9. Infanterie-Regiment Wrede: nach den amtlichen Kriegstagebüchern*, Würzburg, 1927

Franks, N. *Sharks Among Minnows*, London, 2001

Franks, N. *The Storks – The Story of the Les Cigognes, France's Élite Fighter Group of WW I*, London, 1998

Franks, N., Bailey, F. & Duiven, R. *Casualties of the German Air Service 1914-1920*, London, 1999

Franks, N., Bailey, F. & Guest, R. *Above the Lines*, London, 1993

Franks, N. *The Jasta Pilots*, London, 1996

Gengler, L. *Rudolf Berthold – Sieger in 44 Luftschlachten Erschlagen im Bruderkampfe für Deutschlands Freiheit*, Berlin, 1934

Goote, T. *Kamerad Berthold der 'unvergleiche Franke'*, Braunschweig, 1937

Haehnelt, W. *Ehrentafel der im Flugdienst während des Weltkrieges gefallenen Offiziere der Deutschen Fliegerverbände*, Berlin, 1920

Heidelberger Akademie der Wissenschaften (ed.). *Deutsches Rechtswörterbuch – Wörterbuch der älteren deutschen Rechtssprache*, Vol. 10, Weimar 2001

Henshaw, T. *The Sky Their Battlefield*, London, 1995

Hildebrand, K. *Die Generale der deutschen Luftwaffe 1935-1945*, Vol. I, Osnabrück, 1990

Hildebrand, K. *Die Generale der deutschen Luftwaffe 1935-1945*, Vol. II, Osnabrück, 1991

Historische Kommission bei der Bayerischen Akademie der Wissenschaften, *Neue Deutsche Biographie*, Vol. II, Berlin, 1955

Hobson, C. *Airmen Died in the Great War 1914-1918*, London, 1995

Hoeppner, E. von. *Deutschlands Krieg in der Luft*, Leipzig, 1921

Imperial War Museum. *Handbook of the German Army in War. April 1918*, London, 1996

Jean, D., Rohrbacher, G-D., Palmieri, B. & Service historique de l'armée de l'air France. *Les escadrilles de l'aéronautique militaire française: Symbolique et histoire, 1912-1920*, Vincennes, 2004

Jones, H. *The War in the Air*, Vol. II, Oxford, 1928
- *The War in the Air*, Vol. III, Oxford, 1931
- *The War in the Air*, Vol. IV, Oxford, 1934
- *The War in the Air*, Vol. VI, Oxford, 1937

Jordan, H. (ed.). *Blätter der Erinnerung an die im Kriege 1914-1919 Gefallenen der Universität Erlangen*, Erlangen, 1920

Koch, L. *Der Erste Weltkrieg als Medium der Gegenmoderne: Zu den Werken von Walter Flex und Ernst Jünger*, Würzburg, 2006

Lamberton, W. *Fighter Aircraft of the 1914-1918 War*, Letchworth, 1960
- *Reconnaissance and Bomber Aircraft of the 1914-1918 War*, Letchworth, 1962

Langsdorff, W. von. (ed.). *Flieger am Feind, Gütersloh*, 1934

Liddell Hart, B. *The Real War 1914-1918*, London, 1964 ed.

Loewenstern, E. von & Bertkau, M. *Mobilmachung, Aufmarsch und erster Einsatz der deutschen Luftstreitkräfte im August 1914*, Berlin, 1939

Luftwaffe Illustrierte Wochenschrift für die Gesamtinteresse der Luftstreitkräfte und des Luftverkehrs, Vol. II, Berlin, 1918

MacDonogh, G. *The Last Kaiser: The Life of Wilhelm II*, London, 2000

Moncure, J. *Forging the King's Sword*, New York, 1993

Möller, H. *Kampf und Sieg eines Jagdgeschwaders*, Berlin, 1939

Neubecker, Dr. O. *Für Tapferkeit und Verdienst*, Munich, 1956

Neumann, G. (ed.). *Die deutschen Luftstreitkräfte im Weltkriege*, Berlin, 1920
- *In der Luft unbesiegt – Erlebnisse im Weltkrieg erzählt von Luftkämpfern*, München, 1923

O'Connor, N. *Aviation Awards of Imperial Germany in World War I, Vol. I – The Aviation Awards of the Kingdom of Bavaria*, Princeton, New Jersey, 1988
- *Aviation Awards of Imperial Germany and the Men Who Earned Them, Vol. II – The Aviation Awards of the Kingdom of Prussia*, Princeton, New Jersey, 1990
- *Aviation Awards of Imperial Germany and the Men Who Earned Them, Vol. III – The Aviation Awards of the Kingdom of Saxony*, Princeton, New Jersey, 1993
- *Aviation Awards of Imperial Germany and the Men Who Earned Them, Vol. IV – The Aviation Awards of the Kingdom of Württemberg*, Princeton, New Jersey, 1995
- *Aviation Awards of Imperial Germany and the Men Who Earned Them, Vol. VII – The Aviation Awards of Eight German States and the Three Free Cities*, Altglen, Pennsylvania, 2002

Perthes, J. *Ehrentafel der Kriegsopfer des reichsdeutschen Adels 1914-1918*, Gotha, 1921

Raleigh, W. *The War in the Air*, Vol. I, Oxford, 1922

Revell, A. *High in the Empty Blue – The History of 56 Squadron, RFC/RAF 1916 to 1920*, Mountain View, California, 1995

Röll, W. *Sozialdemokraten im Konzentrationslager Buchenwald 1937-1945*, Göttingen, 2000

Shores, C., Franks, N. & Guest, R. *Above the Trenches*, London, 1990

Sloane, J. *Wings of Honor – American Airmen in World War I*, Altglen, Pennsylvania, 1994

Sturtivant, R. & Page, G. *The S.E.5 File*, Essex, 1996

Sturtivant, R. & Page, G. *The D.H.4/D.H.9 File*, Essex, 1999

Supf, P. *Das Buch der deutschen Fluggeschichte*, Vol. I, Stuttgart, 1956
- *Das Buch der deutschen Fluggeschichte*, Vol. II, Stuttgart, 1958

Täger, H., Heerde, D., Franke, H-J. & Ruscher, M. *Flugplatz Grossenhain – Historischer Abriss*, Meissen, 2007

Uebe, F. *Ehrenmal des preussischen Offiizer-Korps*, Berlin, 1939

Ullstein & Co. *Welt-Echo - Politische Wochen-Chronik*, Berlin, 1919

VanWyngarden, G. *Jagdgeschwader Nr II – Geschwader 'Berthold'*, Botley, Oxford, 2005
- *Early German Aces of World War I*, Botley, Oxford, 2006
- *Jasta 18 – The Red Noses*, Botley, Oxford, 2011

Welkoborsky, N. *Vom Fliegen, Siegen und Sterben einer Feldflieger-Abteilung*, Berlin, 1939

Werner, J. (ed.). *Boelcke der Mensch, der Flieger, der Führer der deutschen Jagdfliegerei*, Leipzig, 1932

Wittmann, H. *Erinnerungen der Eisernen Schar Berthold*, Oberviechlach, 1921

Wolff'schen Telegraph-Bureaus. *Amtliche Kriegs-Depeschen nach Berichten des*, Vol. 1, Berlin, (n.d.)
- *Amtliche Kriegs-Depeschen nach Berichten des*, Vol. 8, Berlin, (n.d.)

Woodman, H. *Early Aircraft Armament –The Aeroplane and the Gun up to 1918*, London, 1989

Zuerl, W. *Pour-le-Mérite-Flieger*, München, 1938

Documents:

Allerhöchste Führung des XIV. Reserve-Korps, *Berichte*, in the field, 1916

Armee-Oberkommando der 2. Armee (AOK 2), Tägliche Berichte, *in the field, 1915, 1916.*

Armee-Oberkommando der 3. Armee (AOK 3), *Stabsoffizier der Ballon-Abwehrkanonen Berichte*, in the field, 1915

Feldflieger-Abteilung 23. *Tägliche Berichte*, in the field, 1915, 1916

Jagdstaffel 24. *Kriegstagebuch*, in the field, 1916-1918

Königl. Humanistische Gymnasium Schweinfurt. *Jahresbericht für das Schuljahr 1906/1907*, Schweinfurt, 1907
- *Jahresbericht für das Schuljahr 1907/1908*, Schweinfurt, 1908
- *Jahresbericht für das Schuljahr 1911/1912*, Schweinfurt, 1912

Kommandeur der Flieger der 4. Armee (Kofl 4). *Tagesbefehle*, in the field, 1917
- *Wochenberichte*, in the field, 1917

Kommandeur der Flieger der 5. Armee (Kofl 5). *Meldungen*, in the field, 1918

Kommandeur der Flieger der 6. Armee (Kofl 6). *Meldungen*, in the field, 1916, 1917, 1918

Kommandeur der Flieger der 9. Armee (Kofl 9). *Wöchenberichte*, in the field, 1918

Kommandeur der Flieger der 18. Armee (Kofl 18). *Tagesberichte*, in the field, 1918
- *Wochenberichte*, in the field, 1918

Kommandeur der Flieger der Armee-Abteilung C (Kofl C). *Tätigkeitsberichte der Fliegerverbände*, in the field, 1918

Kommandierende General der Luftstreitkräfte (Kogenluft). *Nachrichtenblatt der Luftstreitkräfte*, Vol. I, in the field, 1917
- *Nachrichtenblatt der Luftstreitkräfte*, Vol. II, in the field, 1918

Kriegsministerium (organisational manual). *Teil 10 Abschnitt B, Flieger-Formationen*, Berlin, 1918

Royal Flying Corps. *Communiqués*, in the field, 1917 (File Air 1/2097/207/14/1)
- Pilot & Observer Casualties, indexed, in the field, June 1915-September 1916 (File Air 1/967/204/5/1097)
- Pilot and Observer Casualties, indexed, in the field, September 1916-February 1917 (File Air 1/967/204/5/1098)
- Pilot and Observer Casualties, indexed, in the field, June 1917-February 1918 (File Air 1/968/204/5/1100)

Royal Flying Corps/ Royal Air Force, Pilot and Observer Casualties, indexed, in the field, February 1918-July 1918 (File Air 1/969/204/5/1101)
- Pilot and Observer Casualties, indexed, in the field, August 1918-April 1919 (File Air 1/969/204/5/1102)
- 19 Squadron, RFC, *Combat Reports*, in the field, 1916 (Air 1/1220/204/5/2634/19 Sqdn)
- 19 Squadron, RFC, *Squadron Record Book*, in the field, 1917 (Air 1/1488/204/37/11)
- 20 Squadron, RFC, *Squadron Record Book*, in the field, 1917 (Air 1/168/15/156/4)
- 32 Squadron, RAF, *Combat Reports*, in the field, 1918 (File Air 1/1222/204/5/2634/32 Sqdn)
- 32 Squadron, RAF, *Squadron Record Book*, in the field, 1918 (Air 1/1493/204/38/3)
- 48 Squadron, RAF, *Combat Reports*, in the field, 1918 (File Air 1/1223/204/5/2634/48 Sqdn)
- 56 Squadron, RFC, *Combat Reports*, in the field, 1917 (File Air 1/1912/204/229/20)
- 84 Squadron, RAF, *Combat Reports*, in the field, 1918 (File Air 1/1227/204/5/2634/84 Sqdn)
- *War Diary*, in the field, February-October 1915 (File Air 1/1176/204/2895)
- *War Diary*, in the field, November-December 1915 (File Air 1/1184/204/5/2595)

Royal Naval Air Service. 3 Squadron, RNAS, *Combat Reports*, in the field, 1918 (File Air 1/1216/204/5/2634/3 Naval)

Articles, Monographs, Periodicals and Texts:

Anonymous. 'Führende Männer im Weltkriege Nr. 8 – Generalfeldmarschall von der Goltz' in *Kriegs-Echo Nr. 66*, Berlin, 1915
- 'Führende Männer im Weltkriege Nr. 18 – Generaloberst von Kluck' in *Kriegs-Echo Nr. 76*, Berlin, 1916
- 'Führende Männer im Weltkriege Nr. 69 – Generalfeldmarschall von Bülow' in *Kriegs-Echo Nr. 129*, Berlin, 1917
- 'Les Héros Disparu: Paoli' in *La Guerre Aérienne Illustrée*, Vol. 1, No. 18, Paris, 1917
- 'Leutnant Grüners Heldentod fürs Vaterland' in *Kamenzer Tagblatt*, Kamenz, 24 November 1915
- 'L'horreur des devastations allemandes' in *L'illustration*, Paris, 9 June 1917

Bailey, F., Kilduff P. & Vanoverbeke, L. 'General Service Unit: The History of Escadrille 23' in *Over the Front*, Vol. 26, No. 3, Dallas, Texas, 2011

Berlin, J. '"Lynchjustiz an Hauptmann Berthold" oder Abwehr des Kapp-Putsches? Die Ereignisse in Harburg im März 1920' in Berlin, J. (ed.). *Das andere Hamburg*, Köln, 1981

Berthold, R. 'Aus hinterlassenen Papieren' in Langsdorff, W. von (ed.) *Flieger am Feind*, Gütersloh, 1934

- *Persönliches Kriegstagebuch 1914-1920* (manuscript), Bundesarchiv Militärarchiv, Freiburg, n.d. (File MSG 2/10722)

Bethge, W. 'Bund Jungdeutschland (BJD)' in Frick, D. (ed.) *Die bürgerlichen Parteien in Deutschland, Handbuch der Geschichte der bürgerlichen Parteien und anderer bürgerlicher Interessenorganisationen vom Vormärz bis zum Jahre 1945.* Vol. 1, Leipzig, 1968

Cron, H. (Transl. P. Grosz) 'Organization of the German Luftstreitkräfte' in *Cross & Cockade Journal*, Vol. VII, No. 1, Whittier, California, 1966

Daçay, J. 'Les Frères Steuer' in *La Guerre Aérienne Illustrée*, Vol. 2, No. 40, Paris, 1917

Duiven, R. 'Das Königliche Jagdgeschwader Nr II' in *Over the Front*, Vol. 9, No. 3, Dallas, Texas, 1994

- 'Das Königliche Jagdgeschwader Nr II, Part II' in *Over the Front*, Vol. 9, No. 4, Dallas, Texas, 1994
- 'Royal Prussian Jagdgeschwader Nr II' in *Over the Front*, Vol. 10, No. 1, Dallas, Texas, 1995
- 'Royal Prussian Jagdgeschwader Nr II Combat Log' in *Over the Front*, Vol. 10, No. 1, Dallas, Texas, 1995

Falls, C. 'Western Front, 1915-1917 Stalemate' in Esposito, V. (ed.) *A Concise History of World War I*, New York, 1965

Grosz, P. *AEG G.IV Windsock Datafile 51*, Berkhamsted, 1995

- *Albatros D.I/D.II Windsock Datafile 100*, Berkhamsted, 2003
- *Fokker E.III Windsock Datafile 15*, Berkhamsted, 1989
- *Halberstadt CL.II Windsock Datafile 27*, Berkhamsted, 1991
- *LVG B.I Windsock Datafile 98*, Berkhamsted, 2003
- *Pfalz E.I – E.VI Windsock Datafile 59*, Berkhamsted, 1996
- 'The Agile and Aggressive Albatros' in *Air Enthusiast Quarterly*, No. 1, Bromley. Kent, 1976

Kilduff, P. 'The History of Royal Württemberg Flieger-Abteilung (A) 252' in *Over the Front*, Vol. 12, No. 4, Dallas, Texas, 1997

Mortane, J. 'Les As Ennemis' in *La Guerre Aérienne Illustrée*, Vol. 4, No. 89, Paris, 1918

Radloff, B. & Niemann, R. 'The Ehrenbechers – Where Are They Now?' in *Cross & Cockade Journal*, Vol. X, No. 4, Whittier, California, 1969

Pearce, M. "Eugène Gilbert – A Great French Fighter Pilot" in *Cross & Cockade International Journal*, Vol. XXIV, No. 2, Farnborough, 1993

Täger, H. 'Die verlorene Ehre des Ernst Freiherr von Althaus' (unpublished manuscript via the author).

Thoms, R. *Invalidenfriedhof Berlin*, Berlin, 1999

Van Dorssen, H., Tubbs, D. & Evans, W. 'Paul Strähle – The War Diary of a German Aviator, 11 August 1917-22 April 1918' in *Cross & Cockade Great Britain Journal*, Vol. XI, No. 4, Farnborough, 1980

VanWyngarden, G. 'Colors: Jagdgeschwader II' in *Over the Front*, Vol. 9, No. 3, Dallas, Texas, 1994

- 'Colors: Jagdgeschwader II, Part II' in *Over the Front*, Vol. 9, No. 4, Dallas, Texas, 1994
- 'Colors: Jagdgeschwader II, Part Three' in *Over the Front*, Vol. 10, No. 1, Dallas, Texas, 1995

Wynne, H. 'Project Aerodromes' in *Over the Front*, Vol. VI, No. 1, Dallas, Texas, 1991

Zickerick, W. 'Verlustliste der deutschen Luftstreitkräfte im Weltkriege' in *Unsere Luftstreitkräfte 1914-1918*, Berlin, 1930

On-line Resources:

Küttelwesch, R. '"Letzte Landung" des Jagdfliegers – Nach 42 Jahre: Grabplatte für den Jagdflieger Berthold wieder auf den Invalidenfriedhof' in *Das Ostpreussenblatt*, Hamburg, 23 August 2003: http://www.webarchiv-server.de/pin/archiv03/3403ob16.htm

Personnels de l'aéronautique militaire / Personnels de l'aéronautique militaire:
http://www.memoiredeshommes.sga.defense.gouv.fr/spip.php?rubrique16

Pietsch, T. 'Bernward Gross 1887-1916' in *Frontflieger*: www.frontflieger.de/3grobe0t.html

Zeit Online. 'Harburg und der Kapp Putsch – I. Teil':
http://community.zeit.de/user/gottesh%C3%BCttenkind/beitrag/2009/07/27/harburg-und-der-kappputsch-i-teil

Other Sources:

Anonymous, *Letter of 24 March* 1920 [about Berthold's death], Stadtarchiv Erlangen, n.d.

Berthold, R. *Lazarettkrankenbücher*, 1916-1918

Keller, F. *Kriegsranglisten-Auszug*, 1919

Kleffel, W. Letter of 25 October 1974 to L. Zacharias via G. VanWyngarden

70 Squadron Recording Officer. Letter of 30 September 1917 to Gould family, courtesy of S.K. Taylor

Strähle, P. Correspondence with the author, 1966-1980

- Interview by the author, 14 May 1967

INDEX

I. MILITARY FORMATIONS

Air Staffs, German

Armee-Abt A Stofl/Kofl 75, 77, 80

Flugzeugmeisterei 120

Inspektion der Fliegertruppen 30

3. Armee Kofl (3rd Army sector) 121, 149, 155, 163, 169, 187

4. Armee Kofl (4th Army sector) 88-90, 92-93, 101, 103, 106, 107, 111, 181

5. Army Kofl (5th Army sector) 80, 89, 103

9. Armee Kofl (9th Army sector) 122, 123, 126

18. Army Kofl (18th Army sector) 110, 111, 115

Air Units, American

1st Aero Squadron 121, 122, 123, 140, 163, 164

2nd Aero Squadron 151

8th Aero Squadron 156

11th Aero Squadron 150, 151, 165

12th Aero Squadron 156, 166, 167

13th Aero Squadron 165, 166

20th Aero Squadron 150, 151

22nd Aero Squadron 151, 157, 165, 166, 170

24th Aero Squadron 170

27th Aero Squadron 157, 165, 171

28th Aero Squadron 151, 152, 165, 166

47th Aero Squadron 163

49th Aero Squadron 157, 166

50th Aero Squadron 156

88th Aero Squadron 157

91st Aero Squadron 170, 171

94th Aero Squadron 151, 157, 164, 166

95th Aero Squadron 153, 165, 171

96th Aero Squadron 156, 170, 171, 172

99th Aero Squadron 170

103rd Aero Squadron 165

139th Aero Squadron 151, 157, 165, 166

147th Aero Squadron 171, 172

213th Aero Squadron 156

Air Units, British

3 Squadron, RNAS 109, 143

4 Squadron, RFC 93, 94, 139, 143

6 Squadron, RFC 93, 139

7 Squadron, RFC 91, 139

8 Squadron, RFC 60, 138, 146, 153

9 Squadron, RFC 59, 61, 72, 91, 138, 139, 178

11 Squadron, RFC 12, 15, 54, 142, 146, 147

13 Squadron, RFC 58, 138, 177

15 Squadron, RFC 63, 147, 148, 160, 162, 169

19 Squadron, RFC 70, 72, 96, 97, 139, 142, 144

20 Squadron, RFC 97, 99, 140, 150

22 Squadron, RFC 96, 139, 146

24 Squadron, RFC 63, 147, 148, 160, 162, 169

27 Squadron, RAF 124, 138, 179

32 Squadron, RFC/RAF 95, 124, 139, 140, 142, 154, 160, 161, 163

48 Squadron, RAF 120, 140, 143, 149, 154, 163

49 Squadron, RAF 124, 140, 161, 163

55 Squadron, RFC 91, 93, 139

56 Squadron, RFC/RAF 103, 104, 124, 154, 163, 164

57 Squadron, RFC 90, 101, 139, 140, 142, 144

60 Squadron, RFC 102, 145

62 Squadron, RAF 124

66 Squadron, RFC 99, 140, 144, 145

70 Squadron, RFC 97, 140, 148

84 Squadron, RAF 119, 140, 148, 149, 153, 160, 162

103 Squadron, RAF 116, 117, 140, 161

104 Squadron, IF, RAF 165

Air Units, French

Escadrille HF 1 179

Escadrille N 3 173

Escadrille MF 7 139, 180

Escadrille N 15 86, 139

Escadrille MS 23 176

Escadrille Sal 27 140, 161, 181

Escadrille MF 32 179

Escadrille F 35 139, 180

Escadrille N 37 69, 120, 138, 179

Escadrille Sal 40 121, 140, 163

Escadrille C 46 158, 164, 179

Escadrille MF 54 60, 138, 178

Escadrille N 73 139, 180

Escadrille N 76 69

Escadrille Spa 77 140, 181, 183

Escadrille Spa 96 119, 140, 162, 169

Escadrille N 103 72, 139, 179

Escadrille VB 108 18, 138, 178

Escadrille VB 110 180

Escadrille Sop 278 115, 140, 161

Escadrille Spa 289 123, 140, 163

Escadrille N 506 80

Air Units and Facilities, German

3. Kompagnie des Flieger-Bataillons Nr. 1 30

Armee Flugpark 2 175, 176

DFW Flying School 39

Etappen-Flugzeug-Park 2 15, 39, 40-43, 176

Etappen-Flugzeug-Park 3 30, 174

Feld-Fliegerabteilung 1b 48

Feldflieger-Abteilung 22 179

Feldflieger-Abteilung 23 14, 15, 30-39, 43-50, 51-56, 58, 59, 60, 61, 65, 67, 70, 88, 121, 173, 176, 177

Feldflieger-Abteilung 24 30, 174

Feldflieger-Abteilung 26 179

Feldflieger-Abteilung 27 40, 48

Feldflieger-Abteilung 29 30, 174

Feldflieger-Abteilung 32 48, 177

Feldflieger-Abteilung 62 51

Flieger-Abteilung (A) 252w 176

Flieger-Bataillon 1 (Döberitz) 30, 174

Flieger-Bataillon 2 (Posen, Graudenz, Königsberg) 174

Flieger-Bataillon 3 (Cologne, Hannover, Darmstadt) 174

Flieger-Bataillon 4 (Strassburg, Metz, Freiburg im Breisgau) 174

Flieger-Ersatz-Abteilung 3 (Darmstadt) 176

Flieger-Ersatz-Abteilung 5 (Hannover) 107

Flieger-Ersatz-Abteilung 6 (Grossenhain) 88, 174

Flieger-Ersatz-Abteilung 9 (Darmstadt) 69

Fliegerschule der Halberstädter Flugzeugwerke 25-27

Fokker-Kampfstaffel Falkenhausen 74

Geschwaderschule Paderborn 176

Jagdgeschwader Freiherr von Richthofen Nr 1 89, 111, 114, 115, 121

Jagdgeschwader 2 109-125, 127, 128, 135

Jagdgeschwader 3 111

Jagdgruppe 7 89, 99, 106, 107

Jagdgruppe 11 181

Jagdgruppe 15 181

Jagdgruppe Nord 181

Jagdstaffel 2 67, 74, 111, 181

Jagdstaffel 3 181

Jagdstaffel 4 67, 69, 70, 72, 73, 89

Jagdstaffel 6 89

Jagdstaffel 7 181

Jagdstaffel 8 181

Jagdstaffel 10 89, 125

Jagdstaffel 11 89

Jagdstaffel 12 111, 121, 123

Jagdstaffel 13 111, 119, 121, 123

Jagdstaffel 14 73, 74-78, 80-88, 104, 181

Jagdstaffel 15 111, 115, 116, 117, 121, 123, 124, 125

Jagdstaffel 18 88-100, 101-112

Jagdstaffel 19 111, 121

Jagdstaffel 20 181

Jagdstaffel 24 89, 100, 106, 117

Jagdstaffel 26 111, 181

Jagdstaffel 27 111, 181

Jagdstaffel 28 181

Jagdstaffel 29 181

Jagdstaffel 30 108

Jagdstaffel 31 89, 100

Jagdstaffel 33 106, 181

Jagdstaffel 35 181

Jagdstaffel 36 89, 100, 111

Jagdstaffel 52 125

Kagohl 1 179

Kagohl 4 179

Kampfeinsitzer Kommando Vaux 56-62, 63-67, 100, 178

Kampfeinsitzerschule Paderborn 89

Kampfeinsitzerstaffel 8 181

Kampfstaffel S.2 179

Kampfstaffel T 179

Riesenflugzeug-Abteilung 501 177

Army Units, Facilities and Formations

1. Armee (1st Army) 31, 35, 36, 37

1. Garde-Infanterie Division (1st Guards Infanty Division) 90

1. Husaren-Regiment König Albert Nr. 18 173

1. Ober-Elsässisches Infanterie-Regiment Nr. 167 176

1. Ulanen-Regiment Kaiser Wilhelm II., König von Preussen 20

2. Armee (2nd Army) 31, 35, 36, 37, 38, 47, 57, 58, 66, 68, 110, 124

2. Grenadier-Regiment Nr. 101 Kaiser Wilhelm, König von Preussen 177

3. Armee (3rd Army) 34, 49, 66, 121, 122

4. Armee (4th Army) 88, 89, 90, 101, 103, 111

5. Armee (5th Army) 89, 103

5. Infanterie-Regiment Grossherzog Ernst Ludwig von Hessen 20

7. Armee (7th Army) 90, 111, 121, 122

9. Armee (9th Army) 122, 123, 126

9. Bayerisches Infanterie-Regiment Wrede (Bavarian 9th Infantry Regiment) 65

9. Württembergisches Infanterie-Regiment Nr. 127 176

10. Württembergisches Infanterie-Regiment Nr. 180 173

13. Infanterie-Regiment Nr. 178 173

17. Armee (17th Army sector) 110, 111

18. Armee (18th Army sector) 110, 111, 115, 118

52. Infanterie-Division (52nd Infantry Division) 48

75. Reserve-Division (75th Reserve Division) 180

Armee-Abteilung A 73-74, 80, 180

Armeegruppe Quast 179

Armeegruppe Stein 179

Armeegruppe Wytschaete (Army Group Wytschaete) 88, 105

Bayerische-Reserve-Feldlazarett 45 (Courtrai) 104

Dragoner-Regiment von Wedel (Pommersches) Nr. 11 88

Feldlazarett 10 (2. Armee) 124, 163

Fliegertruppe 24, 26, 29, 51, 77, 79, 173, 174, 176, 177

Garde-Fussartillerie-Regiment 176

Grenadier-Regiment Prinz Carl von Preussen (2. Brandenburgisches) Nr. 12 177

Grossherzoglich Mecklenburgisches Füsilier-regiment Nr. 90 Kaiser Wilhelm 175

Infanterie-Reg Graf Tauentzien von Wittenberg (3. Brandenburgischen) Nr. 20 22, 24, 27, 173

Jungdeutschland-Bund 22, 24

Kriegslazarett 7 (St. Quentin) 64

Kriegslazarett 19E (Montcornet) 125

Kurmärkisches Feldartillerie-Regiment Nr. 39 175

Leibgarde-Infanterie-Regiment (1. Grossherzoglich Hessisches) Nr. 115 40, 176

Luftstreitkräfte 79, 80, 88, 104, 105, 113, 125, 126, 127

II. PERSONNEL

Alexander, 2/Lt Edmund H.E.J. 58, 138

Althaus, Ltn.d.Res Ernst Freiherr von 17, 18, 53, 54, 55, 56, 58, 73, 74, 173, 177

Arnoux de Maison-Rouge, S/Lt Antoine 139, 180-181

Auffarth, Oblt Harald 93, 95, 99, 182

August Wilhelm, Prince of Prussia 52

Bar, Ronny 8

Barioz, Adj Albert 139, 180

Barlow, AM/1 Thomas J. 182

Barry, Lt Cecil 91, 139

Baumann, Trudy 8

Bayetto, Capt Tone H.P. 99

Beaulieu-Marconnay, Ltn Oliver Freiherr von 108, 115, 117, 135

Becker, Ltn Hermann 112, 145-151

Beetham, Sgt O.D. 124, 140

Bell, 2/Lt Elvis A. 96, 139

Bentheim, Hptm Constantin von 181

Bernert, Oblt Fritz Otto 73, 100

Berthold, Albert Oskar Arno 174

Berthold, Amalia Franziska Ernestine 105, 106, 111, 113, 114, 120, 127, 128, 134, 174

Berthold, Anna Ida Elsa 174

Berthold, Anna Ida Gertrud 174

Berthold, Anna Ida (Hofmann) 19

Berthold, Armin Friedrich Johann 174

Berthold, Friedrich Oskar Bertram 174

Berthold, Helene (Stief) 19, 25

Berthold, Herrmann Armin Julius 174

Berthold, Julius Wolfram 174

Berthold, Oskar 19, 23,

Berthold, Hptm Rudolf: birth, 19; education, 19-22; commissioned as Leutnant, 22; first army assignment, 22; early infantry , 22-24; aviation training, 24-27; awarded Iron Crosses, 36, 38; received Militär-Flugzeugführer-Abzeichen, 43, 46; crashes, 50, 63-64, 124; promoted to Oberleutnant, 51; wounded in aerial combat, 59, 87, 103, 124; awarded Militär-Verdienst-Orden 4. Klasse mit Schwertern, 60; awarded Ritterkreuz des Militär-St.-Heinrichs-Ordens, 61; awarded Ritterkreuz des Königlichen Hausordens von Hohenzollern mit Schwertern, 69; awarded Orden *Pour le Mérite*, 73; receives Ehrenbecher, 80; appointed Kommandeur of JG 2, 110-111; attends 2nd Fighter Competition, 120; last air combat, 123-124; postwar service, 129-134; death, 134; funeral and burial, 134-136, 184.

Berthold's aerial victory claims: No. 1, 17-18, 58, 138; No. 2, 58, 138; No. 3, 60, 138; No. 4, 60-61, 138; No. 5, 61-62, 138; No. 6, 68-69, 138; No. 7, 70, 138; No. 8, 72-73, 139; No. 9, 85, 139; No. 10, 85, 139; No. 11, 86, 139; No. 12, 86, 139; No. 13, 90-91, 139; No. 14, 91, 139; No. 15, 91, 139; No. 16, 91, 139; No. 17, 92-93, 139; No. 18, 93, 139; No. 19, 93, 139; No. 20, 94, 139; No. 21, 95, 139; No. 22, 96, 139; No. 23, 96, 139; No. 24, 96-97, 139; No. 25, 97, 140; No. 26, 99, 140; No. 27, 99, 140; No. 28, 101, 140; No. 29, 115, 140, 161; No. 30, 115-116, 140, 161; No. 31, 115-116, 140, 161; No. 32, 116, 140, 161; No. 33, 118,

140, 162; No. 34, 118-119, 140, 162; No. 35, 119-120, 140, 162; No. 36, 119-120, 140, 162; No. 37, 120, 140, 163; No. 38, 121, 140, 163; No. 39, 122, 140, 163; No. 40, 123, 140, 163; No. 41, 123, 140, 163; No. 42, 123, 140, 163; No. 43, 124, 140, 163; No. 44, 124, 140, 163.

Berthold, Wolfram 21, 65
Bier, Dr. August 105, 106, 107, 127, 181
Billik, Ltn Paul 125
Bischoff, Maj Josef 132
Böhmer, Oblt Fritz 46, 47
Boelcke, Hptm Oswald 25, 27, 51, 57, 60, 66, 67, 74, 75, 77, 82, 123
Boenigk, Oblt Oskar Freiherr von 127
Bohnstedt, Oblt Eberhard 46, 47, 175, 177
Borck, Ltn.d.Res Hans Joachim 124, 162-164
Borgoltz, Lt Jacques V.A. 139
Boumphrey, Lt J.W. 99
Bouvier, S/Lt 184
Braut, Lt Alfred 60, 138
Bredelow, Rittm Heinz Freiherr von 125
Bredow, Vfw 87
Bremer, Johannes 137
Bronnenkant, Dr. Lance J. 8, 10, 81, 87, 131, 136
Bros de Puechredon, Lt Alphonse 44
Buddecke, Hptm.d.Res Hans Joachim 40, 41, 47, 49, 50, 51, 52, 53, 54, 55, 63, 67, 68, 70, 72, 73, 74, 108, 110, 111, 135, 176
Bülow, Gen.Oberst Karl von 31, 35, 36, 38, 168, 175, 187
Buttlar, Ltn Hans von 108

Campbell, Capt John S. 99
Chance, Lt William H.S. 70, 138, 179
Chappius, Lt 121, 140
Coller, Lt Bernard T. 73, 139
Cony, Christophe 8, 84
Coyle, 1st Lt Arthur J. 122
Cornish, 2/Lt William O. 95, 139
Cox, 2/Lt B.H. 59
Crane, 2/Lt C.G. 182

Dangueuger, Capl Henri 69, 138, 179
Deason, Lt Thomas G. 93, 139
Denicke, OB Heinrich 134
Denis, Capt Henri 121, 140
Desbordes, S/Lt Pierre É.F. 139
Deuster, Oskar Freiherr von 19, 20
Dewall, Oblt Job-Heinrich von 175
Dieffenbach, Gen.Ltn Karl 101, 105
Dingel, Ltn Walter 108, 120, 182
Donaldson, 2/Lt John O. 124
Dostler, Oblt Eduard Ritter von 90, 152

Earle, 2/Lt Wallace S. 61, 138, 178
Eben, Gen.d.Inf Johannes von 113, 123
Ebert, German Chancellor Friedrich 129, 133
Edwards, 2/Lt Reginald H. 72
Egerton, Lt R. 59

Ehrhardt, Korv.Kptn Hermann 133
Einem, Gen.Oberst Karl von 122
Eitel Friedrich, Prince of Prussia 90
Ernst August, Duke of Braunschweig 52, 54
Erwin, 1st Lt William P. 122, 123, 140

Faber, 2/Lt C. 59
Falkenhausen, Gen.d.Inf Ludwig von 74
Falkenhayn, Gen.Oberst Erich von 79
Falkiner, 2/Lt Frederick E.B. 91, 139
Farrington, Kimberly 8
Fiedler, Hanns 21
Fitzgerald, 2/Lt John J. 102
Flamming, Lt 184
Fokker, Anthony H.G. 50, 66
Foord, Lt Edward A. 120, 140
Frankl, Ltn.d.Res Wilhelm 73, 74
Franz Ferdinand, Erzherzog 26, 27
Franz Joseph I, Kaiser 26
Freud, Dr. Sigmund 107
Friedrich II, Prussian King 111
Friedrich August III, Saxon King 61
Friedrich Wilhelm III, Prussian King 36
Fyfe, 2/Lt Robert J. 120, 140

Géhin, Sgt André L.M. 140, 181
Genée, Hptm 126
Gerbig, Vfw Otto 84, 87, 88, 181
Gilbert, Sgt Eugène 44, 176
Goltz, Gen.Feld.Mar Wilhelm L.C. Freiherr von der 22, 24, 174, 187
Glaeser, Oblt Gottfried 45, 175
Gnamm, Ltn Walter 14, 46, 51, 173
Gould, Lt Walter H.R. 97, 140, 181
Grade, Hptm Wilhelm 175
Grieffenhagen, Rittm Karl Heino 88, 89
Gross, Oblt Karl von 34, 175
Gross, Ltn.d.Res Max Emil B. 65, 179
Grosz, Peter M. 11
Grüner, Ltn Josef 14, 15, 16, 46, 47, 51, 54, 55, 58, 65, 173

Haehnelt, Maj Wilhelm 80, 89, 173
Hall, Capt D. 101
Halley, 2/Lt Clifford R.B. 182
Hantelmann, Ltn Georg von 108, 116
Hartigan, 2/Lt E. 101
Hartley, 2/Lt H. 124, 140
Hartmann, Hptm Otto 181
Hartnett, Lt Michael Charles 94, 139
Haslam, 2/Lt Herbert 93, 139
Haussmann, Vfw Albert 119
Henderson, Capt Ian H.D. 70, 179
Hennhöfer, Manfred 8
Herman, 2/Lt Robert D. 72
Hindenburg, Gen.Feld.Mar Paul von Beneckendorff und von 79
Hirsemann, Ltn.d.Res Anton 46, 47
Höhndorf, Ltn.d.Res Walter 73, 74

Hoeppner, Gen.Ltn Ernst von 79, 80, 89, 105, 121, 180, 181, 186
Hüttner, Off.Stv 80, 86
Hughes Chamberlain, 2/Lt Robert E.A.W. 15
Humphries, 2/Lt Leslie G. 93, 139, 181
Hutier, Gen.d.Inf Oskar von 118

Immelmann, Oblt Max 51, 57, 60, 66, 82
Inglis, 2/Lt William L. 182

Jackson, Lt William E. 124
Jacquin, Capl Arthur 58, 138, 178
James, Sgt Leonard 120, 140
Jena, Hptm Ferdinand von 174
Jones, H.A. 82, 86

Kapp, Wolfgang 133
Keller, Hptm Alfred 40, 176
Keller, Oblt Franz 43, 44, 175, 176
Kemp, Lt Herbert T. 12, 177, 181
Kilduff, Judy A. 7, 8
Kilduff, Karl F. 8
Kirby, 2/Lt Frederick W. 96, 139
Klaudat, Vfw Gustav 122
Kleffel, Ltn Walther 101, 102, 108
Klein, Off.Stv Johannes 89, 108, 182
Kluck, Gen.Oberst Alexander von 31, 35, 187
Knackfuss, Hptm Normand 40, 41, 176
Koos, Dr. Volker 8, 44, 50, 59, 65, 71, 86, 91, 92, 96, 97, 98, 100, 110, 119, 125
Krieg, Hptm 74
Kuen, Ltn.d.Res Adolf 80

Lambert, Brgd 80
Lane, Capt Cecil W. 12, 177
Langsdorff, Werner Schulze von 113, 183, 184
Lawrence, Capt Thomas E. 54
Lawrence, 2/Lt William G. 54
Lebleu, Sdt Alexandré J. 139, 180
Leger, Sgt 184
Lemmery, Lt Camille 140, 180
Levy, S/Lt Robert 139, 180
Linay, L/Cpl Alfred J. 93, 139
Little, Lt R.H. 183
Littwin, Klaus 8
Loerzer, Hptm Bruno 111
Loewenhardt, Oblt Erich 123, 125
Lohmann, Ltn Paul 108, 134
Loyd, Lt Eric E.F. 93, 139
Ludendorff, Gen.d.Inf Erich 79, 123
Lüttwitz, Gen Walther Freiherr von 133

MacAndrew, 2/Lt Colin G.O. 140
Macfarlane, Lt Peter 124, 140
Mardersteig, Maj.d.Res Georg 174
Margot, Vfw Hermann 88, 108
Marks, Capt Cecil H. 54
Marschalck von Bachtenbrock, Oblt Otto Freiherr 35, 36, 38, 175
Martin, 2/Lt F.A. 101

Maxwell, Capt Gerald J.C. 103-104, 182
McLeod, Lt Norman 96
Meyer, Oblt Willy 175
Michaelis, Ltn.d.Res Georg 85
Miller, Dr. M. Geoffrey 94, 107
Minckwitz, Hptm Horst von 174
Monod, Cap Jacques 140, 181
Moore, 2/Lt G.N. 91, 139
Müller-Arles, Ltn Aribert 34, 175
Munro, Lt F.F. 139
Musset, Ltn Karl 65

Neill, Lt John W.F. 91, 139
Neumann, Maj Georg P. 48
Nielsen, Lt Peter 120, 140
Nivelle, Gén Robert G. 82, 85
Noack, Otto 137, 184
Noble, 2/Lt Harold T. 99
Nowarra, Heinz J. 8, 14, 20, 25, 30, 32, 43, 45, 46, 49, 56, 68, 75, 106, 128
Nowell, 2/Lt Roger E. 96, 139

O'Connor, Neal W. 54
Oertzen, Hptm Jasper von 175
O'Neill, Lt J. 101
Orde, 2/Lt Michael A.J. 60, 138, 178
Orr, 2/Lt Colin G. 101
Ostermann, Uffz Friedrich 38

Palmer, Hptm Hermann 69, 121, 179
Paoli, Sgt Louis 60, 61, 138, 178
Paulin, Ltn.d.Res Michael 181
Payne, 2/Lt Wilfred S.L. 91, 139
Pearson, 2/Lt Leonard J. 58, 138
Pechmann, Oblt Paul Freiherr von 90
Peinaud, Capl Jean 139
Pollet, Sgt 184
Potempa, Oberst.Ltn Harald 8
Powers, Lt Bernard A. 96-97, 139, 181
Pritt, Lt Walbanke A. 99

Quast, Gen.d.Inf Ferdinand von 67

Rabe, Obertsltn.d.Res, a.D Hanns-Gerd 7
Rahn, Lt.d.Res Arthur 95, 108, 160, 167, 168, 169, 182
Ralston, Capt John S. 119-120, 183
Reinhard, Hptm Wilhelm 114, 121
Revell, Alex 8, 103
Richthofen, Rittm Manfred Freiherr von 89, 90, 93, 113, 114, 121
Robeson, 2/Lt V.A.H. 59
Robinson, 2/Lt Edward 15, 54
Roman, Sgt François 72, 179
Rothenbiller, Christa 2, 9
Rothenbiller, OB.i.R Prof.Dr.(h c) Franz J. 2, 9
Runge, Ltn Richard 95, 102, 182
Runnels-Moss, 2/Lt C.G.V. 97

Scaife, 2/Lt Thomas E.G. 59, 73, 139
Schabbel, Ltn Fritz 181
Schäfer, Ltn Hugo 95, 108, 160, 162, 164, 165, 166
Schlegel, Ernst 40, 41, 42, 46, 176
Schleichardt, Off.Stv Richard 110
Schmidt, Oblt Otto 181

Schober, Ltn Otto 95, 182
Schueler van Krieken, Rittm Friedrich 46, 47, 177
Schuhmann, Vfw 77
Schwerd, Dr. Frederich 181
Seber, Hptm Karl 45, 46, 47, 54, 55, 176
Ségaud, S/Lt Pierre 58, 138, 178
Selby, 2/Lt Cuthbert W.P. 61, 62, 64, 138, 178
Seydlitz-Gerstenberg, Ltn Hans-Joachim von 34, 46, 47, 175
Shaw, 1/AM 60, 138
Sidney, 2/Lt Leicester P. 102, 140
Smith, David E. 8
Souchay, Oblt Franz A.P. 46
Spencer, 1/Lt Earl B. 123, 140
Steben, 2/Lt Frederick L. 93, 139
Steuer, Sgt André 72, 179
Strähle, Ltn.d.Res Paul 7, 9, 88, 89, 90, 92, 94, 95, 102, 182
Streccius, Hptm Alfred 112

Tauentzien, Bogislav F.E. Graf von 174
Taylor, Stewart K. 9, 178, 181
Tester, Pvt G. 99
Thomsen, Oberst-Ltn Hermann von der Lieth- 66, 67, 68, 79, 107
Tiedje, Ltn 134
Tomlin, 2/Lt Harry F. 99
Trentepohl, Ltn 46
Turck, Oblt Ernst Wilhelm 93, 95, 106, 108, 182
Turner, Capt Henry 116, 140
Tussing, MdL 140, 181
Tutschek, Hptm Adolf Ritter von 109, 110, 145, 146, 147, 148
Tütschulte, Ltn.d.Res Erwin 46, 47

Udet, Oblt.d.R Ernst 123, 158, 159, 160

Valentin, S/Lt Robert L.A 180
VanWyngarden, Greg 8, 18, 42, 57, 64, 76, 81, 83, 92, 93, 98, 102, 109, 114, 132
Veltjens, Ltn.d.Res Josef 86, 87, 88, 93, 95, 99, 108, 117, 126, 128, 161-166, 182
Vernes, Lt Marcel 139, 180
Vickers, 2/Lt E. 183
Viehweger, Ltn Johannes 31, 33, 34, 175
Vogel von Falckenstein, Hptm Otto Freiherr 30, 33, 34, 38, 39, 40, 43, 44, 45, 46, 175
Volkmann, Hptm Bruno 75, 80

Wallenstein, Gen Albrecht von 21
Walthew, 2/Lt John S. 94, 139

Warter, 2/Lt Joseph G. 99
Way, 2/Lt R.A. 59
Webb, 2/Lt George 116, 140
Weber, Tobias 8, 13, 34, 41, 53, 73,
Webster, 2/Lt Thomas M. 91, 139
Weischer, Vfw Theodor 108
Whealy, Fl/Lt Arthur T. 109, 110, 182
Wilberg, Hptm Helmuth 89, 106
Wilhelm, German Crown Prince 34, 66, 77, 78
Wilhelm I, King 36
Wilhelm II, Kaiser 26, 36, 73, 77, 78, 79, 126, 176
Wilson, Lt G.R. 97
Wilson, U.S. President Woodrow 128
Wintgens, Ltn Kurt 74
Wittmann, Hans 130, 133, 134, 184
Wolynska, Ewa 8
Wray, 2/Lt Thomas E. 91, 139

Ziegesar, Ltn Joachim von 118, 161-166

FURTHER INFORMATION

Readers interested in obtaining additional information about World War I military aviation history may wish to contact websites of research-oriented, non-profit organisations, including:

The Aerodrome
   URL: http://www.theaerodrome.com/
Australian Society of World War I Aero Historians
   URL: http://asww1ah.0catch.com
Cross & Cockade International (UK)
   URL: http://www.crossandcockade.com
League of World War I Aviation Historians (USA)
   URL: http://www.overthefront.com
Das Propellerblatt (Germany)
   URL: www.Propellerblatt.de
World War One Aeroplanes (USA)
   URL: http://www.aviation-history.com/ww1aero.htm

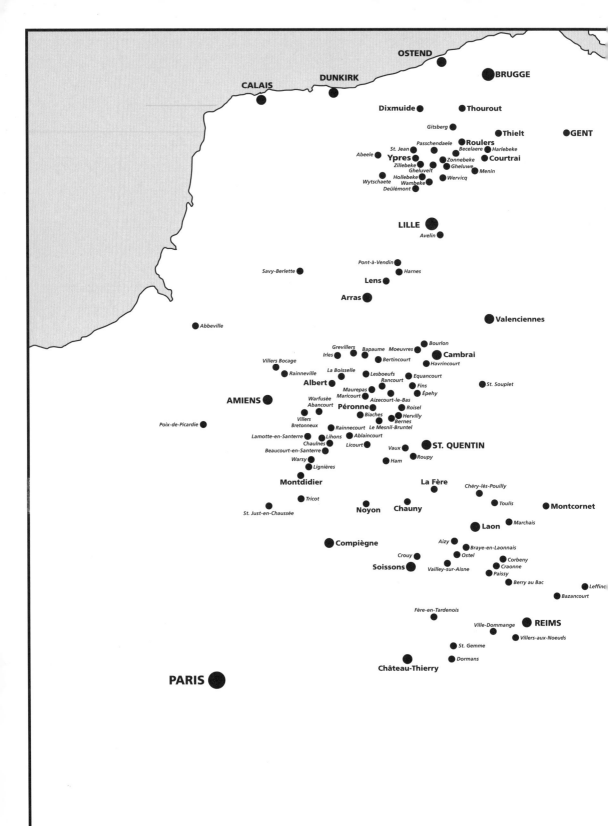